PRA
NO RET   ....KET

MW00583606

Skip Rowland's, "No Return Ticket," is a rollicking adventure story on one hand and a thought provoking examination of why we go to sea on the other. His voyage from California to Australia includes encounters with thieving mechanics that would have derailed a less determined sailor, ferocious storms that will spook the heartiest sailors, and even a south Pacific coup. Rowland writes honestly and openly about his relationship with his son, girlfriend, and various shipmates, using dialog to create a sense of intimacy. He can't seem to get enough of the stars, gazing into the heavens he never loses sight of his place in the universe. It's a nice read indeed.

—John Kretschmer,
**Sailing A Serious Ocean At the Mercy of the Sea
Flirting With Mermaids Cape Horn to Starboard**

Encountering jaw-dropping beauty, exotic beaches, storms, thieves and equipment failures, the author takes his readers across the Pacific in a story which is never less than engaging, exciting and intriguing. A great read for both the experienced yachtsman and armchair reader alike.

—Philip Matyszak,
**Author of "The Gold of Tolosa"
and other adventure books**

Captain Rowland's scenes on deck, especially in heavy weather, are exquisitely rendered and will give even landlubbers a keen sense of the power, beauty, and dangers of the sea. But what's most compelling about this riveting sea memoir are the sailors aboard Endymion, especially Captain Rowland. Their fateful voyage repeatedly tests them, both physically and emotionally. Courage, love, faith, bravado, and endurance all come into play in this compelling tale about the value—and cost—of resurrecting old dreams and living them out despite the risks.

—Tom Peek,
author of the award-winning Hawaii novel
Daughters of Fire

Rowland's debut epic tells the tale of an ordinary salesman who decided to "chuck it all," and sail across the Pacific while he was old enough to afford it, but young enough to enjoy it. From the moment his custom-made sailboat was stolen and put to the torch by thieves—who were subsequently captured in Mexico at the business end of Rowland's revolver—to his attempt to marry off a crewman to a south seas native lady Rowland offers a fast- paced behind-the-sails peek at what happens when the romance of the seas meets the reality of the journey.

"No Return Ticket" artfully balances the many dimensions of a complex sea voyage—harnessing a crew, dealing with bureaucracies and natives, maintaining the vessel, and all the various weather, navigation, health and financial worries—while letting us share in the joy of membership in the seagoing fraternity. Rowland makes the journey at once vast and intimate, relaxing and terrifying, so both the layperson and the old salt can feel both the excitement and the joy.

Not at all a cautionary tale for those contemplating the journey, "No Return Ticket" is a hopeful reminder of why we step away from shore.

—Jeff Josephson,
Marketing Guru and Casual Sailer

No Return
TICKET
Leg One

No Return TICKET Leg One

A TRUE STORY

Captain Skip Rowland

Voyaging belongs to the seamen and to the wanderers
of the world who cannot will not or refuse to fit in.
—Sterling Haydon 1906–1986

CONTENTS

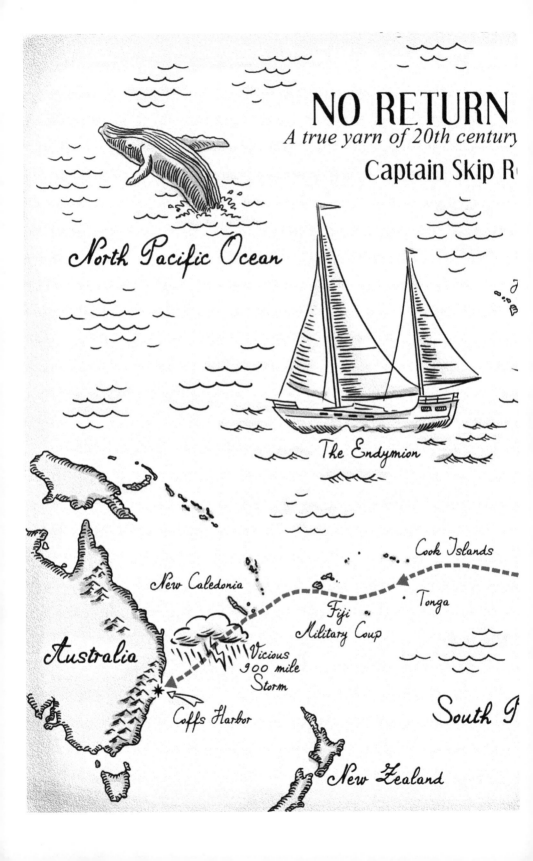

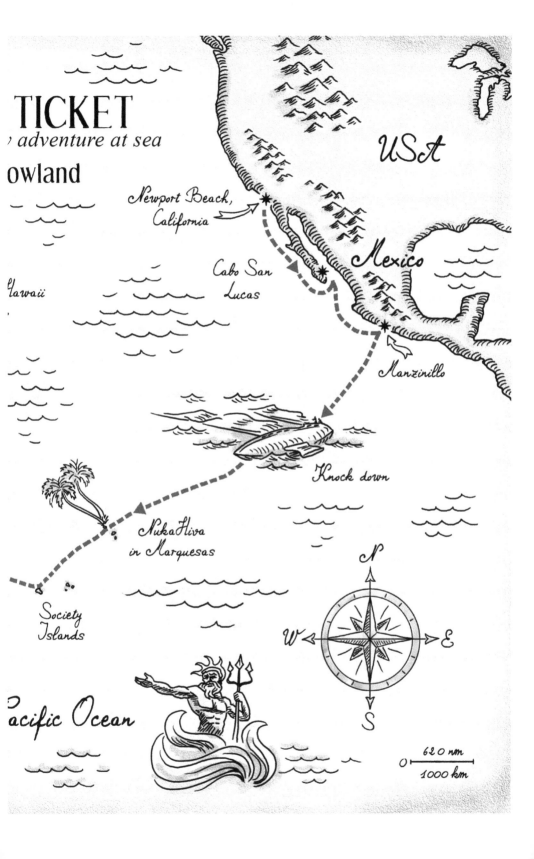

Endymion —
Keats — "A thing of
beauty is a joy forever."

PREFACE

The Ancient Mariner is crowded, as it should be on a Friday night. I look out of place. Dressed in paint-stained work shorts and a faded yacht club T-shirt, I take a seat at the slick mahogany bar to watch the action.

Beyond massive windows facing the harbor are the restaurant's private docks, where my new forty-three foot ketch *Endymion* is being fitted to fulfill my dream of drifting and blending in destinations yet unknown.

Across the bar, waitresses in short, snug uniforms tend to thirsty patrons. Outside, attendants sharply clad in crisp white uniforms race to park incoming luxury cars. Mercedes, BMWs, and Porsches get the first two rows. Exotic collector autos, a Stingray and a lime-green Thunderbird share prime positions directly in front of the restaurant's ornate nautical door. If you happened to arrive in a late model Cadillac, you're probably hoofing it across Pacific Coast Highway from some dimly lit spot behind RadioShack.

It's 1986—before the Internet and sex-inducing spiked drinks. The night is awash with fine-looking ladies dripping in jewelry.

Newport Beach is a granola bowl of California's top achievers and certified whackos, so I'm not surprised when a suit sitting beside me hails a passing waitress, hands her a c-note and coos, "Honey, fetch me some cigarette change?"

In that moment, in a bar full of boozed-up, barley-soaked, high rollers, I confirm that dropping out of this racy lifestyle to become a nobody, sailing my boat wherever I want to go, is a smart career change—and what I truly want to do. I don't know it yet, but I'll never regret this decision.

Well, I'd better get outta here. I'll pay up and climb aboard *Endymion.* Care to join me? I'm about to spin a fascinating yarn, as sailors have done through the ages—except this one is true.

CHAPTER 1

THIS KID WAS NO SAINT

Two prisoners, handcuffed and ankles manacled, sat in Judge Mallory Jones's California courtroom—on trial for stealing my yacht and setting it ablaze off the Mexican coast. (See cover)

The trial was in brief recess for what the District Attorney described as "A more pressing matter"—testimony from a recent liquor store robbery where the manager chased the accused from the single malt scotch section and sent a bullet into his butt. The prosecution wants the bullet—for evidence. The "perp" refuses to give it up, causing the D.A. to request a search warrant. Meanwhile, my stolen yacht case is delayed while the court determines if this is the right bullet, in the right ass-hole.

How in hell, I thought, *did I ever get my respectable self into this situation and this courthouse?*

It started long ago.

Larchmont, New York in 1950 was a sleepy commuter town where everyone knew everyone else—and their business.

On a crisp June evening the senior of four local cops was on the phone with my Dad. "Jasper," he said, "that kid of yours has been popping street lights with his slingshot. He was hiding, believe it or not, in our police station garage—for Christ's sake. Want me to bring him home?"

"Give him a taste of jail. I'll fetch him in the morning," my dad had replied.

I spent the night playing cards and eating spaghetti with Sergeant Paul.

The previous week I had rushed home from Sunday school proclaiming to sleepy parents that I would someday become a saint. Though breaking a few streetlights was surely disapproved of by my God, what kept me from a career in religion was the lure of a vagabond's life.

The desire to go blue water sailing probably started before birth. My Grandpa had raced across the Atlantic in 1905, my dad had been an accomplished inland lake scow sailor, and following my birth, the first place my parents showed off their little "skipper" was the taproom of the local yacht club. When I was 10 and a paperboy I helped my subscribers work on their boats in their backyards. I didn't get paid, but for this kid, holding a can of varnish was as exciting as attending a Yankees game.

One spring day our mailman asked if I would like a ride on his 36-foot "Steel Craft," a rust bucket remnant of a mass-produced powerboat used for coastal patrol during World War Two. Mailman Steve allowed me to steer and stand on the bow, a sort of child Viking. I knew then I would someday circle the globe. By age fourteen I was regularly crewing on racing sailboats out of Larchmont Yacht Club.

My high school buddy Pete Herman owned a 110 class racer called *Cinderella*, a narrow-beamed craft pinched on both ends so it appeared to have two bows. This skinny configuration made the decks almost impossible to walk on, but as sure-footed teenagers we didn't think about danger, or avoid it. Crewing for Pete one damp, foggy summer day, I went forward to perform an end-to-end spinnaker jibe. It's a tricky maneuver on the calmest of days, but this day was nasty. Standing at the mast, I assessed oncoming seas, released the spinnaker pole end attached to the mast, and cautiously walked it forward to attach it to the other bottom corner of the spinnaker. For a moment I was precariously balanced on this stupid, skinny, slippery wet deck, holding a twelve-foot metal pole attached to both bottom ends of the spinnaker but no part of the boat. If all went well, I was to take the end of the pole that was first attached to the sail, bring it aft, and attach it to the mast, thus switching its outboard end from one side of the boat to the other so we could go off on a different course.

All did not go well. We were smacked by a strong puff of wind and *Cinderella* started to heel (tip). Pete was watching me—screaming something I didn't understand. I lost my sea legs and watched Pete struggling to hold the boat steady. *Cinderella* was out of control. Pete scrambled to the high side of the hull as the boat started to turn over. I was hanging onto a wildly swinging spinnaker pole and was no help. Pete jumped for the keel, intending his added weight to help to right us, but he missed. As Pete hit the water, I was heaved from the deck, and skinny *Cinderella* capsized. The spinnaker landed on top of me, as one might imagine a parachute collapsing on a jumper, and for the first time in my life, I was *really* scared. Completely covered by the sail, with a pounding heart and mouth full of salt water, I was smothering and effectively blind. Somehow, I put aside the fear of

3

suffocating, thrashed my way through the sail, and desperately gulped a lungful of foggy fresh air. Around me, fog blanketed everything beyond 100 feet. All I could see were angry, stormy seas and floating debris. I was alone—and frightened.

Turning to look behind me, I saw Pete clinging to a six-foot piece of floorboard that had broken loose. Behind Pete *Cinderella* sat dead in the water, totally swamped and ready momentarily to vanish beneath the waves. Chilled and somewhat dazed, I swam to my friend and clawed the floorboard with him.

"Care for a sandwich?" asked Pete, casually clutching and offering a soggy bag of ham and Swiss on rye he had pulled from a bucket lashed to the floorboard. He wore a comforting smile, but I wasn't hungry.

Our predicament was bleak. We were soaking wet, drained of energy, seriously chilled, numb with fear and lost in thick fog that had swept over Long Island Sound. We hung onto the floorboard, saying little. Doubt was edging into my existence, harvesting my fears.

Suddenly, a miracle burst through the fog, so close that we were showered by the bow wave. *Golliwog*, a beautiful yacht owned by famed sail maker Ernest Ratsey, had come within feet of running us over. Pete and I screamed for help. Our cries were heard and someone tossed a dye marker from *Golliwog's* deck. We swam to it and watched *Golliwog* turn sharply to pluck us from Long Island Sound's frigid clutches.

Cinderella was recovered with considerable damage. When I next saw her, the graceful painting of her name had been removed. In large, sloppy, red letters Pete had renamed her *Ralph*. My friend had a sense of humor.

In my college years I was privileged to crew aboard the famous racing yacht *Ondine*, owned by shipping magnate Sumner Long and skippered by legendary Don Street. Everything aboard *Ondine* was state of the art—even the paint, mixed to exacting specifications, and was flown in from Germany. I recall going with Don to clear the shipment with customs officers, who were suspicious of heavy paint shipped via air. Suspecting something amiss, they strained the paint for hidden treasure. There was none. *Ondine* was once the subject of a *New York World Telegram* newspaper article headlined "$50,000 Buys a Mere Boat." Imagine that—a pedigreed ocean racing yacht with imported paint for only $1000 a foot.

Legendary Don Street and me aboard
Ondine—City Island NY, docks—1954

Gradually maturing, I dreamt regularly of doing something not necessarily worthy, but fun and adventuresome. Vivid visual fantasies of white sandy beaches and swaying grass skirts were integral in eventually making that happen. I was an average person except for my willingness and determination to act on my dreams. Sometimes it wasn't easy, but I have never regretted the decision to make more of my short life than a nine-to-fiver with eleven paid holidays and a half-empty scrapbook.

Whenever anyone would listen, I would shout out my plans to be an adventurer—sailing the world. "Way to go Skip," "Sure thing Skip," and "Good luck Dickhead" were common sentiments, but I didn't care. My dreams welded me to the fantasy I was creating, and the fantasy gradually became obtainable as I gained experience, owning numerous sailboats en route to creating and building what I considered the perfect yacht.

CHAPTER 2

BIRTH OF A LOVE STORY

In the mid-1970s, there was a rush to buy boats built in Southeast Asia. Most were from Taiwan and of questionable quality. Hong Kong yachts were well built, but with prices to match. A few came from China but let's not go there.

Lounging in the cockpit of a friend's boat at Avalon, on Catalina Island, we were watching a gaggle of partygoers aboard a ketch built in China, when, with no warning, the mizzenmast fell over. They had no sails up and there was no wind. The cause was crappy fittings and poor quality stainless steel rigging.

Even so, I too was lured to the Orient by what were often deceptive low prices but high quality teak. George Stadel, an American naval architect, working in Taiwan for the Mayflower Yacht and Trading Company, became my mentor. George had come to Taiwan for recuperation after losing a leg in battle in Vietnam, had fallen in love with his nurse and stayed. George, a handsome muscular Yale graduate, moved better with prosthetic contraptions than most men

7

with God-given legs. I contracted George and the Mayflower gang to build a 48-foot ketch I named *Love Story*, honoring my affair with my wanderlust dreams.

From laying the first fiberglass resin in the mold, I worked side-by-side with electricians, carpenters and finishers, in the process learning to marry the complexities of a seaworthy, well-built yacht with my responsibilities as owner.

It was tropically hot inside the airplane-hangar-sized shed where *Love Story* slowly took shape. Torrential rains added humidity to heat, slowing work and causing sloppy errors, always corrected by the ever-present, incredibly strong George, hopping on prosthetics or doing chin-ups to lift himself aboard the yacht that towered above him as it took shape.

One busy day, while sanding and grinding, fiberglass dust blew into my right eye. George rushed me, in considerable pain, to a creepy-looking native medicine man in a small wood and tin shanty in the midst of rice paddies. Black chickens and dogs were on the loose inside and out. Grizzled men sat and smoked in one of the two rooms while women cooked in the other. A live five-foot snake was carried into the room where I sat, nervous, uncomfortable, and with aching eye. George, seeing the startled look in my one good eye and the way I jumped when I saw the snake, said, "Easy, Skip, easy. I've seen this before. The snake is for you and they're gonna fix you. You're not gonna like it, but it works."

"What the hell, George?"

Strong arms held me in my chair and tilted my head back. Words I didn't understand were spoken and answered by a chant.

"Here it comes!" said George, a devilish smile crossing his weathered face.

8

A tall thin man with a cruel smile and a curved knife held the snake high and slit it down the centerline of its belly and pulled a small, slimy sack from its guts. Poking a small hole in the sack, he squirted the juice from the goiter of the snake into my eye. I erupted in a volley of cursing. Tears flowed like Niagara Falls. I pulled unsuccessfully against the muscular brown arms subduing me – and a minute later the pain was gone. I could see again. Clearly.

"Damn!" I exclaimed to George.

Returning to the boatyard following a tasty black chicken dinner, George told me I was only one of the medicine man's successes, so I thanked George for the quack but not the bedside manner.

After learning of my affection for dogs, George built into the salon a small doghouse as a refuge at sea for a small puppy—one I didn't yet own.

"This is for your buddy and shipmate," George said, proudly pointing to the doghouse. "I think you should name him Bosun."

With copious effort and considerable bribery, we convinced the government of both Taiwan and The People's Republic of China to allow us a sea trial in the Formosa Straits. Launching the boat, everything that could go wrong, did. To reach the road, which wasn't wide enough for the massive truck required to tow *Love Story* to the water, we had to drag *Love Story* by hand, on skids through a monsoon muddy field. The police, who had likely never heard of a "Wide Load Follows" sign, provided extra officers at added extra dollars (mine, of course) to guide our course. We eventually made it to Keelung Harbor, where a huge crane dangled the mast above the docks while officials looked for the proper lucky coin to put below the mast step, an ancient tradition about which I knew nothing.

9

"Calm down, Skip," George explained. "These folks are superstitious and it's an old custom. Afraid of dying at sea, they place coins under the mast so they won't be broke when they enter the netherworld."

Waiting for a coin before stepping the mast of Love Story *in Keelung, Taiwan*

Meantime, the hull was bashing against the stone wharf causing scrapes and scratches, so I asked, "George, why can't they use any damned coin?"

"Do you have any US coins?" George asked. "You may be onto something."

Problem solved.

The mast was fitted. We celebrated with Hsinchu and Taichung, a gastronomically revolting combination of pork balls and sweet molasses cakes.

Our sea trial followed days of begging and graft in exchange for permits to sail in the Formosa Straits, a sixty-six-mile wide, congested body of water separating Taiwan from The People's Republic of China—also called The Black Ditch. We kept vigilant lookout for heavy commercial traffic, and all sorts of odd vessels altered course to look at us under sail—an unusual sight in tightly controlled government waters. Our navigation aids were sparse, causing us to sail too close to the People's Island of Matsu. We were warned away from the Communist island by cannon fire across our bow. Thank you, lucky US coin.

Eventually, I berthed *Love Story* in front of my home on Naples Island in Long Beach, California, and began fitting her for a world cruise—including mechanical work on a new model Volvo Penta diesel with more problems than a used Edsel.

What happened next I could never have predicted.

CHAPTER 3

DEATH ON A DESOLATE COAST

An annoying ringing phone in my hotel room blasted me from my booze-clouded sleep. Following a daylong meeting at the Breakers Hotel in Palm Beach, Florida, I had partied with business associates. The bedside clock told me it was just past midnight. "Hello—who? Yes, go ahead. Matt, it's after midnight. Where are you? How'd you find me?"

Matt Lerner, a good friend, and fine local yacht broker was calling from California. Awakening more fully, I sensed trouble.

"Skip," Matt said, and hesitated, like someone delivering bad news. "What I'm about to say is serious stuff. Better you sit, Skip. Are you sitting down, my friend?"

"I'm in bed, for Christ's sakes, Matt. I'm not sure I could get up if I wanted to."

"I went by your house this evening. Skip—your boat isn't there." My heart skipped a beat.

"I knew you were away," Matt continued, "so I tracked you down. I think I know you well enough to believe you didn't loan out your boat."

"No, of course not."

"So, is it in the shipyard?" Matt asked with a twinge of sarcasm. My thoughts raced. This wasn't making sense. Did the marina staff, for any reason, move *Love Story*? A safety reason, perhaps?

Hopefully? Had I paid my taxes?

"Listen—I'm sorry for being a jerk when you woke me up, Matt. It's supposed to be at my dock, in front of my house. Volvo mechanics are working on that crappy engine, but no one else should be aboard. Are you telling me my slip is empty, *Love Story* isn't there?"

"Yes—I am. Now, listen carefully." Matt, always the levelheaded one, had a plan.

"Here's what we will do, Skip. I'll go to the marine police and report the boat missing. They know me and will know I'm not the owner, so they'll need to speak with you. Give me 10 minutes from our hang up, and then you call this number (which he gave me). Tell them I have your power of attorney, in case I need to act for you. I'm wearing a brown shirt with *Naples Yacht Sales* on the pocket, and blue trousers, if you need to describe me."

As the minutes flew by, I felt rising panic about my yacht but a sense of calm about Matt. I was fortunate to have an observant friend, willing to get involved. There were not many like him. I dialed the marine police.

"Alamitos Bay Marine Patrol, Officer Cunningham speaking."

"Officer, are you in command tonight, or may I speak with whomever might be?"

"I can handle it, whatever it is," he said, sounding a little offended. "Matt Lerner should be standing in your office, he's wearing . . ."

14

"Yes, I know Matt. He's here. What about him?"

"My name is Skip Rowland. I live in Naples at . . .'

"Yeah," the officer interrupted, "I think I know you—aren't you the guy I caught ripping down the 5 mile an hour channel about a year ago in some sort of cigarette boat? That's you, right?"

"Guilty, Sir," I replied, "and I apologize again. You know I paid a hefty fine. Anyway, I'm calling from Florida. Matt's acting on my behalf to report my boat missing."

"Same boat, that fast one?"

"No, it's a 48-foot white ketch, with black spars (masts), named *Love Story*. I'm requesting Matt Lerner, as my agent, file a missing boat report, and your office notify the Coast Guard immediately. He'll also contact Travelers, my insurance company."

"We can do that," agreed Officer Cunningham, saying, "Mr. Lerner will need to fill out some papers. You can sign them when you get back. And Rowland, in spite of our past differences, I'm sorry to hear this."

Hanging up I lay in bed once more but couldn't sleep. The hotel room phone again shattered my reverie. Half dazed, I rolled over and picked it up.

"This is Ryan O'Dell speaking. I'm the insurance investigator assigned to your case, Mr. Rowland. I need to ask a few questions."

"Good heavens," I said, "It's 7:00 a.m. here. Where are you?"

"California," he told me, "it's about 4:00 a.m. and I've been working on this most of the night . . . since the Marine Department called in the missing yacht report. You were wise to handle it that way. You get faster results when it's official rather than a member of the public."

"Makes sense to me," I said.

15

"Here's the good part. We have an informant network, a damned good one, which runs from Vancouver, British Columbia to the southern border of Mexico. If your boat is anywhere between those two points, we will find it."

His voice resonated authority. I felt better. Ryan O'Dell wanted to know exactly the day and time I left home, to help determine the greatest distance the yacht could have travelled. He asked permission to look around my property and encouraged me to go about my regular business and not to worry, that he would be there to help. That was a tall order.

Before hanging up, Ryan said, "I notice your boat's insured for $75,000, but your tax rate is based on $180,000, so I assume this is not an insurance fraud case?"

"Jesus, your kinda blunt aren't you? The reason," I told Ryan, "is because I seldom use the boat now, except to go to Catalina, so yeah, I suppose I'm a dope for underinsuring, but I never thought the whole yacht would be a claim."

"It isn't yet, so don't worry right now, Mr. Rowland. There's a chance it won't even cost your deductible."

He was mistaken.

Following Ryan O'Dell's suggestion, I stayed at the meeting in Boca Raton, but I was morose and inattentive. Mid-afternoon of the following day, I was paged to a phone. Investigator O'Dell informed me, "There is bad news, Skip. *Love Story* has been located on the Mexican coast. There's been a fire. I'm afraid there isn't much left." "What do you mean—not much?" I was shocked. Tears began to form.

"Probably not enough to salvage anything. Your *Love Story* is gone—dead."

"What? Jesus, no, that's impossible!" I was hyperventilating.

"We figure, your *Love Story* was stolen from your residence, probably by the two Volvo mechanics—maybe trying to take it to Australia. We've heard worse."

"Bastards. Really think it was those pricks? Why?"

"They left their truck parked behind your garage, and the Volvo dealer said they hadn't reported for work in a week. Those clues plus an empty slip at your house, it's not rocket science. This morning our plane flew over a vessel matching *Love Story's* description on the rocks, near the blowhole at La Bufadora, a fishing village about thirty miles south of Ensenada."

"I know the place. Go on."

"After the sighting, the pilot flew on for a few minutes, then returned for another look. On his second pass, the boat was ablaze. Our pilot figures diesel fuel had been spread below and above decks, and ignited to torch the vessel. He also reported seeing two men jumping to shore from the boat."

"The mechanics?"

"Don't know. He said they sat on a rock and watched the fire— hardly glanced at his plane. People are nuts!"

"Should I go there?" I asked, knowing immediately it was a dumb question.

"No—at least not now. I'm told the boat burned intensely until it was light enough to float off the rocks and drift to the beach where it burned to the waterline and is now awash in the tide."

"So it was intentional. Arson?"

"Looks like it."

"The two guys, what about them? Did they get away?" I asked.

"I'm sorry Skip, I don't know more, except that when they were watching the fire, one had a large bag, probably of clothing, maybe a sail bag, so we assume they are the same guys first seen aboard."

"Did the pilot get pictures?"

"I don't believe so."

"Damn, I've seen these pricks—one of them was at my house. Not a guy I'd invite to dinner. How about a description? Did the pilot say anything more?"

"Again, Skip," the investigator, sounded uncertain, "I doubt it. The pass was probably too fast and he was flying solo. All he said was that it was two guys."

"I'm coming home next flight!" I said.

"Won't do you any good."

"I'm coming anyway."

After catching the next flight west, I met with Ryan O'Dell in Long Beach. He was a movie screen detective, built like a fireplug, rock hard, self-confident, and missing two fingers, I assumed from some incident long ago. He summarized his findings. The suspect's names, provided by their employer, had been searched. Both had criminal records, one including boat theft in San Diego. I found that odd. I had requested anyone working aboard *Love Story* be bonded, and I had been assured they were. Their photos were being circulated along the border and with the San Diego police—but no sightings so far.

Back in my office, I told my secretary Rhonda what had happened, concluding; "I'm outta here. Get Jimmy Mitchell on the phone for me please—and may I borrow your car?"

"My car? Why?"

"Rhonda, I've gotta see this. I'm going to La Bufadora. Your Honda will be less conspicuous than my Jaguar. I can't draw any attention, so enjoy the Jag. The tank's full and you know I'm good for anything that happens to your car—right?"

She said, "Yes" and I handed her the keys to the Jag.

"Take your time," she added.

Jimmy, my gun collector friend, was less cooperative. "What the hell—you crazy, Skip? I am not lending you my firepower 'cause, the mood you're in, you'll blow somebody apart, and my sorry ass will be hanging with a weapons charge."

But Jimmy was sympathetic. A bit more coaxing and assurance he would not end up in the Graybar Hotel, and I was off to Mexico driving a plain black sedan, armed with a .45 caliber pistol and several dozen rounds. I had qualified with the 45 while serving in the Marine Corps.

I was a determined, angry man, on a mission, with no idea what to expect—and no plan.

My first objective was to cross the international border with a gun in my sports bag. Driving south, I did deep-breathing exercises and rehearsed my story of revisiting Ensenada after the last Cinco-De-Mayo yacht race. I was lucky—no questions asked and an easy crossing. Now in Mexico, I concentrated to recall details about the mechanics. The one I remembered most was scruffy looking, in his mid-twenties, skinny but physically fit. He had abundant facial acne, as if he had repeatedly wiped his sweaty face with a greasy hand and never washed. I wasn't likely to run into him—but you never know. Under the circumstances, I hoped I would and I hoped I wouldn't. I thought about the consequences of my actions and strangely, the more I wrestled with them, the less I cared. I would follow my instincts.

The small picturesque fishing village of La Bufadora would make a good place to kick back had I been coming for vacation.

The rugged shoreline and roads without guardrails were unnerving, but the blowhole, yet undiscovered by tourism, was the area's focal point. I would miss it this trip.

Navigating the rutted dusty road to town, I entered the village about noontime. It was hot and dusty under an unmerciful sun. Not a soul was visible, but these folks didn't need both hands pointing to providence to dial up a siesta in a scorcher day like that one.

Small stores fronted the street, along with several cantinas, from which came the only sound, loud recorded mariachi music. I parked in front of one. A steep hill on my right led down to the beach. At the top of the hill was a pile of rubble. I spotted a heat-seared spinnaker pole and yacht fittings I knew had come from *Love Story* and fought off a strong urge to pick through the pile. On the beach below the hill I saw the charred remains of a hull, horribly blackened by intense fire. My *Love Story* looked like a gigantic dead whale lying on the beach. Cautiously and trembling, I worked my way down the rocky hillside, overcome with tears and despair.

Everything I had worked for, dreamed about, and planned for a future had been burned beyond recognition. I felt so alone—so violated—so depressed. A vision of that lucky US coin flashed through my mind. Yeah. Sure. I thought about the doghouse and the man with one leg whose Vince Lombardi effort built *Love Story*. Despair became rising anger.

Locals gathered quietly to watch me poke again where they had already scavenged.

After an hour on the beach, thinking, weeping, poking, and prodding in the remains—I knew there was nothing, absolutely nothing, worth salvaging.

Charred remains of Love Story

I climbed from the beach and headed for the nearest cantina for a cold beer (a Mexican oxymoron). I felt tired and defeated, and inwardly my anger boiled. A small cluster of youngsters that followed me dropped back—I figured they were not allowed inside, but maybe my expression frightened them. As my eyes adjusted walking through the door-less cantina entry, I felt my heart thump and my hair bristle and broke into a spooky cold sweat.

Two gringos sat backs to me, nursing drinks at the bar—my thieves. The sorry bastards hadn't left the scene. My blood thumped in my temples.

Turning slowly I dashed to Rhonda's car and threw open the trunk with trembling fingers. Opening my bag, I drew a-slow-deep breath to get into my two-foot zone, then headed purposefully back into the cantina, the .45 in hand—safety off. I'd never been so nervous, or so pissed off. This calm, normally rational businessman had gone maniac. I charged through the cantina entrance.

21

"Freeze! Hit the deck –everybody—I mean every fuckin' one of you, everybody—you too lady—this is no drill."

The few patrons may not have understood English, but they understood angry, and did as they were told. A man of about fifty and his younger lady friend actually knelt down, knees on the ground, hands on the floor in front of them. Confusing thoughts raced through my mind: *That's pretty cool. They did what I told them, but then— I have the gun. Am I going to shoot someone? That would be bad. Holy crap—I'm in a mess now. What's next?*

The thieves had turned toward me. "Surprise!"

They were startled, but hadn't put together who I was, what I was doing. My eyes drilled through them. I recognized the acne-pocked, grimy Volvo mechanic and reveled in his scared shitless expression. My intentions were obvious. I was at the point of no return.

"You two fuckers especially—don't move a finger. Hands up high, both of you. Put 'em where I can see 'em, and don't think for a bloody second I won't shoot you, 'cause I will."

"Are you crazy?" one of them asked.

"Yeah—I am, asshole, and you are my target."

"Oh shit!" acne face uttered to his partner—realizing who I was. "Hold 'em up, asshole, high up!" I said again. They were looking for an escape route, maybe a fight. Keeping my cold, somber eyes on his, I moved menacingly toward him, the pistol pointed at his gut, and demanded, "Somebody get the police. You—you own this place?"

The bartender nodded. He had one of the few village phones. "Call the police."

Everybody was still, the cantina deadly silent. I could hear my breathing and wondered if they could see my heart pounding. This was different stuff, exciting, but new territory for me. I had to remain calm.

An older woman began to cry. I told her to leave. She did.

Twenty nerve-wracking minutes later, the police arrived. Two ancient squad cars, red lights suction cupped to the roof, sirens wailing and covered in dust, screeched to a head-jarring halt, spewing more dust into the cantina. The car doors flew open, but only one officer jumped from his vehicle. It was almost humorous. Not knowing the potential danger, they chose to exercise more caution than I had.

One lower grade cop speaking reasonable English entered the cantina first and was barraged by excited patrons, each with their own version. The bartender/owner pointed to me and to the thieving gringos, still in my gun sights. I had lowered my weapon so as not to pose a threat to the incoming officers.

"Drop the gun," ordered the officer.

I didn't. Instead, I turned it slowly in my palm; barrel down, until it was pointed at me. A second officer took it from me. I later learned the cop first through the door was a custodian for the San Diego School District before returning to his native Mexico to join the Wyatt Earp's of Ensenada.

With my weapon surrendered, the Federales took control. I was clearly being detained, but breathed easier when the crooks were cuffed, and I was allowed an explanation. Two elderly men, known to the police, had seen *Love Story* on fire and verified, "Dos Americanos had jumped from the fiery boat to drink and dance with us."

They would dance no more. Maybe I wouldn't either.

With the thieves packed off to jail in Ensenada, the Federal District Attorney grilled me for having a gun—demanding I prove ownership of the yacht carcass decorating their beach.

"OK Señor . . . Now show me about the boat," commanded the cop with the braided hat, obviously in charge.

23

I produced my insurance papers and U.S. documentation, patting myself on the back for thinking to bring them. There followed a great study of my papers. I suspect they couldn't read them.

"Okay Señor, you must pay to clean up La Playa (beach). You must remove the burned remains from La Playa."

I tried, "No es possible, mucho problemo y no tenga dinero." "You must go then, to my jail," the officer said firmly but without pressure or threat. We sat like old friends, finishing our beers. I paid for theirs, and a round for the house, before being led without cuffs to one of the broken-down squad cars. The driver, the former San Diego janitor, explained at this point I was not being formally arrested.

"Tu tenga mordida," he explained, meaning I would pay a substantial fine. Another officer followed in Rhonda's car. We parked side by side in front of the Ensenada police station. The policemen were civil. I could have liked them.

Although I played dumb, this was not a place unfamiliar to me. Years ago I had spent a night here for inebriated conduct unbecoming a yachtsman following a Newport Beach to Ensenada yacht race.

"You stay there." An officer pointed to a first floor office. The thieves had been locked in squalid basement cells.

I sat, waited and thought about my situation. Not so good.

Two hours later an incoming call created visible excitement. The Federal District Attorney had lingered over beers at the cantina, then gone off the road driving back to Ensenada, and was discovered in a ditch, unharmed but shaken.

The squad room was thrown into pandemonium. I recalled a lesson from my USMC training: "If taken prisoner a Marine must always attempt escape, especially early in capture when the enemy is not yet organized" (or something like that).

24

There was no organization. Rhonda's car keys lay on a counter close to me. I scooped them up and vamoosed out the front door, maintaining a steady but quick gait. Shortly they would notice my absence and alert authorities, maybe even at the border.

I drove 200 miles that night, south, away from the border. At a small dingy motel I parked around the corner and checked in as John Dillinger. No shit. I waited nearly a week before daring to return to the States. Were they looking for me? They had no pictures of me, but what about a description? Was Rhonda's car targeted? How would I act? What story would slide from my lips? It was a worrisome drive.

Re-entering the States was a snap. I wasn't challenged or suspected of anything. I returned to Long Beach, a delighted secretary, and an unhappy buddy Jim, whose gun collection was now a pistol short of an arsenal. But I repaid him.

CHAPTER 4

THE TRIAL

There was catching up to do when I got back to Long Beach including work and some beach volleyball with a polyglot mixture of friends keen to hear of my Mexican adventures—old, young, professional and a few unemployed characters who enjoyed a good game.

After matches we gathered for brews at the Sail Inn, a beachside dump beloved by locals. Terry Bailey and Mike Wilcox had heard of the theft. They were Long Beach policemen.

"You're one lucky hombre Skip." Terry summed it up, "You squeezed between the slats of a dock, getting away like that. I'd turn you in myself, if there was a reward'.

"He's kidding you of course," chimed Mike, "what's with the mechanics"?

"I'm clueless," I admitted, "I suspect they're still in Mexico, possibly waiting repatriation. I'm told the police in San Diego will bring them back."

"Better chance they let them go," said Terry. "With proposition 13 none of the services have any extra money—not us, the fire department, or even the courts. Tax cuts are great for property owners but suck for maintaining community services—I'm hoping I don't have to take a pay cut".

"Anyway" chimed Mike, "much as Terry bitches, me and a couple of other friendlies might be able to help."

"How?"

"Like, suppose you supply the gas—we'll check out a squad car, go down there and bring the scum bags back, plant them on your lap."

"Not from Mexico." said Terry.

"Well maybe they're already in San Diego," Mike paused, "my cousin owes me. He's on the force in San Diego. I'll give him a shout. Doesn't hurt to try."

I offered to check with the district attorney, who showed little interest, telling me, "So some fat cat has his boat swiped. You won't get much sympathy."

He got my vote for jerk of the year but we continued to speak. He finally agreed to a grand theft criminal trial, if they were returned to Long Beach.

Mike and Terry, coordinating with San Diego police arranged for a prisoner pick up at the border. The mechanics got a free ride, and I suspect a sound thumping en route north. In jail in Long Beach neither could make the $10,000 bail—a trial was set.

Ryan O'Dell phoned me with a remarkable story about a guy in a jeep who had taken pictures of *Love Story* in flames. Ryan said the jeep driver was showing slides to friends in Laguna Beach a few nights ago and reported he spoke with the guys who jumped from the boat claiming they were delivering it from Honolulu to Los

Angeles, when they went on the rocks and the yacht accidentally caught fire.

An experienced sailor at the slide show said, "That makes no sense—going from Hawaii to L.A. via Mexico. Boats traditionally favor wind, waves, current, and a great northern circle route, heading for San Francisco before diving south to Los Angeles."

The experienced sailor thought something was fishy. Examining the slides it was evident the yachts name had been wiped from the hull but the CF numbers (California numbers for taxing) remained. There followed a call to authorities, which notified Ryan O'Dell, who notified me—the photographer would sell the slides.

But there was a hitch.

The photographer was a drug dealer, both nervous and hesitant.

Ryan offered to negotiate, saying, "Listen Rowland, I deal with every garden variety of low life. I'll make it happen."

And he did. A week later at precisely midnight, I parked behind a specified building on Bluebird Canyon Road in Laguna Beach. A man approached with a box of slides. Not a word was spoken. I handed him $200.00 and he handed me evidence.

The District Attorney was delighted "Now we have a case."

Indeed he did.

The trial lasted only a day. Following the recess to find the missing bullet (with which we started this yarn) the prosecution was victorious, finding both mechanics guilty of grand theft. They had intended to sail the yacht to Australia, sell it and live 'the life'—but they couldn't navigate, had no charts, no skills, no food and no God to guide them. They were sentenced to ten years incarceration, plus fines they couldn't possibly pay. I never saw or heard of them again.

Travellers insurance paid my claim and invited me to enjoin a suit against the Volvo dealer who hadn't bonded his employees. I would receive a portion of any award. However, the employer passed away several months later. I dropped out. It wasn't in my heart to continue a suit against his wife, children, or heirs. They, after all, were as innocent as I.

CHAPTER 5

TWO BEAUTY QUEENS

Two years following the trial I still reflected on what had happened, and believed if luck and value in personal life was measured on a one to ten scale, I would check in at 11.5. My two sisters and I were blessed with parents who loved us equally. At a time when divorce rates were climbing, and mom's left home for careers, our parents had been role models. I was always encouraged to do the best I was capable of—to explore everything of interest. At the University of Denver I relished fraternity life and ROTC with equal enthusiasm. Following a combat free tour in the United States Marine Corps, I took a sales position with 3M Company in their business products division. With my folks encouragement, Marine Corp's discipline, and hard work, I won the salesman of the year award my second season with 3M.

But I wanted more. Southern California life style had a lock on me. Cars, boats and a waterfront home became my focus. I was so motivated I pasted pictures of Jaguars and sailboats around my bathroom mirror. While washing I would aggressively say to my mirror image, "Skip, someone's going to sell something in your territory today—it had better be *you*."

I knew yachts and Jaguars weren't obtainable in the corporate structure, so I resigned to form my own manufacturers representative company, where I would be the sales rep for multiple non-competing companies, working strictly on commission. It was a bold move because my only product was a line of flimsy fake flowers, with a limited retail audience. Facing a buyer as a former Marine, holding a bouquet of artificial flowers took courage.

Luck tapped my shoulder again. Chip Carter, a sales rep I seriously admired was relocating from San Francisco to southern California. He represented Lee Nails, a line of fake fingernails. We teamed up, purchased another folding chair for my tiny one room, one phone, windowless office in a law library, and we went to work.

Several months, and several loans later, we were offered exclusive representation of Krazy Glue, a product in demand. "Money," we were told, "will change us."

We were ready. Our business, staff, office space and bank account grew. Chip and I became incredibly close friends, had fun and worked hard. We were determined to be 100% ethical in a business that sometimes attracted fringe players. From the day we met Chip and I never had a signed agreement, and for seven years we worked side by side with never a disagreement. I had met my *soul mate* in a business suit, a relationship that will continue for our lifetimes.

Chip always knew of my dream to someday drift and blend. It wasn't an easy conversation, but we developed a plan for Chip and an associate to purchase my half of our business. Things were falling into place.

I had also learned the value of proper insurance—if you have it. I did Travellers paid without question.

In 1985 I commissioned Henri Wauquiez, a quality French yacht builder to build *Endymion*, as a slightly smaller, more sophisticated, version of *Love Story*. The Wauquiez factory, in the small French village of Mauvaux was an ordinary looking, family owned old building that, at one time had been a shoe factory. The building was badly damaged and occupied by the Nazi's during World War Two. Bullet holes and twisted remnants of once deadly killing artillery remained, scattered around the property.

The disaster at Chernobyl, several hundred miles north by crow, occurred only a few weeks before *Endymion* was scheduled for shipment from the French factory.

As freighter deck cargo, 43 foot *Endymion* arrived in Los Angeles tightly shrink wrapped, an unusual sight, even to seasoned longshoremen who watched with curiosity and caution as the bubble wrapped yacht was set from freighter to dock with a huge crane. Before we could board, or remove the wrapping, US authorities had to carefully Geiger counter every inch as a precaution against the same Chernobyl contamination that had frightened Europe.

The name *Endymion*, meaning 'beauty is forever' came from the English poet John Keats. My grandfather had raced his 130-foot schooner *Endymion* from Sandy Hook, New Jersey to Germany in 1905 hoping to claim a cup from the Kaiser of Germany. *Atlantic*, another famous yacht won the race in a record time, and Grandpa placed fourth. He didn't win a cup, but passed to me a vintage watch fob with granddad's name inscribed below crossed burgess, one his personal flag and the other, the New York Yacht Club.

With my *Endymion* under construction, I listed my house for sale. Even doubtful friends were becoming reluctant believers in my dream. Soon *Endymion* was fully outfitted, I had no car, no mortgage, no bills and could have packed my remaining possessions in a shoebox. No keys and no fixed address sounded good.

Original Endymion *off Long Island, NY–circa 1903*

Pleasant sleep came easily in these days. Dreams were frequent, often including flying over treetops or gliding high above the earth, sometimes swooping from mountain tops, maneuvering among trees and buildings, never hitting anything or touching overhead wires. It was effortless, soundless, and joyful dreaming, related I am confident to the freedom approaching. It was time to get outta here.

Endymion's owner's quarters, where I spun this yarn, were more a stateroom than a cabin. A sturdy but comfortable teak desk was to starboard entering the cabin. A long settee gracefully curved from the end of the desk, around to the centerline of the transom. Well-proportioned bookshelves were above it, and two generous port lights in the transom provided an incredible view aft. A queen size extra comfortable berth, with Tempurpedic mattress, was fitted to the starboard side of centerline. Ample reading lights, stereo speakers and a polished teak table that pulled out from under the berth provided a romantic touch when the sea was calm.

Opposite the desk was a head (toilet) with shower, and two portholes opened to the cockpit enabling me to always be aware of instrument readings. They also made voice communication with the helmsman a cinch. Had these been pirate days the ports would have made a keen listening post to overhear plots against the skipper.

Below deck every inch wood was quality teak, air-dried for seven years before being carefully fitted to the yacht. The grains matched throughout, so a piece with a drawer in the center, for example, carried the same grain features across the drawer facing, as would be found in cabinetry on either side of the drawer. Every wood piece had been meticulously varnished and was covered by an astonishing thirteen coats of beeswax from a French monastery. (Talk about having nothing to do!) Two extra gallons of wax were aboard had we chosen to "wax on – wax off" during lazy hours.

I wrote much of this book in this aft cabin I so loved.

Endymion was fitted with the best of equipment-Brooks & Gate-house instruments, Furuno radar, three anchors, Robertson autopilot,

Hood boom furling system, Avon inflatable, Givens survival raft, and Sony sound system, to name a few.

I was particularly proud of the sound system. Music had always been important to me. Custom deck speakers, easily removed in inclement weather, were housed in handsome teak boxes and would fill the cockpit with surround sound from 300 cassette tapes, stored in a drawer below deck.

I loved this boat. And if it's possible she loved me back.

Endymion was my fourteenth boat, including an Islander 36, Cal 40, Columbia 52 and of course, *Love Story.*

Luck and fate had one more present for me, a gift that would never have occurred, had the *Love Story* tragedy not delayed my voyage. I met my opposite sex soul mate. Denise was the nurse supervisor, and right arm, for my good friend and neighbor, Dr. Joe Noble. Being Joe's patient, I knew Dense casually, and had seen her at social gatherings. Always attracted to tall blondes, I hadn't paid proper attention to this beautiful young lady with long, thick auburn hair, deep soulful eyes, bright smile and body that committed men to sins in their minds. This was not 'Nurse Sluggo.'

One day while siphoning blood from my arm, Denise said, "Nice tan Skip. Been on vacation?"

"Sort of," I said offhandedly. "I sold my business and bought a boat to sail around the world."

"Really!—Sounds interesting," replied Denise just as casually, "I'm wrapping up a divorce myself, and plan to buy a live aboard at Marina Del Rey."

The flirt was on! She had my attention. This beauty would not get away. The cobra coiled. "Well, if you'd like to see my yacht's plans, you may get some suggestions for living aboard."

Denise shortly after our first date.

"Sure! Sounds good to me."

Two dates later Denise and I were committed and I never (seriously) looked at another blonde. We went to France together to visit *Endymion* under construction, attended the Los Angeles Olympics and soon became life partners, nearly causing me to lose my doctor friend for swiping his prized nurse.

Denise had her own ideas about what should be aboard *Endymion*. She won on two specific items. We built in a washer-dryer; much against my argument for tradition, claiming a good sea bucket with a little soap and two able feet pounding the contents had worked for centuries—why not now? Denise would have none of it. She wanted convenience.

The survival raft, a compulsory item for going off shore was Denise's second target. These highly technical rafts, capable of self

37

righting themselves in breaking seas, contain carefully measured medical supplies, food, desalination equipment, repair kits, fishing gear and more. Speaking light heartedly and seriously in the same breath (because she could) Denise rationalized a rescue at sea would involve another vessel coming to our aid. She wanted a few extra items custom packed, to give the false impression when rescued, that life aboard the raft was routine. They included make up, deck of cards, score pad, visor and champagne. The raft manufacturer thought the idea novel enough he acquiesced, even producing an official inventory document including those items that we later presented to skeptical customs officials.

With the outfitting of *Endymion* and relationship solidly in high gear we set our departure date for early January, 1987 and sent abundant invitations to our combination christening and bon voyage party. The world was smiling that Christmas season.

Then fate intervened.

Early evening, the fifth day of Christmas, a fist pounding on the hull brought bad news: "Denise had fallen on the gangway. 911 responders were en-route."

Denise had slipped on the steep low tide gangway and tumbled ten feet to the dock below, seriously fracturing her tibia and fibula, bones that support our weight and are important to knee and ankle joints—a skier's fracture with no snow. In agony, she was taken to Hoag Memorial Hospital in Newport Beach where Denise was fitted for an ankle to hip cast. Her leg would have to be re-broken twice to heal correctly. She would not sail with us.

Denise put up a brave front hearing the news, but was broken hearted. Me too. She could go only on the short first leg to San Diego, then return to her parents home to further mend, and hopefully join us in Tahiti. It all seemed so distant.

CHAPTER 6

THE CHRISTENING

Sunday, January 4th, 1987. What a party!

In a sense, this day, and this party, had been in the works for nearly forty years. Everything was perfect except for Denise's painful struggle with her new full leg cast and the mental torture of saying goodbye, though temporarily, to a boat and its captain whom she had so come to love.

So many people were crowded onto the Ancient Mariner Restaurant docks I was concerned they would slowly sink, or break loose and float away. Champagne wasn't hard to find and several departure gifts were serious, while most were 'parting shots.' My ex-wife, who had always felt I dreamt beyond my budget, was sloshing free champagne and advised Denise, "What a fool you are, going anywhere with Skip."

Denise needed assistance swinging the christening bottle from her dockside position on crutches, but managed a bull's-eye. Minutes later, those still lingering aboard returned to the dock, we cast off our lines, reversed slowly from the dock, made a smart pivot in Newport Harbor, and pointed our bow outbound. Thrilling!

An armada followed us through the harbor, yelling slurred wishes, giving charitable advice and occasionally mooning us. Fortunately, none of our well wishers collided with anchored boats or seawalls. It had been a fun, gratifying day. We dissolved into the dusk-beginning, at last to drift and blend.

Sunday, January 4, 1987
between 11:00 am and 1:00 pm
you are invited to attend a
very special occasion
aboard the world class cruising yacht

"Endymion"

At 12:00 noon she will be
officially christened
At 1:00 pm she will depart
Newport Beach on her
epic 'round the world voyage
Please join us at this memorable time
to inspect Endymion, witness her christening
and celebrate with a champagne toast.

Denise Wharton, Tony Rowland, Skip Rowland

Escort vessels to the harbor entrance will be provided
should you desire to participate. (Weather permitting)

R.S.V.P. Regrets only 714 · 631·7657

Christening Invitation

40

CHAPTER 7

GOODBYE GLITZY CALIFORNIA

It was a simple overnighter to the Coronado Cays Yacht Club in San Diego. As I was a member, my crew, guests, and I could enjoy one last day of comfort and everyone at the club would make us welcome as we ticked off various departure loose ends.

Two short hours south of Newport Beach, while sailing in balmy, relaxing conditions for a January night, and with remnants of champagne still pouring, we had our first "test under fire." My 26-year-old son Chip, who was along only for this short leg because of business obligations, screamed from below:

"Awwww CRAP! Who bought these lousy knives anyway?"

A hungry lad since birth, and using a knife with an extra sharp blade, he had sliced into a gift cheese ball, taking a generous portion of his finger along for the ride. Denise, crutches supporting her, managed to hobble down the companionway, to suture and wrap his painful, bloody finger. I wondered—had God sent a message to have a nurse aboard for all time? None of us craved the cheese ball painted with Chip's blood, so he alone packed it away in a few hungry mouthfuls, continuing his bitching, which diminished as Nurse Denise added scotch and aspirin as a nautical pain reliever. Chip dozed off leaving cheese consumption his one and only contribution to his short voyage. We would shortly be parting for a long time, perhaps forever, we just didn't know. This made for quiet reflective times where all of us, Denise, Tony, his girlfriend Kim, Chip and I, tended to be in different places mentally and emotionally.

"I love you, Skip," whispered Denise.

"You're reading my mind," I replied. We were snuggled in the cockpit in the wee hours, holding and comforting each other as people do when they are in love.

"You made me proud today, Skippy."

"Thank you, Denise. It's bittersweet. It's wonderful, the feeling of satisfaction in getting to this point. It's wistful though, and I feel out of sorts at leaving you, my love."

"You'll miss me?" Denise asked, and held my hand slightly tighter. I kissed her. She returned the pleasure. We had our answer.

My other son, Tony, who was to sail with me, was busy telling his brother Chip, older, by one year, about the treasures he would find and the girls he would meet. Chip claimed the girls in Tony's life worth knowing were all in California and assured him, "Don't worry, Tony, while you're away I'll take care of 'em for ya."

Denise and I overheard the quip. We were both somewhat pleased only Tony would sail with his dad. The "boys" (as Denise referred to the duo) have colliding personalities. Chip is the more aggressive, demanding, my-way-or-the-highway kind of person, who can be a handful in close quarters. Tony, on the other hand, is in many ways the opposite to Chip, caring, thoughtful, and can be counted on when the chips are down (so to speak).

As sons, I loved them both. Denise did as well. As a choice for crew, it was Tony—hands down.

Thus, on the morning of January 13th, Tony and I said our final uncomfortable goodbyes to Chip, Denise, and Tony's girlfriend Kim. We made a quick stop at the last fuel dock in San Diego harbor for Tony to rake the junk food from the shelves.

Clearing Point Loma in a light nor'easter, we were surprised, and somewhat awed, by the size of the huge rollers running with rhythm below and with our southbound hull. In his best rendition of the King's English, Tony exclaimed, "Jeez, Dad, I never seen no waves like these ones." Even a navy destroyer was rolling as she slipped silently past. They were big waves indeed, long slow ocean rollers bred of a storm in some distant quadrant and telegraphed ahead to give sailors fair warning.

By noon we saw our first of many whales. These were a real spirit lifter at a time we were huddled in foul weather gear and gloves, to guard against rapidly falling temperature, gathering heavy clouds, and dwindling distance between those "long slow rollers." We shortened sail.

Tony again, "Jeez, Pops, are we nuts—leaving in January?"

I wondered.

Late in the day we passed into Mexican coastal waters, but could still receive San Diego radio. The weather news was about a rapidly moving storm dubbed "The Yukon Express." We had heard of it the previous day.

"Cool name for a cold storm, and I have a feeling it wants us," Tony commented.

"It might. I checked the chart against the last weather broadcast. It's packing a lot of wind and could catch us. Are you ready?"

"Yeah, I guess so," Tony said lamely, but picked up tempo, adding, "My music is in my sea dry pocket and the Lord is on my shoulder. What could be better?"

"Try your English."

Night fell fast and heavy. The last network evening news was history when we passed seven nautical miles (nm) west of "Roca's Soledad," a nasty collection of rocks, hidden except in extreme tides, and a known collector of "near miss navigation" trophies. We were headed for Isla San Martin in increasingly heavy seas and a rocking ride that had me concerned.

By midnight we had breaks in the sky, a glimpse at a stunning moon, and a chorus of chattering porpoises leaping and clowning within inches of our bow.

"Awesome, freezing but awesome," said Tony.

Both of us were wide-awake. We wondered if we had outrun the Yukon Express. Tony snapped pictures of the moon darting in and out of ominous clouds, and I nervously noticed a few distant waves now had a crest and small break to them. We were not free.

By 1300 January 15th we had our hook (anchor) down at Isla San Martin. It was an uncomfortable first anchorage to the lee (away from wind) side of the island but with minimal shelter from increasingly angry waves. Following a short nap, a 'cuppa Joe,' and a can of Campbell's allegedly 'best,' we caught a scratchy weather alert from San Diego: "Coming waves and cold will set records."

"That sucks," Tony said as a wave rolled *Endymion*, knocking his spoon from his mouth.

"I agree Tony—sounds ominous—let's move."

With weather deteriorating by the minute we upped anchor to strike out for the more promising shelter of Islas San Benito, 133 nautical miles south. Though experienced, we hadn't given enough consideration to something we well knew—sailing yachts couldn't outrun a storm.

Shortly after midnight our radios took a dump—shut down. At 0200, the "Yukon Express" found our little spot on the Pacific and hit with winds gusting to forty knots. Raging seas shot fingers of icy spray throughout the January night's 13.5 hours of blackness. At 0300 Tony wrote in the log: "One cold mother tonight."

When morning broke we could see mountains of water crashing on rocks ahead, we believed marked a channel between the two islands of San Benito's. It looked terrifying, and treacherously narrow. We'd made good time. The sea waves chasing us from astern were fifteen feet with angry breaking crests, and dark against the dawn sky. As they caught up and swept below, they would send us screaming down into the trough, where we would stall, and the wave would race ahead, towering once again to obscure the horizon. It was scary—yet fascinating. Tony reminded me of the Pacific sailor's adage, "Going south . . . sail it. Going north . . . mail it."

Tony and I, in our yellow slickers, looked at each other. We were closing rapidly on the narrow, wave-battered passage.

"Whadda ya think, Dad?" Tony asked, his eyes wide and face flushed from the pounding wind and stinging salt spray. "Looks crappy and narrow gettin through there. I didn't come here to get my body pounded on yonder guano-crusted rocks."

We opted for the longer route around and anchored safely by mid-morning in a reasonably protected bay, again exhausted, yet intrigued by the small fishing village nestled in protection of the otherwise barren and forgotten rock. A nip of whiskey for our souls, and again we slept—first I wanted to thank God. I sat at the desk space in my aft cabin, pen in hand to write to Denise, and quietly offered:

"Dearest Lord" (I always think of God as my friend), "Thanks for keeping us safe in this ball buster Yukon stuff. I owe you, and promise to be back atcha finding good in people and making a better world, one of peace—and by the way God, we could use warmer weather, maybe a little sun? And thanks to French yacht builders. They did well. We didn't take a single breaking wave over the cockpit—but you were watching, so I guess you know that. Thanks again, God. Skip—out."

Actually, the only waves that reached deck were smaller quartering seas that posed no threat other than a soaking. *Endymion* didn't have the sleek lines and gracious overhangs of bygone generations, but her design had two appreciated advantages—more interior bulk and added safety with her higher freeboard (measurement from water to deck). *Endymion* tended to rise on the seas and not take green water from behind. The separation of keel and spade rudder provided great downwind tracking even in dicey weather.

Anchored and settled in, we were approached by a skiff full of waving Mexican teens with a trade deal we couldn't refuse. Eight live lobsters soon scampered around the cockpit in return for a six-pack of Budweiser. Ahhh—Mexico was grand.

46

CHAPTER 8

CLOSE CALL

Mild hangovers accompanied us as we continued south in light winds with a spinnaker flying for the first time. Tony made a case for Cedros Island, passing slowly to our port, as the place we should drop anchor so he could surf.

I was enjoying my son's company and had never felt closer to him. Tony was energetic, a good sailor, conversationalist, and a skilled politician when close to surfing beaches, but required retraining to understand large surfing waves do not equate to safe anchorages for expensive cruising yachts.

For southbound sailors, January 18th was a cold night. I stood watch wearing both of my only two pairs of socks and my feet were still cold. We listened to a ham radio operator near Phoenix, Arizona declaring his soft drink bottle, left outside, had frozen. We concluded, to our delight, that the weather gods had taken to punishing others as well as us.

The next morning, with warming temperatures, Tony persisted. "Come on, Dad. Just a couple hours anchored along the beach. I need to surf!"

"Tony, you've earned it, but I can't acquiesce." "What the hell's that mean?"

"It means no," I said, unhappily. "I won't chance it with big waves."

"OK, Pops, I understand. Let's get underway."

We set anchor later that day in Turtle Bay. Ashore, Tony and I climbed steep hills with astonishing views of vast empty beaches and an endless blazing blue ocean, so calm, so serene, so empty. We looked in awe at the magnificent, perfect, gentle curve of the earth.

"Thanks, Dad." "For what?"

"For taking me here. For letting me share life with you."

"Yeah, Tony," I said thoughtfully. "You're good company, son. This is a remarkable moment—this view and trying to comprehend what makes us function as living souls, able to realize how finite we are in this big picture—and then to share it with those you love. We are lucky indeed"

Tony and I were in harmony.

We came across two gravesites marked by rocks piled meaningfully. We wondered how many years ago death had taken them, and what had caused their demise. We called them "Jack and Bill who went up the hill," and said a prayer for them.

A pleasant seasonal twelve-knot breeze whisked us offshore for the next few days. We didn't care about time or what might be happening in the world we'd left behind. Nor did we consider the future except for reaching Cabo San Lucas in time for Super Bowl Sunday.

"Winds come aft of 120 degrees. What say you to a spinnaker?" Tony asked as he peeled away his last layer of shirt.

"Are you nuts?' I asked. "The spinnaker is work. This is easy—tranquility."

"Come on, Pops, let's crank her up and see what we can do. I'll get the lines." Tony was on a mission.

Working together we flawlessly set the big, red, white, and blue sail, picking up an impressive three knots so we moved at almost the exact speed of the wind. We were happy, relaxed, and sufficiently lazy—a father and son, sailing south, drifting and blending on a vast empty sea.

The reverie was short.

"Look Dad—look up, quickly," Tony shouted as he lay prone of the cockpit on cushions.

Above us, two large hawks disputed landing rights on our masthead.

"Get outta here! Screw off!" Tony yelled, waving a winch handle. "Sonofabitches!" I screamed, shaking my fist.

The intruders were unimpressed. Birds can effortlessly damage delicate instruments, antennas, or other gear mounted on the masthead—their preferred landing strip. And they crap a lot. One had settled high in our rigging, while the other circled noisily.

"The pistol, Tony, get the gun," I urged.

Tony dropped down the companionway, re-emerging seconds later jamming shells into our only weapon, an ageing .38 pistol. He shouted, "Take that, you poachers!" and fired several rounds skyward.

The birds, quick to get the message, propelled salvos of guano as they lifted off. No direct hits for either team.

We spent the afternoon pondering the wisdom of having a gun aboard. Surely, we would be outnumbered if ever we were attacked, and history shows guns at sea are often the owners' guns turned against them. All weapons must be declared in any port of entry, worldwide. Some yacht owners hide them, but consequences are severe, and expensive. If you want to reclaim a confiscated weapon when leaving the country, you must sail back to your port of original entry to fetch it. So, for example, if we declared the gun in Cabo San Lucas and later departed from Acapulco, we would need to sail back to Cabo, just for the gun.

Worse could be confiscation of your yacht if the authorities find an undeclared weapon. We were a documented vessel, meaning if *Endymion* were to be detained, anywhere in the world for any reason, we would receive the same privileges as a U.S. Navy ship. If it helps the crew avoid a nasty foreign prison, it's a good deal, but if they hate America, it may not work so well. Countless vessels are documented, so this, in theory anyway, must work. The flip side for the owner is if war is declared, the U.S. Government can seize your yacht to defend the country.

"Now, there's a knee-slapping chuckle," declared Tony. "What defense could they expect from a 10-knot sailing vessel against an incoming missile?"

Most cruising yachts are documented, and we decided not to do anything about the gun except clean it and stow it—in a better hiding place.

One smart thing I did before leaving the US was on the advice of my navigation coach Capt. Swede Jensen.

Swede, always blunt, had asked, "Skip, is your boat clear with the bank?"

"Yes," I replied

"Well then, you're a dumb shit! If you get into trouble in some distant land and they confiscate your boat, there won't be anybody stateside who will give a shit about you or your crew; but if your boat has a sizeable mortgage, the bank will find the boat, and the chances are good you'll get released along with the yacht."

The problem is banks don't like to loan large sums against boats that will be sailing over the sunset. So, you have two choices—first, don't tell them, and second (more advisable), have a sum equal to the loan amount on deposit with the bank in another form of investment. One can offset the other if absolutely necessary.

We held Turtle Bay abeam at sunset January 21st. With a wink of life left in the western sky we dropped the chute, our work on deck aided by powerful mast lights installed to illuminate the foredeck when needed. We set a lightweight, masthead 150% jenny (large sail forward) and sailed into a magical night of stars with not a care in the world.

"You're up, Dad." Tony was barely audible telling me it was my watch. I grabbed a quick cuppa Joe, gloves and jacket, and was on deck to relieve Tony when the clock struck eight bells for midnight. I was pleased to see Tony properly harnessed, though the sea was calm. "She's cold again tonight, Dad, but Father dearest, look at the sky." Tony pointed out the constellation Orion, adding, "I think that's Jupiter low on the horizon. It's like God placed every star and planet perfectly to shine right at us. This is so cool, Dad."

"Tony, it is. I agree but I'm only half awake. Can you give me what I need to know to carry on, and you go grab some shut eye." I was not conversational.

"OK, Pops," he said, stepping aside to give me the wheel. "Course is 135 degrees, speed 7.5 knots, wind steady at 12 to 15 knots, moderate sea, and nothing unusual to report."

"OK, thanks, Tony." I took the wheel.

51

"Oh yeah, Pops, I almost forgot," added Tony. "I have one unidentified point of light bearing 05 degrees to port, just starting to rise."

Tony held his arm over the compass, indicating 05 degrees. "I can't make it yet, whether it's a star or planet, but it's coming up a bit fast, so Dad—you'll want to keep an eye on that one."

"I will, sir," I said proudly, mentally noting Tony's comprehensive report.

"And have fun, Dad," he chuckled, taking a parting shot over his shoulder. "With so many stars, it will be hard for your aging eyes to track a single strange one."

"Roger all that and go below. Get some rest," I said to Tony and repeated the bearings back to him, as sailors have done through the ages.

Tony dove below and curled up in the spinnaker on the starboard settee in seconds. I strained into the darkness to find the errant star and basked in the sheer joy of being at sea on a John Masefield, "I must go down to the sea again," kind of night.

So many stars, I thought, literally millions of points of light. I would never see this from anyplace on shore.

Sipping my second coffee, I checked again the rising 'star' Tony had mentioned off our port bow. As he'd said, it was coming up fast—too fast. My nerves triggered a slight tingle.

Within twenty minutes the rising light split into two, one above the other—range lights on a freighter. In navigational language the lights told me the vessel was 100 meters or more in length. Soon I could distinguish a faint red portside light, meaning that she would pass us from starboard side (right), to port side (left). Just to be sure I bore off to starboard twenty degrees, adjusted sail, and set my course at 155 degrees. No need, I tried to convince myself, to have intruders compromise our spectacular night.

Type of freighter encountered that January night (Not the specific vessel)

Worry and vigilance are both sailors' companions, and I couldn't keep from assessing those lights every few seconds. There was something disturbing about the situation.

Then, only for a second, I thought I saw a pin prick of green light. Then it disappeared, and returned a second time. I was certain I saw green. A cold shiver raced down my spine.

Green and red together could mean only one thing!

The vessel was coming straight at us! If his lights were regulation, we were five to seven miles apart. *What the hell?* I thought to myself. "*Could we be on a collision course?*"

No way, I thought. We're well seaward of the shipping lanes. I'll just watch.

And I did, but for insurance, I took *Endymion* off course another 25 degrees, sailing due south. Again I saw only his port side red light.

OK, that's better I thought, relax Skip.

The green appeared again.

"What the fuck," I muttered. "Tony, get up here! Be quick! Tony!

Wake up, damn it!"

"Jeeze, Dad, I'm just nodding off."

"Well get up—I need you *now* Tony—and flip on the radar. We've got a situation."

"OK, Pops, radars on," Tony said, poking his head from the companionway, wearing tussled hair and a look of concern. "What's the radar target?"

I showed Tony what his "rising star" had become.

"I'll scope it." And he disappeared into the cabin, his voice trailing behind.

"Shit!" I heard from below. "This isn't right!"

Like me, Tony was worried. On this vast ocean with no conceivable reason for vessels to even come close, the freighter appeared to purposely have altered course to come close—maybe even hit us. It doesn't happen often, but the coast of Mexico is known for suspected collisions of ships with small yachts. Sometimes the watch is asleep. Sometimes both vessels are on autopilot—and sometimes it's murder! "Dad, give me the wheel and you look at the radar." Tony pushed past me, sounding concerned and determined to change places.

"You're better at the radar than me."

I set the range to ten miles and stared into the screen. There was no question. We were on a collision course, two blips on a radar screen aiming to bump into each other in this whole empty ocean.

"Go starboard another 20 degrees." I yelled to Tony. "Starboard 20 she is," he repeated.

I watched the scope intently. It took a minute, but ever so slowly the invader also altered course. There was no mistaking that he was changing course with us—aiming for us. I struggled to remain calm. To the freighter, we were wingless, helpless sitting ducks.

I picked up both the VHF and High Seas radios: "Vessel northbound at 27.58 degrees north and 115.32 degrees west, this is the southbound US flag sailing yacht *Endymion*. Do you read me?"

Silence.

Concentrating to remain calm, I repeated, "Captain—do you read me? Acknowledge please."

Only awkward, empty silence. Then from my radio came one hair-raising word:

"Yes," followed by painful silence.

"Captain," said I, "we have altered course by 55 degrees to avoid you. My radar has you inside five miles. I am switching on our strobe light for further identification. Your intentions, please?"

No reply.

Tony and I were both visibly frightened. I read it in his face and eyes. I was shaking, thinking to myself, *Could this really be happening?*

"Tony, I don't know what to tell you. We don't have many choices here."

Handing me a life jacket and flare packet, Tony said, "Put this on, Dad. Stay calm."

We put the jackets on. Tony verified the freighter's course by holding our hand-held compass over the ship's binnacle. They matched.

We jibed over and bore off another 20 degrees. A slowly rising wind had us plowing through choppy seas with some rolling. The freighter stayed with us. I gave the radio another try.

"Captain of the northbound freighter at latitude 27.58 north, longitude 115.32 West, I repeat—what are your intentions?"

In a thick foreign tongue came a chilling response: "What are *your* intentions, *captain*?"

All I could think was *we're doomed*. No matter our course change, this mammoth vessel, one hundred times our size, showed clearly his red and green running lights even with the more choppy sea, meaning he had altered course with us, and could shortly run us down.

On deck, Tony and I struggled to figure how to avoid collision, including using our engine for easier maneuverability. The Perkins was on, idling smoothly, unaware of demands to come. Tony removed the locking pin from our survival raft. We knew the raft would be our last resort—we should stay with the yacht if humanly possible.

The high seas radio shocked us, bursting to life with a crystal-clear Yankee voice: "*Endymion—Endymion—Endymion*. This is the Shell Oil tanker, *Sea Shell*. I have you in my radar. I believe you will miss, but it will be close. *Sea Shell* standing by channel 16."

Comforting.

"Thank you *Sea Shell*. Any advice?"

"Beware his wake, and being sucked in if you pass close. *Sea Shell* out."

Every sailor who has crossed shipping lanes knows the low *whomp whomp whomp* noise of large propellers turning beneath the sea. It's concerning to hear it coming, and relieving to hear it pass. We heard it closing on us.

I went to the radio, "*Sea Shell, Sea Shell, Sea Shell*, what do you think? How close?" I stammered into the radio, while Tony attempted to drive *Endymion* further off course.

Concentrate, Skip, I told myself, stay within your two-foot zone. "Check your harness, Dad. Check the quick release—we could get rolled." Tony's voice quivered.

We could see the outline of this huge shadowy hull coming toward us, bearing down on us like impending doom—the closer it came, the less sky we saw.

Tony worked the sails for every ounce of speed he could squeeze from them. I put my hand on his shoulder.

Whomp, whomp, whomp. Getting louder—closing on us.

I worked the wheel, swung hard and jammed the Perkins to full throttle. The monster seemed to move with us.

Seconds away, the stars completely disappeared behind the massive mountain of the freighter.

"Endymion, Endymion, Endymion. This is Sea Shell. I think you will miss."

"That's bullshit! Hang on, Dad," Tony shouted over the rising noise of the freighter's engines. All reference to the horizon disappeared as the phantom ship slid by a mere 100 feet from us, violently rolling *Endymion* in its powerful wash, drenching us in the stench of burning diesel and throwing me hard into the lifelines.

Tony harnessed to the mast, yelled, "You OK, Dad?" "I'm fine Tony, but I took a spill. Did you get his name?"

"Can't read Arabic or whatever the fuck it was. But I saw plenty of scrapes on the hull."

"Yeah, I dropped the spotlight when I fell. I wanted to see a hailing port on his transom."

"Win some, lose some, Dad. At least we're alive." She flew no flag. She made no apology.

Our masthead is six stories high. Our intruder, at least ten stories, missed sending us to the bottom and certain death by a field goal attempt. "*Why,*" I asked myself, "*in this vast endless ocean where we are thirty-three nautical miles offshore, far from shipping lanes, did this behemoth vagabond freighter latch onto us?"*

I called *Sea Shell*. "Captain, our thanks, Sir. We're shaken, but OK. Could you identify the vessel?"

"No, she maintained radio silence except that short passage with you. There are gypsies at sea. Be careful and safe passage, *Endymion*. *Sea Shell* clear."

Sunrise the next day hushed my nerves and I awoke with a prayer: *"Thank you Lord. That was a close one. Tony thinks you've sent us on a training mission. You have the controls up there, my friend. Be kind to us please."*

Munching cereal, Tony said, "Maybe God was testing us again, and two questions, Dad. You didn't see the Shell tanker on the radar? Why was he out of the shipping lanes?"

"Nope," I answered, "I didn't see him because I was using the 10-mile radius ring or closer and he must have been further out. To your second question, I have no idea."

"Consider this," chirped Tony. "You were looking at roughly 5 of 60,000,000 square Pacific Ocean miles, and this ass wanted the same quarter square mile you did. Blow your mind Dad? It does mine."

We sailed on, believing the unknown captain of a Shell oil taker saved our lives that star-bright, terrifying night.

CHAPTER 9

CABO SAN LUCAS

At 1130 January 25th we rounded the legendary, much-photo-graphed rocks at the tip of the Baja peninsula, to enter fabled Cabo San Lucas on Super Bowl Sunday. We sensed a party!

Later, neither of us was able to remember watching the Denver Broncos or New York Giants. It had been appropriate, perhaps compulsory, for us to release steam following two weeks of no alcohol voyaging. Tony had been a splendid first mate in every sense, and I needed to express my gratitude. We had an abundance of fun in Cabo, as friends as well as father–son. Tony, once moderately bashful, had become self-confident and assertive. I loved it.

In the days to follow, we bonded with other party-minded souls. We couldn't be as laid back as our Mexican hosts, but we tried by limiting ourselves to one daily chore like scrubbing decks or changing oil. We lathered up with two genuine fresh water showers a week. Every other night, duty included cocktail hour in a different cantina, where we chose to stay reasonably responsible, though I doubt either of us would succeed at tending bar. An exceptional place was "Pappy's." We never discovered who exactly "Pappy" was, but we enjoyed his inexpensive food, hospitality, and unreliable TV, a tube model, I believe.

Tony met his first 'cougar,' a blonde hair stylist on holiday, more than a few years his senior. She hounded Tony incessantly for a chance to rearrange his handsome, curly, sun-bleached locks. Why it required her staying aboard several nights I'm not certain, because even the slight motion of *Endymion*, made her violently ill, assuring Tony's one chore the next day—a slop clean up. There must have been some chemistry though. She cut and styled his hair. Black & Decker could have done a better job.

Tony with his catch of the day.

By the time we sailed on to the small fishing village of Los Frailes on February 4th, we were a relaxed and tanned father–son team enjoying an uncommon bond and an enviable, spirited lifestyle, including some great fishing.

CHAPTER 10

LAID BACK IN FRAILES

The airstrip for both Cabo and Los Frailes was located halfway between them and would be a terrifying place to land—even sober. Flights arriving and departing were mostly ancient Douglas Aircraft DC-3s from the 1930s and 40s. They once revolutionized air transport and made a significant contribution to the Allied campaigns of World War Two.

For me, seeing this dusty airstrip was personal. My Dad had worked for American Airlines at LaGuardia airport in New York City during the war. As a child, I visited Santa Claus in a DC-3 cockpit every Christmas. I wanted to see the vintage trophies to aviation ingenuity fly one more time, check to see if Santa was still hanging around.

I got my wish watching one clattering in from the sea. I was amazed the relic had been able to get airborne in the first place. The prop wash created vast clouds of ugly fine dust on approach to the dirt runway before it bounced eventually to an uneven, restful stop, surrounded instantly by a human sea of hawkers.

Equally ancient as the flying machines were the multi-colored taxis that barreled through the dust and rushed down the runway chasing the still-rolling plane with engines still sputtering, to introduce the newcomers to their first taste of Mexican hospitality. It served to remind Tony and me, watching from our rented motorbikes, just how far the world had come since World War Two.

We had come to Los Frailes to case it out, and it was worth it. Back aboard *Endymion* and approaching our anchorage, we passed incredible homes teetering on rugged rock cliffs overlooking the sea. We suspected they were grand but inexpensive, at least by U.S. standards. This was a remote area with dense vegetation. Sea breezes developing daily carried moisture to assist the thriving plants. Views over the sea from these lavish brick and tile haciendas, we observed, would surely attract wealthy weekenders—those brave enough to hop aboard one of those DC-3s, with tin galleyware bearing the logo of defunct airline TWA and seats marked 'property of American Airlines.'

This was a miniature slice of semi-tropical low income living, where prices, I was confident, would advance over time, eventually catching up with the world. The indigenous population were poor by our standards, but wealthy compared to their cousins on mainland Mexico. The locals were gentle, smiling, courteous—but not industrious.

Sailors aboard other sailing craft anchored at Los Frailes invited us aboard for cocktails or dinner. Generally speaking, however, we were the odd couple, being just a couple of guys. It was good for Tony and me because we continued to bond in a way I suspect many parents never get to enjoy with their children. We were referred to as 'characters,' and we liked that.

Barry and Catherine Zimmerman, aboard their 34-ft. steel cutter *Saskia,* named for Rembrandt's first wife, were standouts for Tony and me. I guessed them to be in their early thirties, consistently cheerful and wanting to share their joy. Tony left some expensive film at a processor in Cabo. It was to be forwarded to us, but that didn't happen. The Zimmerman's picked it up for Tony and carried it all the way to Manzanillo, where we saw them next.

Los Frailes was also where I caught up on correspondence. Several letters from my folks had found us, and a healthy stack from Denise. Dad and I were close, and had written regularly since I left home 28 years ago. Lately, with frequent address changes and dubious postal services, Dad had started numbering letters so I'd know if I missed any. Denise had written wonderful letters daily, brimming with love and support, though I feared she was terribly lonely, being here only vicariously when she longed to be here in person.

It didn't seem fair that Tony and I basked in sunlight and sipped margaritas served by pretty young Mexican girls (though often pregnant), while Denise lay at home in pain suffering through doctors' appointments during a cold and miserable Southern California winter. Her cheery letters always carried an embedded keepsake whiff of her favorite fragrance. The mail carrier must have enjoyed them. The challenge with Denise's messages, were the intimate romantic phrases, which sorely reminded me that it had been two months since my last female contact, kissing Denise goodbye on a fuel dock. That hardly satisfied my desires, but if her leg healed well enough, she would meet us in Manzanillo before our Pacific crossing in early April. Privately, I suspected her doctor might discourage travel because of the possibility of complications with a hip cast. But when her mind is set, Denise is not to be lightly challenged. We would face that later.

65

For the time being, we had to face the lovely mahi-mahi Tony had brought home for dinner.

Before leaving Los Frailes, and because it was so beautiful, Tony and I spent another day hiking the beach. We stumbled upon a scruffy gaggle of Americans who claimed they had been camping at this beach site for twelve years.

"Sorta strange," mumbled Tony, low and privately. "Very strange," I responded.

They possessed a shambles of a mobile home, and that was a generous description for the rubble they called home. Though invited, neither Tony nor I chose to go inside. Robinson Crusoe was likely better dressed. There were six in all—two men, four women, and no children. They were friendly, even though we didn't venture inside, and invited us for lobster on the grill, so we rowed out to fetch a couple of sixers of Budweiser for the occasion.

"I seen better hair on a wholly mammoth, but least they don't stink!" Tony was skeptical.

"I dunno Tony, strikes me it could be a cultural evening. Maybe they have been here that long. I'm curious. Why, do you think they're dangerous?"

"Naw, they're too damn skinny—probably hopped up on something we might like," said Tony, smoothly guiding our inflatable alongside *Endymion's* boarding ladder.

That night we spoke of worldly things with six pleasant, highly unusual, well-educated individuals, who had simply opted for another lifestyle. One was a former accountant; two had been teachers, and one an operating room RN. They hadn't drunk the Kool-Aid. They had decided a future in the competitive American workplace wasn't their choice. In truth, their thinking and mine travelled on parallel rails.

We drank our beer, sampled some homegrown 'stuff' from a local plant, liked it, and had more. The word 'drugs' never entered the conversation.

Back in the inflatable, I slurred, "Whadda ya think now, Tony— still thinking drugs?"

"Yeah, I'm thinking there's a connection."

"Their choice, their world," I offered. "It takes a village."

"Easy there, Pops," Tony remarked as we boarded *Endymion,* anxious to weigh anchor for Mazatlan .

"Perfect morning!" exclaimed Tony at sunrise. "Today, somewhere in the Sea of Cortes our log should roll over 1000 nautical miles."

"Let's get at it . . . up anchor!" I chimed in.

It was Sunday, February 8th, a perfect day with winds at 10–12 knots from 60 degrees apparent. We fell into what had become a Sunday ritual. Tony dressed only in shorts and me with not much more, under the sun, at sea, with Reverend Chuck from Calvary Chapel Church, telling us as it is, from our on-deck speakers. We prayed for all those in suits and ties, sweating it out back home, while we lived for the moment in the truly perfect world our creator had prepared for us. It wasn't a serious prayer.

We had a problem. I had noticed, not for the first time, our engine was overheating in the short period we used it for getting underway. It concerned me.

A shark swam lazily alongside for a few minutes and a six-foot-wide sea turtle, plentiful in this food-rich warm water, dazzled us with its amazing speed when we sailed close. But no fish, on or under the surface liked our bait.

"Hey Tony . . . how about next time we stick a hook through you and give you a toss?"

I was awarded a finger.

Sailing into a dark night with Tony asleep below, I was again reminded of the majesty of the universe. With calm seas, a slight breeze, warm night, and crystal-clear skies, I had it all. I felt a little sad for everyone who dreams of doing something like this, and doesn't. I understood why, though. It's one thing to have dreams and quite another to make them real. My advice—toss the stress. Get free. Go cruising, mountain climbing, ballooning, or whatever. The harmony you'll discover drifting and blending in with whatever area you choose will be mind-bending. "I wish tonight," I whispered to the wind, "that every living person, may have just one night like this one."

And God answered—at that moment, there was a burst of shooting stars brilliantly lighting the dark sky. The sound of nothing was overwhelming!

"Thank you, God."

I wondered then about city folks who maybe, never in their lives, had heard the powerful sound of silence. I have been *so* lucky.

My log entry, in fact, for 0430 said, "God was here tonight— Thank you God!"

The lights of Mazatlán winkled on the horizon as the sky began its morning awakening, and I turned the helm to Tony for his watch. "Something stinks!" Tony exclaimed as he handed me my morning cuppa Joe.

A moment later he was yelling from below "Shut-er down Dad-smoke in the engine room."

Turning off the Perkins I noticed the heat gauge and wondered two things—why hadn't the alarm sounded and why hadn't I noticed. Had I been that tired? Tony replaced a faulty impeller and we were underway a half-hour later on flat seas and with a light breeze. We gave the Perkins a rest.

"What's that?" I asked Tony, cocking an ear, "Sounds like a motor."

Tony listened for a moment. "No problem. It's a plane, father so stupid."

High above, sunlight illuminating its wing, a jet to somewhere was boring a hole in the sky—the first jet we had seen or heard since leaving San Diego. Two hours later, we found its destination when we entered the filthy, noisy, unimpressive harbor of Mazatlán, Mexico.

CHAPTER 11

PRETTY GIRLS
AND POLLUTION

O ur disappointment with Mazatlán's commercial harbor conditions was immediate. Attempting to set anchor we repeatedly
pulled up twisted pieces of rusty metal with oily

rags and debris clinging to them. I had the sense every move was
watched by dozens of eyes, causing me to suspect thievery in these
parts. I decided not to leave the boat at night.

Once anchored, we locked *Endymion* down tight, securely stowed
everything of value below decks and set out through sultry, humid air
thick enough to wear it, to find customs and immigration check in.
As dictated by Mexican logic, neither was located in or near the port,
so we walked two blistering hours before finding the Port Captain.
Fortunately, our clearing went smoothly.

We next checked out the beachfront, an end-to-end collection of
brassy-looking hotels. The saving grace in the sea of humanity was

sighting a bounty of apparently well-heeled female tourists in skimpy (thank you, Lord) swimming suits.

"I gotta think," mused Tony, "all these people are blind to the poverty surrounding this street."

"I dunno, son, I doubt even the blind could miss it. Some pickpocket will find em—for sure."

"Yeah, crime is probably the leading economic provider." Looking around, I surmised Tony had pegged this one. We stopped for a couple of cool drinks in a beachfront bar, grabbed some groceries, and took an exhaust-belching cab back to the harbor.

Tony and I decided to take deck watches, at least for the first night. "I'll swing the first one," volunteered Tony, also suggesting four-hour watches. We settled on two hours to keep us more alert.

I spent most of my first watch wondering about the people aboard the jet that had flown over us that morning. What had they been talking about up there? Was there a delicious in-flight meal? How many were businessmen under pressure from an employer in a distant city? Did they see the little yacht sailing toward Mazatlán in the dawn's early light? *Hey, that was us*, I thought. Could they have wondered what our life was like, floating on a vast sea, where careers and city life were unheard of, distant considerations? Probably not, but it gave me a perverse secret joy to consider it.

Tony took over at 0200, and we shared a cuppa Joe.

"You know, Pops," Tony opened a dialogue, "I'm excited about tomorrow."

"Yeah, what's up?"

"Kim will be here mid-afternoon. I just wish we had a more romantic anchorage to start her visit."

"And what do you mean by 'start her visit'?"

"Well, she quit her job, Dad, so there's no pressure to go back. Maybe she can just hang with us—(long pause)—and be part of the crew?"

I felt blindsided. There it was, our first difficult discussion since San Diego. Kim, as cute a California blonde as any movie or joke ever created, was also as flakey.

Attempting to mask my disappointment by sounding considerate, I said. "Gee, Tony, I hadn't thought about it. I'm guessing she's flat broke. I know you don't have much, and I'm not sure I'm keen to assume care and feeding responsibility, as well as her general safety. Remember, this is Kimmy."

"What's that supposed to mean?"

"Well, she's your girlfriend, and you call her bonehead. Right?"

"Yeah. I'm joking, though."

"Well, Tony, she's not a brain trust. Boats are complicated. How about we welcome her tomorrow and figure it out over the next couple of weeks?" I was confident a couple of weeks with Bonehead would take the wind from Tony's sails.

"Sure, Pops, that works—and she has letters from Denise."

Tony appeared happy with the results of our short talk, so I excused myself, but was halted dead in my tracks descending the companionway.

"Dad, is this real love?"

"Is that a serious question, Tony?"

"Yes. You're in love with Denise. How did **you** know it's real?"

"Oh boy—you are serious, aren't you?" I said reappearing on deck.

"Well, Tony, first thing—I can't say for sure I'm in love with Denise. I think so, but I can't say for sure."

"Could have fooled me," said Tony, "the way you act together."

"Let's see, Tony, if I can explain. With Denise and me, we went through a pretty short period of infatuation. You know what that is?" "Yeah, Pops, sex, parties, and rock n roll!"

I let his comment go. "Well, if your definition is right, infatuation continues for Denise and me, and that's terrific, but infatuation is still a time of doubts. For us it took only a couple of months to build a truly abiding friendship. I believe that's because planning this trip drew us closer. Anyway, we started acting and feeling more like one, perhaps as soul mates might. We're at the high end of that curve now, and the deep love we all want so much, is, for us, right around the corner."

"Meaning what?" Tony grumbled.

"Meaning you asked a damn good question. I'll say infatuation is different than deep friendship and the deeper meaning of love doesn't come without first having the abiding friendship. Where are you and Kim in this, Tony? Infatuation?"

"I was just asking a question, Dad, but thanks. You're probably right. Infatuation. Can that also mean obsession, because that's what I feel."

"I'm going to bed, Tony. Goodnight," I said, thinking of the early commitment Denise had made to sail with me, to entrust me with her life and future. A remarkable young lady, and yes, I believe in love.

Tony and Kim met in high school and found romantic attraction the summer following graduation. Kim became a mostly unemployed hair stylist, and Tony had rescued the tall, thin, attractive blonde. I liked Kim and believed they cared for each other in a dreamy, youthfully exciting way, but I put the brakes on calling her "bright." Tony had become a splendid crew. He did anything I asked, but normally didn't look for things to do. With Kim aboard, I sensed things would be different, that Tony would likely be less focused. I fell into an uncomfortable sleep, wondering if maybe I was a wee bit jealous of this bright-eyed perky blonde who would soon be sharing my son's attention—attempting to pickpocket his heart.

Tony shook me awake for my watch. Kim was still on my mind, and I hadn't slept well. Tony was going ashore to pick up Kim and needed money. Tony managed money poorly, spending every cent he had as quickly as he got it. But, when we were in places like the open-air market or around underprivileged children, he always reached for his pocket to give what he had. The world was a better place because of people like Tony. I gave him what he wanted.

Kim and Tony were late from the airport. It didn't matter much on 'mañana' time. They had obviously stopped for her semi-official introduction to Jose Cuervo. I knew this because she fell out of the inflatable trying to climb aboard *Endymion*, but managed with wild thrashing, and a strong lift from Tony, to keep her head above the harbor sludge and get aboard. Her backpack carried mail from Denise and luckily it was in the second, more secure transfer from the Avon, so I too, had a pleasing end to my day.

We allowed Kim a day of sobering up. She wanted to go fishing. Imagine that! We went, and learned it was a mistake to fish during or just after a full moon because fish feed continuously in moonlight and had no interest in our bait. We also learned professionals like the one we hired don't do much different than we do. Most important, we learned never to hire a guide again because we didn't catch a damn thing.

"Well, that was fun. Let's hit the bars, Tony!" Bonehead had spoken.

That night the two partied while I read and reread my letters from Denise, one of which offered a timely fantasy for being alone on Valentine's Day. Good therapy—but a long night's deck watch.

75

The following day I invested in a call to my parents in Florida, who were concerned because they had not heard from me for almost a month. I gave them a slow burn explanation about Mexican Postal Authorities and what might have gone amiss. We came to a conclusion, which worked well for many years. We started numbering our letters on the envelope. In the end, a few letters were lost, and confusion took hold as Dad gained years and mixed up the numbers. No problem, especially if it was to be our worst—which it was not.

The next day, Kim and Tony were taking pictures in Old Mazatlán, giving me precious time to be alone. I noticed the anemometer beginning to rise. I took a couple of bearings to be prudent, and went below to tackle morning dishes. Standing in the galley, I felt we were heeling (tipping or leaning). I jumped topside and found us nearly broadside to almost gale force winds whistling through the rigging.

They call these Mexican winds a Chubasco. On steamy hot days like this one, they race down from the mountains to cool over the ocean. They are capable of havoc.

Endymion was dragging anchor—moving toward a pile of slippery rocks.

I jolted the Perkins diesel from its snooze and dove into the tiny locker housing the remote control for the anchor windless, something I was really glad I had added as an accessory. As I screwed the remote into place, I put the engine in gear and *Endymion* rode up on her anchor, enabling me, alone with the remote, to get the anchor off the bottom and away from the harbor's debris field of rusty anchor chains that had become the death knell of decaying freighters. I moved a quarter mile out, dropped again and seemed to hold. Wind was down to 30 knots, having dissipated as rapidly as it had arisen. When we started to drag I had out seven times scope—all chain. Had I been ashore with Tony and Kim, we could have been seriously damaged. I just accepted what had happened and put another check mark on my growing list of respect for nature.

Sitting in the cockpit, measuring my good fortune at being aboard the last half hours' near calamity, I bowed my head: *"Dearest Lord,"* I offered, *"I owe you another one for guiding me to purchase an anchor remote. By the way . . . did I say my thanks for the masthead strobe light? It's handy . . . keep it working for us and I'll do my end. Your buddy Skip—out!"*

The wind dropped to a twenty-knot breeze. Chubascos can be fickle, though. I hoped Tony and Kim would choose a lull in the wind to row out to their mother ship. The Honda outboard wasn't on the Avon (because of theft), so it could be a tough row against 20 knots trying to keep Tony's expensive photo gear dry.

Fortunately, they spent the night ashore. Fun for them and worry for me, but all was safe and forgiven in the morning. Cruising is not for those who keep schedules.

CHAPTER 12

UP THE RIVER

Forsaking the noise and clutter of Mazatlán with its wall-to-wall tourists was a pleasure! Something had been toxic about the mixture of overheated tourist sweat, bargirl perfume, and exhaust, both mechanical and human. Clearing the polluted harbor, we felt invigorated—plus we were anxious to further blend with the real people of Mexico. For this segment of our journey, we welcomed aboard good friends, Art Taylor, and his partner, Laurie. Perhaps this gave Kim a feeling of seniority, as she seemed to take to her 'fluff' duties with renewed vigor. Kim was amusing to observe, assuming the self-appointed role of leading lady by showing our guests around. But, I admit, fluff and fold Kimmy was slowly finding a place in my heart as a pleasant young soul with intoxicating spirit and energy.

Art and Laurie had been with Denise and me when *Endymion* arrived in Los Angeles as freighter deck cargo. We had all worked to remove the shrink-wrap around the yacht, while sipping champagne—to relieve fears of nuclear poisoning, we told each other.

Now these nice folks were aboard. Two fishing lines instantly appeared. Art claimed fishing as his area of expertise.

"The lines will get a varsity workout," Art boasted, "Mine will have the trophy catch."

"You're fulla crap, Art!" Tony replied, testing the pull on his Penn reel. That evening, with gentle seas, a soft breeze and setting sun, we dined on mahi-mahi. Ditto the next breakfast, and next lunch. All landed by Tony.

We arrived at Isla Isabella at dusk. All except me were anxious to go ashore to do some trading for lobster. I never knew which of our ship's supplies were going up for barter. Usually beer was in the equation, and if Tony could slip one past me, I would lose a couple of my coveted Billabong T-shirts. Flashlights, magazines, and candy were hits as well—and Krazy Glue, believe it or not, fetched top lobster, but it required a demonstration to make the point and for this, we called again on Kim.

"Watch this!" Tony would say as Kim held out a hook, to which Tony would then attach squirmy bait by using Krazy Glue. The stunt, repeated frequently, earned us a lot of the tasty crustaceans.

Our intended next port of call was San Blas. Art read with interest from the sailing directions: "Located on a river flowing through dense jungle to the Pacific. River entrance shoaling can be dangerous due to shifting. Yachts entering this remote area are urged to exercise extreme caution."

"Cool," said Kim.

Tony looked skeptical. "I was talking with those guys from San Diego, on the charter boat in Mazatlán, remember them?"

No one did, so Tony kept going. "They were up this river . . . I think it was this one, anyway, and they told me there's a whole bunch of Mexican marines in the area and they search everyone who passes."

"Yeah, so big deal," said Art. "Your dad was a marine and look how harmless he is!"

"Thanks, pal," came from me.

"My sentiments, too," Laurie added, lifting the pen from a letter she was writing. "Once this cop pulled me over, an asshole, it took forever for him to search my car. He just wanted a date, I think . . ."

"I can see that," Interrupted Tony.

". . . and I know I personally don't want some sweaty Mexican pawing through my things!" continued Laurie.

"Or pawing you either," Kim proudly declared, like she had made a major contribution to an international debate.

"I'll make this decision for everyone," I said, rising behind the wheel to demonstrate authority. "Kim—Tony—anyone else with contraband, toss it or smoke it. We came to see this part of the world, and that's what we're going to do. As your Captain, I'll be cautious. We shouldn't be worried."

"So we can't have smokum on board?" Tony interrupted again.

"Right, Tony, and we can't be influenced by rumors from semi-sober charter fishermen who may, or may not, have been where they say they have been."

My little speech caused everyone to leave the salon. Shortly, I was bathed in the familiar blue haze of 'private stuff' being disposed of.

We entered the San Blas River at daylight with Tony and Art standing bow watch, pointing out shallow areas to avoid or changes in water color, indicating shoaling. We had no problems, nor did we experience overly curious military checking us out as we passed their marine base, dropping anchor in fifteen feet of river water with a slight current taking us seaward, thus aligning and holding us broadside to a tiny village. Only a modest 20-foot anchorage separated us from a sullen, tired-looking group of village women, laboring over laundry on the river's edge. I counted nine small mud and timber hut dwellings, several goats, and limitless chickens against a backdrop of truly forbidding, dense green jungle.

It was a setting of contrasts—my carefully maintained sailing yacht from another country anchored in the midst of what could only be described as Mexican poverty—happy poverty. We had hardly set anchor before a scruffy group of laughing children were swimming around *Endymion*, offering to be our guide or run errands. They were cute, and the laundry ladies, seeing us wave at them, waved back—broad smiles lighting dark faces as if to made their burdens lighter, whether it was heavy wet clothing being sloshed through the current, or baskets of drying fruit stacked atop heads sitting on shoulders made firm by years repetitious toil.

"This all makes me feel so lucky," Laurie said, looking toward the shoreline wash rack.

"Yeah, me too," came from Kim.

You don't know the half of it, I thought.

The girls chose one particularly handsome youngster, a strapping teenager named Pedro, to be our guide, interpreter, and local friend. His mother taught in the one-room school. His father, grandfather, and three brothers had been lost at sea as fishermen—all in the same storm. It was tough to listen to the story or imagine its impact on these gentle people. Our lives, so gadget-oriented and complicated, were so different than their simplistic, straightforward, and too often tragic existence.

Pedro offered to take us up the river in his 'ponga' to see monkeys. We were delighted. The lad proved a skilled skipper of his small boat and an informative guide—and the family breadwinner. We later met the family, all seven surviving children and mom, none of who gave the slightest hint that tipping Pedro would be appreciated. But we did and Pedro earned his keep, taking us to places where wild pigs ran loose, and Art and Laurie ran after the wild pigs. Fools! Kim had a horseback ride on what looked like a donkey; while dozens of brightly colored cackling parrots eyed us from trees along the river's edge.

We also learned that a crop favored by Tony, and illegal in America, was grown just a short hike from the village. We hardly missed Tony and Kim when they disappeared for a few hours.

With the girls promising Pedro they would write, we sailed from San Blas on the morning tide, going southeast to a picturesque, obscure little cove called Chalaka, fifty miles distant, another semi-safe anchorage with sparkling white sandy beaches on which rested two inviting restaurants. Certainly they would have lobster and chilled beer.

That morning being a Sunday, the girls requested to dress up for a meal ashore. However, an obvious, tricky shore break was going to make landing the Avon difficult. Tony and I held a brief management meeting.

"OK, here's the plan," I announced. "Tony and I will swim ashore, check out the restaurant, and then help you guys bring the Avon through the surf. Art, you drive. Kim and Laurie, you'll be passengers, one on each seat forward of Art. Carry your shoes because you could get wet to the knees, in the landing."

We were unintentionally misleading. This shore break was wicked. The girls, dressed to the nines, placed themselves in the Avon as instructed. Art, we knew, was not an experienced inflatable driver. With the girls looking every bit like Easter Sunday parade participants, they came roaring toward the shore, kamikaze Art at the helm—girls hanging on. The first wave to catch them sent the Avon into a broach, and the second wave sent them all, arms flailing and hair flying, into the surf. Tony and I had a chuckle. The others were pissed off.

Another day blending.

CHAPTER 13

SKY SNAKE

The first storm Tony and I encountered shortly after exiting San Diego was due to our own stupidity. We hadn't given attention to multiple reports about the Yukon Express and took unnecessary risks, not wanting to delay our departure again, which had been stalled by Denise's unfortunate accident. Now we had no reliable weather forecasts, and depended on pilot charts, common sense (now there's an oxymoron), and informative books relating to weather for the mariner.

Puerto Vallarta sits inside a 24-mile bay called Banderas Bay. Some reading this may recall the movie, *Night of the Iguana*, filmed here, where crusty ugly iguanas are in ample supply. We found them docile, shy, and reclusive, unless cornered, which makes them angry—like any cornered creature.

The entrance to Banderas Bay is narrow and congested. Massive, threatening, angry black clouds chased us as we sailed close to land approaching the narrow entrance—it's seaside marker just visible three miles distant. The wind rose steadily and quickly.

"I'm not liking this!" said Tony, gripping the wheel and looking astern as the water began to froth and the wind played tunes in the rigging.

"I don't feel so good," moaned Art, appearing ghostly pale.

The sudden squall hit fiercely. Within minutes seas became confused, steep and close, as they do in shallow water, but *Endymion* performed beautifully. We reefed the main at twenty knots apparent wind and were sailing fast: "Nine knots," shouted Kim . . . just hit ten—ten there, you guys!"

The wind was abeam and we were in an exhilarating groove that couldn't last because we needed a course and sail change at the harbor buoy now a half-mile away.

Next came lightning, followed immediately by deafening thunder, telling us the storm was imminent. We had caught a fierce chubasco by the tail, and that tail was shaking us.

Then came rain so intense we could hardly see the bow from the cockpit. Tony and I, acting as a team, leapt back and forth checking instruments, radar, radios, and headings.

Art was having a hard go of it. Wretchedly seasick, he lay in a lee-side salon berth, firmly clutching a bucket. Laurie had the humor to toss him a teddy bear.

Like most chubasco storms, this one ended as it started—fast. We dropped sail and headed for Nuevo Vallarta, a new marina with new docks a few miles north of the city.

"Docks . . . really! We'll be connected to land for the first time since San Diego. Nice!" Tony was excited. "Fresh water, electricity, a real shower . . . We're stylin it."

Art and Laurie had jobs so they headed back to the States. Kim didn't face work issues, but she also left. There were typical goodbyes, but I believe Tony was ready for this. His eye had begun to wander. Was his infatuation perhaps declining?

Nuevo Vallarta was home for eight blazing hot days. With summer still months away, several yachts planned to make this their permanent home, and one Canadian chap had set up a ham radio net.

One morning a yacht's skipper was on the VHF radio complaining: "I have no idea in hell how it got there, but this morning I nearly stepped barefooted on a coral snake wriggling his way aft on my deck."

"Bullshit!" answered another boat. "Coral snakes are not swimmers—especially in salt water."

The snake boat owner promised to meet curious nature lovers at the customs office at high noon. Tony and I went, and sure enough, there was a colorful, now deceased coral snake in a Jiffy peanut butter jar. We concluded the poor fellow had been snatched by a bird, which lost its passenger flying over the anchorage, and dropped the little critter on the yacht's deck, still alive and able to strike, perhaps like a cornered iguana.

Generally speaking, Puerto Vallarta was a destination with plenty of activity and a wide assortment of vessels. I was impressed the way cruisers helped each other. During our short stay two rescues took place involving our marina neighbors. A desperate cry for help from a small 23-foot sloop sailed by a young California couple said their boat was breaking up in rough seas twenty miles off the coast. A large Mexican powerboat from Nuevo Vallarta, with a group of volunteer yacht owners from the marina, went to their rescue. The relieved couple tied to the dock next to us showing high spirits by pledging to continue their adventure. Truth be told, not many quitters get this far south. Most, who become overwhelmed by the rigors and danger of cruising, tend to turn north no further south than Cabo San Lucas.

The second rescue involved *Encore*, a 57-foot, high-tech racing sloop, also from Newport Beach, that lost its keel while slugging it out sailing north from Acapulco against wind and sea. (Remember, going north—mail it.) Taking on water, *Encore* was in grave danger of sinking. A Coast Guard plane, actually dispatched from somewhere in Alaska, had parachuted a pump and raft. The pump failed (can you believe it?) and the same group of guys from this marina went to sea again, put a temporary patch on the leak, and towed them in.

CHAPTER 14

CHOOSING OFFSHORE CREW

Wherever boats are moored, crew is available. While in Puerto Vallarta, Tony and I made progress selecting additional crew for the upcoming 24 to 30 day haul across the Pacific to the Marquesas Islands.

The question "who do I take," had as many answers as "how do I carry my inflatable?"

Leaning toward taking strangers aboard for our offshore voyaging, we had important factors to consider.

We didn't want an addict, drunk, thief, or murderer. The chances of these occurring were slim, but possible—and I'd already lost one boat to thieves. Yachts are frequently in places where it's not easy or practical to check resumes and references, and the "perp" himself could have scripted glowing referral letters.

Our practice was to lay low and observe. Sometimes I would cruise an anchorage by dinghy, trolling for breakfast or cocktail invites, but never announcing a need for crew. I also watched where crews changed, and asked why. These are not always for negative reasons. Many times, destinations aren't convenient; time available is a question; maybe even personal goals. For certain, we learned quickly which ships were "happy" ships and which ones were not.

In one port, to illustrate unhappiness, we watched a fist fight between a well-paid engineer and captain of a large sailing yacht. The disgruntled mechanic was told to leave the yacht immediately. He was angry and possibly shorted a few severance pay dollars.

This mechanic knew the yacht's route and by phone alerted authorities in the next port that the yacht would arrive with hidden drugs. His argument was convincing. The yacht was stopped and searched keel to masthead for three days before being allowed entrance to the country, and no restoration work was done to bring the vessel back to its former pristine condition. All aboard were detained for the duration of the inspection, perhaps strip searched as well. The wealthy owner had nannies aboard for his children. Imagine that dilemma. The moral there, difficult as it may be, is to remain level headed, and kind, even to those you feel should walk the plank. A lesson I could later use myself.

We developed a superb crew selection plan that bore consistent results. When we located a likeable individual, we arranged the first interview away from the boat, perhaps for a lunch, where we could do more of that important observing. I wanted to know if they smiled, laughed, were easy going, and, most importantly, did this person seem happy. We would be living in close quarters where conditions could go from super to shit in seconds. Crew I could relate to and trust (that's a big one) was significantly more important to me than crew with skills. We could teach the skills.

If the prospective crew member showed promise, we invited them aboard the following day, telling them to show up in just a bathing suit and to bring nothing else—no handbag, wallet, sports grip, etc. This way Tony and I could show them *Endymion* without fear they may plant drugs or a weapon for future use. It had happened to others.

If we were confident a person would work out, we elevated the discussion to duties, sailing plans, meal preparation, and so forth, and then said something to the effect of, "We'll sail Tuesday morning. Please come by Sunday or Monday for a photo shoot. We take Polaroid's of our crew and send them to people expecting us in the next port."

We generally didn't know anyone in the next port, but even the dullest thief, pervert, or murderer would likely avoid that picture session. Damn cheap insurance that always worked.

For the most part, strangers who became our crew also became great friends, and those friendships have endured for years.

But sometimes, we made mistakes.

CHAPTER 15

BEYOND VALLARTA

A sloop in the Nuevo Vallarta marina had been sold, leaving crew to find another vessel. Jim 38, and his 27 year old mate Denise seemed to fit our criteria, were able, and agreed after interviews to a sea trial before the crossing. First they had unfinished business in Acapulco, so they would meet us in Manzinillo.

Jim was a licensed Captain and claimed to have operated Caribbean charters over the last five years—hard to verify from Mexico. Denise, a big woman, claimed to be a gourmet chef with a degree she couldn't produce from some fancy French school. They both presented resumes. Tony and I agreed Denise would have adjustments to make because we take turns as chef of the day, and anything more complicated than a burger crimps our style. The couple only wanted a lift to Tahiti and was willing to post bond, which comforted me. Always cautious, I faxed their references to my Denise in California with instructions for as thorough and speedy a background check as possible.

Sailing out of Vallarta with only Tony and me aboard was refreshing and we felt normal again. We had chuckles and fun with guests aboard, but Tony and I had developed a relaxed synergy that came from being together, and working together. We knew what each other was thinking, knew what to do when things develop suddenly, as happens aboard boats. We'd even worked out 'private time' privileges for remaining socially acceptable aboard a sometimes very short 43 foot yacht. Tony threw himself into a large beanbag chair we enjoyed having aboard. It was permanently positioned on the aft deck where its occupant needs not be involved in ships operations, unless required. When I wore a beat up, old favorite Los Angeles Rams ball cap my crew came to understand it meant 'don't bother me!'

Tony quipped it meant, "me and the Rams—two losers hanging out."

We were in perfect sailing conditions, moderate following seas, wind aft of abeam and the spinnaker pulling its load. Tony was asleep, content after beating himself in a hard fought game of backgammon. Sitting at the wheel, steering with one hand, my thoughts drifted again to Jim and Denise, our prospective trans-Pacific crew. I wasn't happy with myself. The guidelines I'd developed for crew selection were sound, so I asked myself why, in some vague way, was I already marginally uncomfortable with having them aboard. I couldn't put my finger on it specifically but sensed I had missed a warning when Denise didn't show evidence of her fancy cooking school completion and Jim hadn't produced a captain's license. It was more a caution flag warning in my mind than a red danger flag.

I moved to adjust the jib, allowing Tony to continue sleeping. I was nagged with the sense there's more to the couples story than I've been told.

"Damn…what is it?" I muttered to myself, gazing across the empty ocean still bothered but confident my Denise will do a thorough job checking resumes. We need extra hands for the crossing but there are so many stories floating around about crew who refuse to leave the boat after arrival. Some don't post a bond so immigration officials won't let them leave the boat, forcing the skipper to keep them for another passage, until some port authority relents, or looks the other way as his palm is greased. I won't let this happen. I'm not known for the patience it would require.

Anyway, we had time to work it through. There was hope too, my Denise would have her sea legs—but I doubt it. Denise, as a nurse, understands the importance of being healthy and fit when medical care may be hundreds of ocean miles away, or simply non-existent. Trusting her good judgment, I abandoned my defeating thoughts to get back to reality.

"Chow time Tony—get up and get busy!"

And so it went. We ate, slept, fished, exchanged chuckles and marveled at the balance of nature God had created for our pleasure. The radios were quiet except for one often repeated broadcast looking for a seventy eight year old single-handed sailor two weeks overdue reporting in by radio. He, too, had been sailing from south to north along the Mexican Pacific coast.

Tony, after one missing man broadcast, suggested "His family should be concerned, south to north at that age. If they ever find him he should get a gold 'dumb shit' card."

Our second night out we dropped anchor in a small cove between Cabo Corrientes and Ipala, Mexico.

We took a look around and there, a quarter mile away, was a dismasted, rough looking small sloop, sea grass clinging to its hull and decks a mess, answering precisely the description of the missing seniors boat. Minutes later there was a knock on our hull. Sitting in a beat up dinghy and hanging to our rail, was an able bodied, snowy white haired senior sailor, with a twinkle in his eye and a question on his mind, in search of a cold drink, someone to talk to and someone with a working radio. He was disabled after being dismasted and loosing his antenna.

"Name's Charlie. Would ya have a working radio—and maybe a cold drink?" he asked.

"You bet we do, Charlie," I said inviting him aboard for all the drinks he could ever wish for, plus todays catch, mahi mahi for dinner. "Damn chubasco caught me," explained Charlie, with fresh fish and a shot of scotch warming his innards. "Happened so fast. Pitch dark, couldn't see er comin. One moment everything was hunkey dorey, next I'm on my ear (sailing term for tipped way over). I couldn't get the sails loose fast enough and the damn mast snapped." "Anyone with you?" Tony asked.

"Naw, just me. Had a hellava time draggin the rig aboard and cuttin the rest free."

"The radio's been broadcasting about you a week now." Tony said, looking at the seasoned senior with awe, "when did it happen?" "Don't know how many days fer sure. I drifted—seemed like forever. Food was gettin sparse when this anchorage popped up. Used my outboard to get here. Be nice a you to radio my position."

We talked well into the night. Charlie was mentally alert. He didn't complain of injuries and we didn't see any, so we arranged a ham radio link to his greatly relieved family in Oregon, notified the Mexican authorities and arranged for an early morning tow into Ipala, the nearest port with medical facilities. Tony escorted Charlie back to his boat, making certain he was safely aboard before reassuring him help would arrive shortly after sunrise.

"That was a good thing we did," said Tony "but what I can't figure is what was he trying to prove by solo sailing as an old man?" "Maybe nothing," I replied, "and possibly a lot. We are all different. We all have our challenges. Maybe he liked solitude or was proving himself to his family. Heck Tony, a lot of people thought we were crazy, and what's our reason for being here?" "Because we want to!"

"Point made."

Shortly after dawn we watched Charlie be taken into tow by a Mexican naval vessel. All was well, so we headed south to our next coastal diversion, a tiny cove housing the only Club Med to be found on Mexico's West Coast. By carefully maneuvering in shallow waters and narrow channels marked by flimsy buoys, we were able to anchor less than two hundred meters from shore, and within easy view of a constant parade of bikinis, a sight we believed we had earned. Club officials allowed us to purchase colorful beads used as money at their venues. We stayed several days. Had we wished we could have had some topless escorts to Manzanillo. It would have been tough to explain the crew list to Immigration. So again we sailed alone, but feeling good—really good!

We left on a setting sun and by morning were sailing very close to shore, just outside the wave line. The wind was taking a vacation, the temperature had risen, and we ghosted on a flat sea toward our final Mexican destination, Las Hadas Resort in Manzinillo.

Our solitude was interrupted when, out of the north a giant commercial airliner appeared, flying so low it skimmed the tips of palm trees lining the shore. Tony and I looked on in horror but heard no crash. We looked at each other, bewildered. Strange things were certainly happening, but this wasn't the Bermuda Triangle. Then we heard the whine of jet engines being reversed, indicating a runway completely hidden from view, a major airport, undoubtedly serving Manzinillo.

"Imagine," Tony grinned, "we are SO relaxed we didn't notice an airport sneaking up on us."

We entered the anchorage at Las Hadas resort under engine power and at low throttle and were assigned a "stern to" European style berth, meaning our bow would be pointed out and our stern facing the dock. Maneuvering to this assignment was tricky, especially with some fifty other yachts, mostly larger, watching and waiting for us to screw up. But we didn't. We smartly dropped anchor in the middle of the small, tightly packed harbor at low throttle and backed with precision into our designated position in front of a ladies apparel store and a cantina with ample outdoor seating. Patrons intently watched our approach, possibly expecting us to screw up. We did a proper maneuver though, securing our lines to the concrete wall just as the sun went down and the music came up.

"This" said Tony, "is going to be fun." Too much fun.

CHAPTER 16

THE MODEL AND
THE BEER COMMERCIAL

Las Hadas was a phenomenal place of extraordinary architecture, and it was all built by hand. Sprawled in the cockpit, rum and coke in hand, Tony and I drank it all in, savoring our destiny, certainly our luck anyway in finding such a place.

By mid-morning we met our first resort official. Señorita Melinda, the dock master, was no type A muscular gorilla man, slinging lines and barking orders. Melinda was the first lady dock master we had met. She checked in at six feet and was stunning with perfectly etched cheekbones highlighting enormous smoldering black eyes hidden behind Ray-Ban pilot sunglasses. Her coal black hair hung thick below her shoulders and sparkled in the sunlight whenever she walked the docks.

"Surprised?" She asked, turning provocatively to catch my wide-eyed amazement at our introduction. I sensed late payments for dock space were rare.

Ninety yachts were housed in the marina when it was at capacity. We'd been assigned a choice position in front of a colorful cantina with a scant twenty feet separating its dockside tables and our stern. Our neighbor to port was a Cal 47, a comfortable though sluggish sailing yacht belonging to an arms dealer from Mexico City. Comforting information.

"Whoa . . . this is a bit dicey!" was Tony's contribution.

To starboard our neighbor alongside was a fifty-foot sloop from Los Angeles with three men aboard whom, taking Tony under their wing, helped to polish his already well-defined skills for living life in the moment.

Tony thrived with the young people in a similar age group. Most crewed on mega yachts with owners who were captains of industry and flew their personal jets in for the weekend. The crew, who likely had been playing volleyball or sleeping, got busy polishing silver or scrubbing decks. A few days later, when the jets lifted off with the crew being handsomely tipped, they would go back to sleep—or volleyball. Other young people were stretching low budget holidays, a few worked in the resort, and most all shared a common goal of a good time. It didn't take long before Tony had flawlessly inserted himself into the good time beach volleyball crowd.

"It's an all-day, everyday activity, Pops. You know I gotta keep in shape, right?" Tony said, tossing aside his work schedule to devote his energy into creating his own volleyball squad, the 'Tony's Late Night Bar and Grill' team.

His team came complete with attractive young Mexican ladies as groupies. The girls, Tony explained, were models for the various dress shops scattered around the resort. One in particular had caught Tony's attention.

"It just happened, Dad—she was on me like a duck on a June bug!" Indeed, it appeared that way. She was a lovely young lady whose angelic smile topped a dynamite body. I was happy for Tony. Work could wait. He had earned a pleasure break, but any potential relationship was doomed anyway because he would be sailing away. Stuck in Pasadena, Denise listened by phone as Tony and I raved about Las Hadas, the food and the fun. Sadly, she reported she would not be sufficiently healed in time to cross the Pacific with us. As courageous and stalwart as Denise was, I sensed her tears. While I couldn't see them with my eyes, they rained down in the uncertain, hesitating delivery of her near term fate.

"Skip," she had said, "my leg isn't healing properly. I desperately want to be with you—but I'm really scared of what is happening here."

"I understand," I had replied, attempting to sound encouraging. "It's a long voyage and a big world. This is only a glitch."

"I could end up with one leg shorter than the other," Denise had openly sobbed. "I might limp the rest of my life. I can't do that." She had paused to catch a breath, and continued, "Like, Skip, like . . . can you picture me walking around mountains in the same direction forever so it looks like I'm level?"

She laughed, and I laughed with her at her sense of humor, probably inherited from her show business dad. (Senior audio engineer on the Ed Sullivan show and later the Academy Awards) Denise went on, "Twice, I asked my doctor to reposition my break. It hurts like hell Skip, but I'll get a perfect healing and won't limp—at least I don't think I will." Her spirit lifted as she added, "The doctors agree, too. Spiral fractures are tough. I want it right!"

We talked it over. The disappointment was painful for each of us; mine easier because I had a full agenda while Denise had only a TV to occupy the numbing days ahead. I pledged to stay at Las Hadas long enough for Denise to fly down for a high quality, spirit-lifting, fun-filled visit. This would put our departure on the edge of the safe weather window for avoiding Pacific storms, so I cancelled sailing to Acapulco as originally planned, choosing instead to head outbound from Las Hadas. It's called flexibility—an advantage of drifting and blending.

With her plans made Denise called me back. She had heard from Kim, who complained she hadn't heard from Tony. Kim invited herself to join Denise for the trip. Denise felt badly but had no control over Kim's apparent jealousy. Tony wasn't happy with the news. He'd been thriving with his new adventures and had no desire or intention to share them with Kim. In Tony's mind, his earlier questions about the depth of their relationship had been finalized before she had left the boat several weeks earlier.

Me? I just waited for the explosion.

Most of my relaxation time and all of Tony's was spent under the blistering sun around the resort's largest swimming pool. A bridge, separating two sections of pool touched down to a small tropical island in the middle. The forty-foot-wide island housed two nasty-looking iguanas that stared sinisterly at startled tourists swimming by. Although harmless, we gave them space.

Each night a live group at the cantina next to our berth played happy Mexican tunes with serenading and storytelling. One night an accomplished wood f lute artist played the most enchanting, haunting music I had ever heard. It came from a newly released movie *The Mission*. I lay in the cockpit, or *Endymion's* hammock, closed my eyes and listened—perhaps even dreamed—as the wood flute's mystical sound transported my mind to the dense jungles from which I imagined it originated.

Back in my real world we were seriously preparing for our crossing. We tuned rigging, greased winches, created a 'flight plan,' worked our radios, and carefully inspected safety and survival gear—all page one of many on my checklist.

I hoped for a smooth crossing but was mindful of my navigation mentor, Captain Swede. On a calm uneventful night far at sea, he had lost a leg because a fatigued bolt snapped suddenly, causing a massive spool of towing wire to tumble free, crushing his leg. Three hours of my prudent preparation now could prevent a disastrous, life-changing, split-second situation somewhere in our future. I was determined to be prepared.

I set early April for departure. Leaving from Manzanillo would give us a more favorable angle through the doldrums approaching the Equator, and Manzanillo put us 200 miles closer to the northeasterly trades, while also distancing us from the 'normal' tropical depression path. I liked this plan, which had us looking for landfall at Hiva Oa in the Marquesas Island group, around the first of May, which was also when our French visas would become effective. Perfect—and I was content to provision at Las Hadas. It was hot, however, so the tedious work was done in a constant sweat, ever searching for the next cold drink.

In the quieter evening hours, usually at the hinged cocktail table forward of the wheel, I had also written a set of "sailing rules" for my crew, when finally assembled. When gathered, we would again go over the boat with a fine-tooth comb looking for potential problems. I planned to actually practice "man overboard" drills, practice 'heaving to' and have Tony make an inspection of the masthead via the bosun's chair, usually Denise's job, as she was the lightest.

Blessed with the tranquility of a noiseless night, I sat alone contemplating my life. Tony had crashed below deck, the musicians had packed up their instruments, and the bar staff had gone elsewhere. We were past the two-month cruising mark. I was firmly convinced that, while it might not work for others, selling my business and my lovely home, which I said I would never leave, and walking away from my possessions was the toughest but smartest decision I had ever made. Magazines and pundits say travel is a great educator, but for me it was more—it was the people we met who influenced and built our character. Most we met didn't have the comforts or toys available in America—and they didn't need them. Well, maybe they just didn't know they didn't need them. An uncluttered, relaxed, simple lifestyle, I'd discovered, equates to abundant happiness. It was easy to like the local Mexicans with their close-knit families.

Delivering a message about family values, lovely Señorita Melinda strongly criticized me. "Skip, how much did you pay that boy?"

She was referring to a youngster who had helped me pack supplies from town while Tony had suffered through a big league resort volleyball tournament.

"Six dollars," I said. "I gave him six Yankee dollars."

"Please, Captain Skip, you are so stupid. You mess up the economy and destroy family values doing this."

"How so?" I asked, hairs rising in spite of her glamor. "Alejandro makes a quick six American dollars from you in fifteen minutes, and his father works a full day, maybe two full days, for the same amount—at hard labor! Then his son flashes this easy money and the father is shamed!"

I said I understood. I did. She made sense. I agreed to be more conservative.

One of Tony's new volleyball friends, Kyle, struck me as extra value. I guessed him to be in his mid-twenties. I liked that he was courteous and well spoken, and was impressed that he appeared, anyway, to refrain from the heavier drinking applauded by a hefty number of peers, and of which Tony was occasionally guilty. Kyle had no fixed plans or pressing agenda, so joining our crew was soon a done deal.

Tony and Kyle, now good buddies, would make a good watch team under sail. Kyle, by the way, said Tony's new nickname was TR. Maybe I could substitute TR when I would otherwise call him dickhead.

Tony called Kim, requesting she please not come with Denise. Though I wasn't privy to the conversation, I believe he broke the relationship as cleanly as he could. Tony was normally a gentle, sensitive person. I imagined he felt appreciable guilt, and I had no doubt Kim felt blindsided. There obviously had been difficulties. Best, I felt, not to interfere.

Having morning coffee along the quay, I was approached by a man in a suit jacket, sans tie, who appeared nervous and extraordinarily out of place, being so well dressed. Moving tentatively, he requested to join me by asking if I worked on *Endymion,* the yacht he had been looking at.

"It's a fair assumption," I replied, hardly looking up from the coffee I was pouring. "I own her."

"Ahhh—good," he said, already pulling a chair from the table. "I represent a professional photo crew from New York, here to shoot a bathing suit catalog for a major retailer. May I sit?"

"Sure . . . may I offer a coffee?"

"Thanks, I'd like that—no cream, no sugar," he continued in an accent as out of place as his suede shoes. "My name is Joe. I'm a New Yorker."

"No shit, Joe? I would a never guessed! Call me Skip."

Turning his head to the harbor, Joe said, "I've been looking at all these boats. Where do the people get the money?"

"Half of 'em probably come from the Big Apple," I said sarcastically.

"Anyway, I saw yours . . . that's it, isn't it?" He pointed over my shoulder to *Endymion*.

"Yup . . . she's mine."

"Your wide decks and big cockpit—that's whatcha call it, isn't it—cockpit?"

I confirmed his amazing accuracy.

"Good then. I have a proposition for you. Would you be interested in renting *Endymion* for a two-day photo shoot?"

My response was slow, intended to sound tough. "Not sure," I replied. "What's the pay, and more important, how badly will you screw up my boat?"

"The pay is $500 a day. That's the whole prop budget. We shouldn't make a mess, though the models will need to change below, but we have clean up people." Then he added the clincher: "And you or one of your crew must be available if we need to move anything or need answers to nautical questions."

"What are they modeling?"

"Oh, sorry—I shoulda told you. Bathing suits."

I was chomping at the bit. A grand in cash—*Endymion* in magazine pictures. I was stoked. "You talkin' Yankee dollars there, Joe?" I asked.

The city man mopped morning sweat from his brow and nodded affirmatively, so I pushed on. "And, when you're finished, some of equipment stays as insurance until I inspect for damages?"

He paused, and looked vacantly across the harbor, as if searching for alternatives.

"Sure—it's agreed then?" he asked. "We need to start right away. The girls arrive in an hour. This is a dazzling day."

"It's a done deal, Joe from New York," I offered. "And I'll take the money up front, thank you."

Joe got the last word. "We'll pay you half in advance, right now if you like, and half when finished."

"You're on," I said. "I'll round up my crew and we'll get the yacht photo ready for you. By the way, what catalog's this for?"

"JC Penney swimsuit edition."

We shook hands. I went to tell Tony and Kyle, who were already knee deep in Mexican models. I caught up with them preparing to go water-skiing.

"You're shittin' me, Pops," said Tony with Kyle silent but smiling on. "Why now? Kyle, Greg, and me are goin' water skiing with the crew from *Butterfly* (a large motor yacht). Besides, Dad—I got all the senoritas I can handle."

"Your call, Tony. I'm surprised you'd choose water skiing to a professional shoot, never mind models—but it's up to you." To my surprise, Tony opted for water skiing, leaving me to chaperone the models.

I quite enjoyed it, as I did the attention I drew from other yachts, and a small group of the ever curious who gathered to watch. Several times I was asked to provide binoculars, a yachting cap, or some line (rope) as props. I moved freely amongst the models, some half my age, who referred to me as "Capt." They were respectful of both my property and me. As the man from New York had affirmed, they were seasoned professionals.

That night I was eating alone in a small waterfront cafe, keeping an ear cocked for wood flutes and thinking about Tony. As a photographer, I felt he'd been a fool because he could have absorbed buckets of knowledge about his trade at this shoot, yet he chose to water ski. What a dope.

"Hi Capt. Skip, remember me?" A striking young model from the bathing suit shoot stood beside my table showering me with her effervescent smile. "I'm Lisa. I was on your lovely boat today."

Her voice, her presence was electrifying. I was instantly aware I had known this person before, but how—where?

"Sure, Lisa. Didn't I fetch you a ball cap from the America's Cup races? Care to sit?" I asked, admiring her bubbly personality and lithesome body and was still puzzled by the magnetism.

"Yes, the cap was great," she said, sliding into the chair across from me. "I have a question for you, Skip. I'm auditioning for a commercial for a new beer in the northeast called Schooner. Casting is next week. Do you know about schooners, anything you could tell me to make me sound knowledgeable for my interview? With so many girls modeling these days, I need whatever competitive edge I can get."

We spoke briefly about different yacht rigs. She wasn't getting it, so I suggested, if she felt comfortable, we should return to *Endymion* where I could show her pictures of schooners from books I had aboard. Walking the short distance to the boat, Lisa lightly took my hand. I was surprised. *What's this?* It felt natural and comfortable. *OK, be honest, self—it's electric.* I hadn't been touched by anyone since parting with Denise what seemed ages ago, and I was experiencing a mysterious, emotional feeling drawing me to this young lady in a powerful slow surge. I wanted it, but I feared it. There was a hauntingly familiar sense to every move she made. I was positively certain

I knew her and I imagined—*could it have been from another time, or another place—another life?* Powerful thoughts. I had always believed in such things.

Aboard *Endymion* we sat across from each other at the salon table and discussed pictures from books. Lisa showed keen interest. I took in her sculptured facial features, the blonde streaks in her stylishly short hair, the casual motion of her arms as she made a point, and listened to her voice, which was mysteriously sensual. I'd never been attracted to women with short hair, so what was happening? Was I impressed, maybe, because she was sitting with me, someone twenty years her senior, when there was a marina full of handsome men who would find her fetching? Nothing seemed special—but everything was special. I wondered, *What's happening here?"* I was on a high I couldn't understand and loved every moment.

About when the conversation should have ended, Gary, from a neighboring boat, stuck his head through he companionway. "Skip, you coming, buddy? It's getting late. Time to get a move on or we'll miss the good parts!"

"Good parts of what?" Lisa wanted in.

"A crew member on another yacht is leaving," I explained. "He's a musician, plays horn and banjo, and the club at the next resort down the beach is hosting a party for him. Gary and I are going to check it out because music played by musicians for musicians is the best!"

"I'm coming, too. OK Skip?" she asked, pulling a brush and lip gloss from her clutch bag.

"Yeah, of course," said Gary. "Matter settled then," I added.

We walked to the neighboring resort along the beach, on what turned out to be a night of moon and stars lighting our way through this tranquil setting so distant from home, yet filled with music, good company, and the intoxicating scent of flowers everywhere. I had a love partner in California, yet I felt untroubled.

The party was all we expected, and we left riding high on the infectious spontaneity of the moment. Lisa returned to *Endymion* with me, where we lay side by side in the huge hammock until sunrise, speaking freely as one might to their barber or bartender, about our loves, fears, and dreams. Lisa whispered her concerns at never pleasing a man, not being able to trust, while I shared the joy Denise has delivered to my life. Eventually, we drifted into a light sleep . . . knowing not how this moment had come to be, but that it was comfortable, and somehow uniquely special.

But, like Tony and Kim, a future with Lisa was unlikely. I loved Denise deeply. I was about to sail across an ocean. There was that substantial age difference, and Lisa was nearing the peak of a promising career, in distant, noisy New York. We both knew this was only for the moment—to live fully and to cherish.

The next day's shoot wrapped at noon. The crew would depart the following morning. Watching the photo session, I asked myself if there was something wrong with me because I reveled in last night's good time and didn't feel guilty. I didn't plan to tell Denise, at least not right away, because it would genuinely hurt her. It hadn't at all minimized my love for Denise. This was one of those occasions novels describe, where if you're honest with yourself, you turn the pages, read more, and wish it were happening in your life.

Lisa and I spent the afternoon at the beach, in the water, and sailboarding. We made love that night.

Tony about fell over, meeting my new friend the next morning. She cooked a pan melt breakfast for us. Tony and Lisa exchanged awkward banter, as people do when meeting for the first time under unusual circumstances. Tony handled it well. I didn't. I was already feeling terrible for having betrayed Denise's trust.

Lisa made a surprise announcement: "This is where I belong. I know it! I'm calling my agency, canceling everything, and I'll stay with you. Maybe forever."

That made my heart pound. "Lisa, it sounds wonderful but be practical. You know I have a girlfriend who will be here in three days, and you have a career, and . . ." I was losing it, and sensed the edge on my voice.

Tony interrupted, "Hey guys—you just met. Be calm—OK?"

"OK! OK! I get it. I understand rejection." She was angry, her voice wavered as she slammed a pan on the galley stove.

Best I see this side now, I thought.

"All my life people have loved me for my looks, but not for who I am! Not for me." Lisa held back a sob but mist clouded her eyes.

I felt inadequate. My constitution was reminding me of failing Denise, while my heart unequivocally wanted to comfort Lisa—but I couldn't find the right words.

Tony stepped in to save the moment. "Lisa, something righteously cool happened between you and my dad. I know it was unexpected or spontaneous because I know him. I know he'll never want to lose this memory, or the magic you obviously have charmed him with, but he is serious about Denise. They have a good thing—really! You seem super, like really nice, Lisa, but you guys travel truly different roads."

"I'm staying until SHE comes," Lisa said, almost defiantly.

Though wracked with guilt, if ever I was to be positive or encouraging, it was now.

"Lisa, you are a warm, wonderful soul," I said, taking her into my arms and gently wiping her tears. "You have, in the most positive

111

sense of possession possible, taken this man's life, enriched it, and given me joy. You're incredible." And I meant it.

She sobbed. "Thanks, and I love you."

"I love you too, Lisa, but I'm not IN love with you, nor, I suspect, are you with me. Think about it, Lisa; love means the full unification of our spirits, our personalities, and souls. Whether it was God or fate that brought us together, it's been the best, the very best, and I love you for it."

"I didn't trust men much when we met, Skip. And I didn't like you a few minutes ago, either." Lisa, still in my arms looked up, squeezed my hand lightly, and added, "But I feel your kindness, and I admit when I came to you with the dopey schooner beer story, I felt something special."

"Kinda strange, isn't it?"

"Yep, and I have a plane to catch if I'm going to be the Schooner beer spokes lady."

Powerful feelings had been woven under Mexican skies, but sanity won. Whatever euphoria had pulled us together for a few moments, it was not the substance of sustaining love. I put Lisa aboard her flight at the hidden airport the day before Denise arrived. Amidst promises to write, no tears were shed, but a connection had been made between two people who just happened to be in the right place at the right time. Or was it the destiny of our souls?

As this superb young lady stepped onto the boarding ladder, she stepped out of my life. I never heard from her again, nor did I ever see her picture in any print ad. I did, however, write one letter.

And I wish I had not.

CHAPTER 17

HURTING THE ONE YOU LOVE

Returning to *Endymion* from the airport, my mind shifted back to reality. I needed to complete arrangements for Denise #2 and her mate Jim, if they were to crew on the crossing. First I had to find them. When last we spoke they were making a yacht delivery and retrieving passports that, somehow, they had left in Acapulco. This wasn't comforting, but I let it pass.

Much-needed parts for our Robertson autopilot, affectionately called 'Harvey,' after a friend who could never find his way, needed to be forwarded from Newport Beach, but to where? Figuring a destination address in Mexico, where the package wouldn't be stolen, was challenging. Denise would be arriving tomorrow. That was exciting, except that my emotions and normally strong sense of loyalty had been hammered by my behavior. I needed Denise's easy way and boundless love to comfort me—but I didn't deserve it. My family came from blue-blooded New England stock where loyalty was expected and honesty was a way of life. I had violated both covenants, and didn't like myself very much.

So, with all this self-deprecation to redirect me, what did I do? I went back to my cabin and wrote a romantic letter to Lisa. Stupid idea. Tony flatly refused to come to the plane for Denise's arrival because he didn't want to see Kim. Kim felt otherwise and was on the tarmac in spite of a boatload of encouragement for her to stay home. This could get ugly.

Stepping from the plane, Denise looked elegant. She wore a red sundress I had gifted her from Nordstrom once when we stopped for a quick 'shopping fix' that took several hours. I'd been told women liked to shop, and Denise earned a black belt that day. She embarked the plane practically glowing with a deep tan. A live flower in her hair and a hint of jasmine fragrance added to the brightness that matched her smile. I could tell that her cast, still present from toes to above her knee, was causing discomfort, though she moved with grace, seeming not to notice the evident pain. I felt warm all over. Denise always had that effect on me. Kim, finding no Tony to greet her, went into a 'snit,' refusing to come to the boat. She found no argument from me, so we dropped her at a motel. Kim stayed in her cramped motel room for days expecting Tony would come to her. When that bore no fruit she would saunter up to the boat, flaunt her bitterness and linger below decks waiting for Tony. Her timing was bad; Tony was never there and she left eventually, never spending a night aboard.

Denise and I got along famously. She had checked out potential crew Jim and Denise #2 as best she could. What few references they had were acceptable, though I'd always been skeptical of references because you never carry them from people who disapprove. With Denise present, we went into party mode, casting responsibilities aside as we wandered among the many yachts sharing stories and cocktails. In Denise's handbag, there was, however, a problem.

Denise carried a letter from my former business partner Chip Carter, advising me a financial problem needed my attention, even after selling my share of the company. I needed to fly immediately to Los Angeles, leaving Denise, in crutches, on *Endymion* with Tony.

Denise had an urge for lobster but couldn't get off the boat in her cast without hauling the stern closer to the quay and then jumping the remaining distance to the pier. To her surprise, a sharply dressed waiter appeared beside *Endymion* delivering a festive lobster dinner, white linen service and all, compliments of Tony, demonstrating some class. While Tony and Denise bonded, the common enemies remained Kim, for arriving, and me, for leaving.

I was back in two days. Denise had two stories to relate. The first demonstrated her sense of humor. A tourist walking the quay, gazing at the assorted yachts, spotted Denise alone in the cockpit with her crutches and cast. He looked at the boat, paused, walked away, and returned for a closer inspection. The hailing port on the transom of Newport Beach, California, got his attention and he gathered his courage to inquire, "Pretty lady . . . Did you actually bring this boat all the way from California?"

"No," said Denise. "It's a kit."

I thought this incident funny and demonstrated her quick wit. Her next story, however, stung.

"While you were gone, Skip—I found this!" Her eyes were flat, her voice somber as she held aloft the letter I had written to Lisa and carelessly left on the pad on which it was penned. I could not do or say anything. Hurt flooded Denise's eyes and the quiver in her voice stabbed like a driven nail. Although we were not engaged or married, I had broken an unspoken trust with the one person on earth who meant the most to me, and I was both ashamed and disgusted with myself.

"I'm sorry, Denise, I don't know what else to say. You should never have seen that, and I should never have let it happen. I am *so* sorry." Tears were in my eyes. "Hurting you is something I would *never* knowingly do. I can only ask your forgiveness and understanding."

Denise, being the bigger person, said, "Let's go to the pool and have some fun. You've made me cautious about our future, but it won't ruin the good time I came for."

We went to the pool, where a fashion show was in progress, including Tony's current flame, modeling clothing and swim suits from resort stores. I filmed it. We sat with friends from other yachts. It was almost like nothing had ever gone amiss. We got a little 'popped up' and I accidentally spilled rum and coke down Denise's cast, rendering it sticky and more uncomfortable inside the plaster. Thankfully, being diet coke, she had only to cope with the army of ants attracted to rum. Somehow, Kim got wind of the video, which also contained footage of other portions of our trip. Denise was to carry it home for friends and family to view—but it came up missing. Enraged, I suspected Bonehead Kim had stolen the tape, first because of her burning desire to see it, and second—she had been alone below decks. I asked politely if she had seen the misplaced tape.

"Go to damn hell, Skip," she defiantly shouted. "I didn't take your tape, and I don't give a damn where it is either! Tony and me are finished and I'm leaving."

"OK!"

"And you can tell that bastard son of yours, and his Maria—or whatever the skinny bitch's name is," Kim stopped there, her eyes like fire, and stormed off the boat.

116

We searched every inch of *Endymion*, never finding the tape—but several months later, Kim delivered it to Tony's house in California, hurling a few parting shots as she threw it on the lawn. Finally, closure. Jim and Denise #2 appeared one day, ready to work, and there was plenty to do. Denise #2 was a big woman, over six feet, lithe, with a practiced tan, strawberry shoulder-length hair and no fat. But she carried a hefty attitude—the "I'm superior" type. She would tote luggage like I might lift a six-pack. Jim was a hand's length shorter, rather skinny, and spoke through a tangled jungle of jet-black mustache and beard, though he was generally on the quiet side. I'll stop short of branding him meek, though I thought so. I started calling Denise #2 'The Amazon,' adding the noun 'lady' if addressing her, directly. She considered this a compliment.

My Denise convinced me the Amazon's trained classic chef background would likely prove useless for our provisioning. We hadn't considered 'classic food essentials.' My Denise pointed out items on the Amazon's preferred list: pâté, frozen lobster (which would never keep), Peruvian mushrooms, capers and more, causing my Denise to quietly comment, "Crapola, Skip; you can't afford such luxury—and you'll get fat!"

Denise went to town with the Amazon. The budget withstood the shock. When finished, we had piles of sensible provisions awaiting assigned storage. Each crewmember was allowed one bottle of liquor.

We were otherwise a dry ship, except for a limited stock of the king of beers, Budweiser (light style) to accompany our traditional Sunday church services with Reverend Chuck.

We had also put ourselves against a scheduling wall. While the purpose of this new life was drifting and blending without pressure, the world's weather patterns wait for no one. Every April day we delayed sailing west increased stormy weather potential one or two percent.

Laying in supplies for Pacific crossing

Denise had already delayed her return to Los Angeles, but an important appointment with her surgeon was looming. It was time to go.

Tears were in all eyes as Denise boarded her flight. We would meet again in Papeete, and we would stay in touch during the crossing by ham or high seas Single-Sideband (SSB) radio.

I deeply missed Denise, her smile, her laugh, and her love from the moment she disappeared in the airport's passenger lounge. But with time short and to insure safe passage, we needed to get underway. Storms could already be building along the Equator. We don't want to meet them. My nerves were showing.

Crossing the Pacific would be my life's biggest undertaking. I had many offshore miles under my keel, but this voyage could take 30 days before landfall. Our intended track would take us to the Marquesas Islands of Hiva Oa, Fatu Hiva, and Reynolds Bay. From there, we would cautiously traverse the low elevation, reef-fringed Tuamotu Islands, sailing eventually to Tahiti in the Society Islands. Denise would join us in Tahiti for Bastille Day July 14th.

At least that was the plan.

CHAPTER 18

PACIFIC
CROSSING-OUTWARD BOUND

Sunday, April 12th 1987. *Patriot Games* is the best selling book in America and the world is listening to *Nothings Gonna Stop us Now* by *Starship*—and nothings gonna stop us from heading out today.

This is it! Departure day! Outward Bound!

Repairs and maintenance are complete—we hope! Provisions are aboard and stowed. Crew have said their mournful goodbyes, and what 'goodbyes' they were. Tony and Kyle had partied till dawn's early light at Club Myeva. My wake up call came as a soft feminine Mexican voice cooing, "I love yooouuu Tony, I love yooouuu Kyle, please come back, OK? Please—for me?"

Sure little lady, I thought. Be right back.

Settling our two-week monster marina bill, the lovely Harbor Mistress Melinda, gave me a bottle of champagne and called us "her friendliest, most fun yacht since taking this job."

We were down to hours and minutes. My overworked mind felt dull, yet I willed it to be sharp, because it had to be. I was firmly in my two-foot zone, where nothing could escape me. I'd never felt so ready, so prepared or as excited. Crossing the Pacific was a big deal. I sat on a plastic cantina chair on the quay studying *Endymion*, reworking how many times I had inspected the decks in the safety of the Marina. Or how many times had I run my hands and fingers across the lifeline turnbuckles searching for weakness. I'd re-examined every grommet in every sail, checked each clevis pin and strength tested every fitting on deck. All part of an endless checklist I have been over more times it seemed, than I've had birthdays.

Tony has been aloft to check the rigging and given a thumbs up. We had left the Marina once to vigorously scrub our bottom to rid the hull of lecherous growth. A nasty job. Creatures I hadn't known to exist, grew in the stagnate Marina environment and had clung to our hull. Kyle, our best swimmer, handled the ugly removal chore. Jim handled everything connected to the engine and generator, reporting it well.

I asked myself if I'd been overthinking this? Were all these checks and rechecks necessary? I thought so. We were about to point the bow around the breakwater, leaving protection, becoming outward bound for as many as thirty days where there would be no outside help.

Then, I found myself talking to God again and asking—*"one day when on the horizon we see the first blur of land—will it be the right land? Will we smell land before we see it?* They say sometimes, the fragrance of an island is powerful enough to travel great distances with the wind, and linger many hours. *Will we be aimed at the right tiny island, after mostly hand steering a twenty-two ton vessel through waves, wind, doldrums and possible storms, with less than one degree of error for as far as 4,000 nautical miles? So many questions Lord! I admit some fragmented doubts and fears co-mingled with my normally brimming confidence."*

"Forget it! We're committed," was the message I got and repeated to no one in particular, putting my chair aside and climbing aboard *Endymion* for the last time in Mexico. "We've made our choice. We are ready. What say you God?"

A big, open, awesome ocean and unknown future await us. My job was to deliver us to the pin size target island safely. All jobs, I reminded myself, have degrees of danger. The guy, who climbs towers to replace blinking red warning lights, has a more dangerous job than a store keeper, for instance, and passage making should qualify for some sort of hazardous duty pay—I would think!

Some experienced captains called this "The Milk Run," but I don't think so. I believe for any first time adventurer, this passage would be a life changing challenge. But, who knows, some day, I too may say, "No sweat, it's a milk run."

A polyglot mixture of yachts, bar girls, hippies and tourists, blew horns, shouted good wishes and told us to 'get lost' when, at 1050 that Sunday morning, we cast off our last confining lines, to head triumphantly outbound from Las Hadas, a place we so enjoyed.

Forty minutes later we were hove-to, sending Kyle over the side to see why the speed interface with our other instruments wouldn't work. This important gizmo calculates just where, in this big pond we are. Jim could find no problem on the hull, so still within sight of Las Hadas, we removed several months of stored canned goods from the bilge, disconnected the thru-hull fitting, and removed a torn condom hitching a ride on our speed indicator.

Four sweaty hours later we were again underway, trying unused sea legs, and adjusting to ocean vagaries. Tony and Kyle carry the extra burden of varsity hangovers from the previous night. With the wind forward of abeam at 15 knots *Endymion* surged ahead. I know she felt good to be at sea!

"Fish on the line!" Kyle sang out. A big sturdy reel shrilly screamed as line raced out. Behind us a huge black marlin angrily broke the surface, launched skyward and slammed down to the ocean—wildly fighting for freedom. We were not skilled, nor quick enough. The Marlin shortly broke free, taking with it 1,000 feet of line and a fine lure. I was secretly pleased. We couldn't possibly have landed the monster fish, they are not good eating, and soon enough the fish would spit out or shake off the lure. Also just as well, because the sun, on it's way to tomorrow, was fading into our first of countless picture perfect sunsets.

My crew consisted of Tony and Kyle on starboard watch, Jim and the Amazon taking port watch and myself as Skipper and navigator having no specific watch assignment, but the privilege of inserting myself into any watch I chose, maybe of necessity, but also, because sometimes I too wanted wheel time.

All of us took turns in the galley. Each day's lucky winner planned and created meals and performed cooking duties for 24 hours. This encouraged friendly competition, and creative meals, especially when the seas got rough or the equatorial days became furiously hot below deck. Tony, drawing the short straw in competition, rigged by his Dad, went below to assume duty as our first chef. Not to anyone's surprise his first creation was enchiladas—so bad Kyle tossed them overboard and dove for the peanut butter jar.

By 2130 of night one *Endymion* was a quiet ship. Port watch was on deck, Jim at the wheel. I was nodding off in my cabin when I heard a light "clink," sounding like metal against fiberglass.

"What the heck?" Shortly the clink was followed by a much louder "clank." I was thinking something heavy was out of synch when Jim called through from the cockpit calmly saying, "Skip, I think we have a problem. I have no steering!"

"All Hands...All Hands!" Less than a day out we had our third problem—this one substantially more serious.

Taking the helm I balanced the sails to self-steer *Endymion* on a reasonable course. Kyle and Tony followed my sail trim commands, helping to keep our balance in order to sail straight in gentle seas without any steering. Jim went to the engine room, with the Amazon passing the required tools. Jim isolated the problem; a broken shiv on the steering quadrant had rendered the steering cable useless. Jim made repairs with seizing wire in less than a half hour.

I couldn't get back to sleep so I wandered topside.

We were well offshore now. The rest of civilization is someplace else. "Beautiful night." said Kyle, at the helm. He seemed confident and supremely happy. I went below to the chart table and continued plotting our course across the Pacific Ocean on a very small-scale chart. This was my comfort zone. I liked this work because I felt it tied us to our pin point on the chart, even though the seventy nautical miles we had made, looked on this chart to be the same 'dot' as where we started.

"*Big ocean*" I thought again to myself, and went topside to chat with Kyle, who was now sitting behind the big wheel steering with his feet.

"So, what occupies your mind this hour Kyle?" I asked. "The moon." He replied. "I've never seen it so clearly."

The cloud cover had dissolved and a brilliant moon shimmered across the sea. Searching above I found the stars Betelgeuse, Rigel, and Capella, each ready to guide us perfectly along our path. "Nice job guys, pleasant voyage to us," I said looking to my star friends high in the night sky.

"I'm surprised you could see em," Kyle remarked, "With the moon so dazzling."

Kyle was right. With the moon aglow at sea, it's similar to street-lights in cities, making it more difficult to see the total beauty the skies present. It saddens me to think nearly half, maybe more, of the worlds population has never seen the luster of the Milky Way, perhaps never seen a shooting star blaze a path across the sky. At sea we get to appreciate dozens of them.

I headed below deck, my mind sensing the wonder of how it is we are so finite in this infinite universe, yet we possess minds that figure, bodies that move as directed and eyes, wow—eyes that serve up these wonders for the length of our lives. I so wish that everyone, could be in my shoes now, if only for a minute.

On deck for my watch again at 0300 I find two "booby birds" gliding in the slipstream of our sails, silhouetted against puffy night clouds outlined by moonlight. Picture perfect, they moved effortlessly, never landing in the rigging. I sensed I was with them, lost in the magic, that ethereal spot between reality and dreams.

We were averaging a solid eight knots, with wind abeam (from the side), steady at 18 to 20 knots—close to our best sailing angle. A firm hand was required on the wheel. Yeah, the best! We had small reefs in the main, mizzen, and jib. I could see and project how every coming wave would cause us to pitch and roll, or if I would get a spray bath. *Endymion* was part of me and I wanted this first night at sea to last forever. "*This,*" I thought, "*is what life is about.*"

Whap!! Something wet, slimy and sticky slapped my leg and dropped to the deck. Score one direct hit for an ugly flying fish and a couple of missed heartbeats for me. As I reached to toss it back to the sea, I thought what a strange prehistoric creature it was, with tiny wings beating out survival, supporting a heavy submarine shaped sea creature body, a throwback to Darwin. I return it to the sea, hopefully alive and able to scare the crap out of another voyager in earths 220 million square miles of ocean.

At 1300 on our second day at sea Tony suggested, "let's up the chute (spinnaker) Dad". Because it was a first with this crew, we were 'all hands' getting the big sail flying properly. Conditions were perfect. *Endymion* surged forward like a sure-footed jaguar after it's prey.

An hour later Jim said, "I don't feel comfortable with this Skip. I still have wheel control, but she's fighting me, and the seas are up."

I locked my eyes to the Brooks and Gatehouse wind indicators for a few minutes. It was gusting twenty-four knots which, adding boat speed, approached thirty knots actual wind—way too much for our spinnaker. "O.K all hands" I called again, "Lets bag this chute and take a reef in the main."

The spinnaker had been up less than an hour. Isn't that the way. Conditions were better the next day so we set up a competition. Everyone chipped in $10.00 to go to the person turning in the best one-hour distance at the end of the voyage. Luck, of course, would play a major roll because one person could have more favorable wind conditions than the next. It also helped keep crew alert and responsive. Chiding naturally started immediately with Kyle telling

Tony, "Hell man, I've sailed more miles with no sails up than you have with everything flying."

Tony, actually the youngest in experience turned in the best run for the first day, telling Kyle to "Sit on that!"

I had avoided steering for the most part, choosing to spend my time observing the crew and working up ideas for a more enjoyable voyage. My senses, however, were tuning in troublesome vibes. The Amazon tended to question everything I, or anyone else said, and acted too authoritatively to suit me. I hoped the tension was only in my mind. I needed to be careful and keep harmony.

Chef of the Day Jim created a tasty chefs' salad for dinner. The wind dropped and we set the spinnaker again in 10-12 knot breezes with a calming sea. The spinnaker would remain aloft longer than anticipated.

CHAPTER 19

PACIFIC KNOCKDOWN

We slowly settled into a routine life at sea. Sleep came readily, in fact so easily we could stumble over each other napping on deck, in beanbags at the stern, or stretched out on plush cockpit cushions. I had ordered them 'special,' as Tony put it, for sleeping under the stars, and we were getting plenty of practice. We functioned more like a team, though playful moves were made when the helmsman wasn't looking, to mess up a competitor's logged hourly run for the spinnaker competition by quietly easing the spinnaker sheet—especially if the helmsman was nearing championship distance. I found the aft cabin I had bragged about had disadvantages at sea. The high bunk created uncomfortable motion with the wind up and boat rolling. Also wide, it was more appropriate for two people when motionless, like tied to a dock, but at sea a big wave could flip me out, possibly causing serious injury.

My cabin was also insanely noisy. The trailing generator, on deck right above my bunk, whirled, whined, clicked, or screamed, depending on hull speed. The manufacturer of this costly little item failed to mention noise in his sales pitch. All lines, including main and spinnaker, were led to big, heavy turning blocks above the port and starboard sides of my cabin. With slack wind like the previous night, these blocks banged and clomped when sails luffing in windless skies raised the blocks and slammed them down against the deck. And there was the beloved propeller. It turned and freewheeled just below me, causing the cutlass bearing to shriek like a banshee if we did more than seven knots. The steering quadrant, also under the bunk, interfaced to the autopilot, which, with its bum bearing, pierced my pillow with mournful, ear-shattering screeching.

All said though, sleeping in the wonderful aft cabin while underway in gentle seas was one of life's ultimate pleasures. With practice, I was able to ignore the noise, relegating them to my unconscious, and there was a totally amazing view out the two large port windows in the stern. Watching the endless sea was mesmerizing provided timeless pleasure—and was luxuriously relaxing. I couldn't get enough. For the rest of my life, when under stress, I will take myself back to this time and this place of peace.

As bitchy as I was about the noise, I wouldn't have traded that racket with anyone, anywhere, for anything. If folks can adjust to the endless street noises of city life, I could certainly get in tune with this chaotic symphony at sea. When I was topside on *Endymion* I was essentially alone in a world known to few, and so tranquil it defied description. I highly recommended it. The trick was to get there.

On April 15th, we tuned in the Pacific Maritime ham radio net for the first time. Our closest contact was in Hilo, Hawaii. Around midnight we saw our first moving lights at sea, stimulating a lively debate between Tony and Kyle. Tony insisted the steadily growing lights were a passing freighter, while Kyle insisted it was a floating 7-11 store.

Our fourth day at sea found our batteries near death. Refrigeration was responsible. We couldn't generate enough power to run the ship and luxury items together, without running the diesel engine, and that was reserved for needs more serious than ice for drinks. And since there were no service stations in this neck of the sea, we came to have adoring fuzzy feelings for warm Diet Pepsi. We didn't mind; we were solidly into the trade winds and the sailing was superb! We just pointed the bow at the Equator and felt the days unhurriedly getting warmer. We'd averaged slightly more than 150 nautical miles daily, good for a cruiser using no power.

The next dawn we saw something few humans ever see. Most people wouldn't give a hoot, but it was inspiring to us, being alone and close to the Equator on the 'big pond,' as Tony called the Pacific. The sun rose as a ginormous red ball creeping into the sky, due east while the moon was setting due west. Polaris (the North Star) was where it should be, and to our south, barely touching the horizon, was the Southern Cross, a bright but small constellation not seen above 20 degrees north. Both are major navigation aids, and to see them at the same time was awesome. I thought about God and the ancient Christian belief that the disappearance of the constellation was linked to the crucifixion of Christ.

Sailing day and night with a spinnaker flying takes meaningful effort and concentration. I believed we'd been overworked. We'd been five days and nights without dropping the spinnaker, but Saturday morning, April 17th, it lay in a tangled clump on the foredeck, a victim of concentration gone astray, causing the big sail to get wrapped around the head stay. Actually, it was one of two errors during the previous night. The scariest occurred just past midnight.

We'd been sailing in winds of 17 to 20 knots, in pitch dark under a solid deck of low clouds. A glimpse of any star would have been reassuring. We were pushing the margin of safety for flying a spinnaker. Tony, at the helm, found it exhilarating but difficult to manage. Lying in my bunk I heard an annoying grinding noise coming from the cursed trailing generator and went topsides to check it out. We were making 7 knots with the wind at 120 degrees and a moderate chop.

"How's the helm?" I asked Tony.

"Little tough to hold," he replied, "but I can handle it."

I knew from his expression that Tony was in his element, loving every moment.

"Tony, we need to inspect the trailing generator. To reduce pressure on the generator, you'll have to head into the wind enough to almost stop us so I can drag it in. Whadda ya think?"

Kyle, half asleep, listened from a curled-up position under the dodger. He interrupted: "The problem, and a major one, is keeping the spinnaker from collapsing. I'll help."

We didn't want to go through the laborious process of taking the spinnaker down properly, as we should have, repacking it and later resetting it. We devised a tricky shortcut plan to slow the boat enough to drag in the generator line with propeller. I thought we could pull it off, though it required momentarily collapsing the spinnaker while simultaneously bearing off to shield the powerful sail from filling again too quickly. Tricky stuff! Tony would drive the boat, and I would luff the main and mizzen while releasing the fore guy to let the spinnaker pole go forward against the head stay—and ease the spinnaker sheet—all in perfect harmony—all done quickly. Kyle would haul in the generator. Everything had to be flawless, considering we were 22 tons in motion on an open sea in total darkness. We would act on my signal. Jim and Denise were off watch. Let them sleep. For practice we talked it through three times.

Preparing to let the pole go forward, I asked Tony, "Ready to let her luff?"

Thinking I gave the order to "take her up," Tony misunderstood and threw the wheel over hard, heading into the wind before I could release the pole or spinnaker sheet. The massive sail grabbed all the wind in the sky that night, putting thousands of pounds of tension on the line I was trying to set free, lifting me suddenly off the deck. *Endymion* bolted forward, starting to heel dangerously as the spinnaker's full power captured the wind, and I fell hard into the cockpit.

"Take her down . . . DOWN!" (Away from the wind) I screamed at Tony. Within seconds we were in a complete knockdown. *Endymion*, out of control, at night, in mid-ocean, slowly lost forward momentum and lay over on her side in a do or die moment. We all held on. Time stood still and I thought, *No—not like this. This can't be happening!*

"Let go the fuckin' sheet!" Tony was screaming, "Damn it, Dad— let go! Release it!"

I snapped to, but I had taken a bad wrap (turn) on the winch and couldn't release the sheet. The 5/8th-inch, 10,000-pound test line was fouled around the winch and we were going over. Five men wouldn't have the strength to untangle the wrap!

"Take her off! Off, Tony—off!" (Away from the wind), I screamed back at Tony, who with both feet braced against the leeward cockpit rail, was using his full weight and both hands straining to turn the wheel. I saw shock in his wild eyes. He couldn't match nature.

Terror set in. I reached for my rigging knife.

133

"All hands—all hands! Now! Kyle, some help here!"

Jim and the Amazon had scrambled from below. Kyle had thrown his weight with Tony to turn the reluctant wheel but it wouldn't budge. I prayed to God the steering cable wouldn't snap.

Endymion was in the last throws of the knockdown. The boom's outer end was in the water, and the huge spinnaker also touching the water, dragging us over. *Endymion,* her spreaders inches from the wave tops, was slowly stopping. I sawed the line with all my strength, but was running out of steam. My arms ached, my heart beat wildly and blood flowed from a leg gash caused by a flying winch handle. Kyle was bleeding above his eye.

Water lapped at the edge of the cockpit. With forward motion gone, *Endymion* was settling in the dark seas—*My God,* I thought, *she's going over—we're going to die—she's going to sink.* Though spent, I sawed like my life depended on it! Jim had pulled bolt cutters from the black hole and was crawling toward me when the impossibly strong line parted with a deafening *crack,* jerking the knife from my hand and slicing my forefinger.

The loose end of the spinnaker sheet became a lethal, deadly weapon, snapping wildly back and forth. But *Endymion* ever so slowly began to right herself. The spinnaker, no longer a threat to survival flailed crazily to leeward.

It wasn't over. I released the spinnaker pole and guy. Jim reached the mast to release the spinnaker halyard, ducking the savage bite of the spinnaker sheet slapping at him, lucky to escape broken bones from the line nearly wrapping around his body and throwing him against a lifeline.

We eventually gained control. I thanked God publicly that no one had gone overboard. The Amazon brought up our comprehensive first aid kit Denise had prepared prior to leaving California. She stitched

Kyle's left eye before tending to my leg and finger. Tony and Jim nursed minor cuts and bruises.

Still shaking, we straightened up the mess on deck, untangled the spinnaker and its lines, attached a new sheet, and put the big kite in the sky again. It's what sailors do.

Kyle returned to his generator chore, wearing gloves this time. Earlier, in a dumb move and prior to the knockdown, he had taken a wrap of the trailing generator line around his wrist. Had this caused him to go overboard in the knockdown we would never have recovered him. Kyle was our strongest crewmember, however, and he retrieved the tangled mess of the generator failure, while the rest of us Monday morning quarterbacked the knockdown.

"I feel like a pilot," Tony offered; "fly through a thousand hours of nothing and then a minute of total panic!"

"Yeah, I hear that. I'm sitting here wondering what I'm getting Denise into," I said, looking proudly at my son. "That was damn scary, what we went through!"

The near disaster had been the captain's error—mine alone. We clearly tried to do too much with too few people. Our timing was bad and though I'd done it thousands of times, I had failed releasing the sheet. The whole experience plainly illustrated what I have drummed into my crews for years—this is an awesome sport harnessing powerful forces, and when something goes wrong, it can often be sudden and deadly. For me it was a stern reminder that a fully loaded, 45,000-pound yacht plowing through the ocean demands my best skills and constant attention. Being 1,200 miles from shore, it would be difficult to find a doctor.

While assessing my own culpability there was one thing that had pissed me off. Only I had been wearing a harness and been connected.

Kyle had one at his side but not on, and Tony had left his on his bunk. It's well known that over 50% of males lost at sea went overboard while taking a leak. Had a harness been attached, that simple device would have kept them from floating away in darkness screaming for help. Tony or Kyle could have been lost during the confusion that night. I couldn't imagine the difficulty explaining that to Kyle's loved ones, who hadn't wanted him to go offshore in the first place.

Soon it will be Easter. We had planned a major meal, beer, and church services with Reverend Chuck. And, oh yes, a giant Easter egg hunt for which Kyle and Tony had been creatively decorating eggs.

Tony was playful Easter morning, using the ham radio to invite our nearest neighbors to the egg hunt. He had responses from Bora Bora in Tahiti, one from Hawaii, and one from a charter operator in the Galapagos Islands near Ecuador. The only yacht to respond was *Renaissance*, a sloop from America 300 miles in front of us, who said, "You supply the eggs and I'll bring the hollandaise. We can meet halfway."

CHAPTER 20

A LETTER HOME

I wrote home:

Mom & Dad,

As you read these words you are with me aboard Endymion. She is performing beautifully. I couldn't ask for more. It may sound foolish, but I think she knows. It is Good Friday. Tony and Kyle are sitting in bean bags on the foredeck consumed in a championship game of chess. Everything here seems to claim the title of "championship" something, but it's all in fun. Jim is at the wheel and the Amazon is throwing together some sandwiches. In so many ways it's just another day at sea, yet no day is "just another day."

I, too, am sitting on our amazingly steady foredeck, with pen and paper on a borrowed piece of floorboard, indelicately wedged between my knees. The spinnaker flies high above me, waves are crashing all around, and we are taking a high-speed sleigh ride across the Pacific. This morning on the ham radio net our nearest neighbor was an Argentine Naval Frigate 600 miles SW of our plotted position. Can you imagine that?

We are nearly 2,000 miles west of Panama, 1,800 miles SW of San Diego, and still days from landfall at Hiva Oa in the Marquesas Islands. Soon, maybe tomorrow, Easter Sunday, we will cross into the Southern Hemisphere, fulfilling in this tiny boat, my big long-time goal. Aside from God, who is always on the seas with us, we are totally alone in this gigantic expanse of open ocean. For an average guy like me, it certainly fulfills my dreams for adventure, peace, and what I happily sense is becoming a more meaningful life.

Remember Dad, when you told me as a kid, the Pacific is larger than all the landmasses of the world put together—well, it's hard to believe but here we are—smack dab in the middle. Except for the Navy boat out there somewhere, there isn't a living person within 1,000 miles—360 degrees around us!

Nature is a fascinating companion. The wind blows constantly, dolphin race alongside often kissing the bow as they roll and go airborne to look up at us. We have learned how to mimic their call hoping to keep them close for longer periods.

Flying fish play around us all day and night, while huge Pacific rollers rocket us down their fronts and into the night, often with a phosphorescent glow. The Heavens are awesome. We know the stars now. They are our friends, guiding and greeting us as they have mariners through all of recorded time. I hope you can feel my humility.

Our bodies are bronzed, our muscles toned, and minds sharpened. The routines of the day are simple, but there is no room for mistakes. We've made a few, and there's no one here to help us. I have never been so self-sufficient, so gratified, or so thankful, and I like it this way.

Thank you Mom, Dad, for your wisdom and guidance that are so helping me achieve my goals.

I love you dearly!

Skip

CHAPTER 21

PROBLEM IN THE NIGHT

The sun dipping beyond the horizon, on what had been an incredibly clear day/evening that accentuated the earth's curve. It was Easter eve. I felt spiritual and shared my thoughts with God, though he didn't respond to my request to see the 'green flash,' a phenomenon that occurs at the last instant the sun sets on the horizon. The sky must be clear, with no clouds or obstructions such as land or other vessels. For only an instant, prisms of color respond to water or impurities in the atmosphere, resulting in what mariners call a brilliant green flash of light. OK—another night perhaps?

I was chef tonight and attempted to create beer bread as an extra treat for tomorrow, but it flopped. I also made a high seas radio call to wish Denise Happy Easter, and let her know how much I missed her. I tried on these infrequent radio calls to make Denise feel like she is with us vicariously. We talked about weather, meals, the beauty around us, and small slices of life I hope would cheer and comfort Denise. I didn't mention the spinnaker kerfuffle.

As I hit the bunk after our call tonight, the ship's log rolled over 1,400 nm. Slowly drifting to sleep, pleasantly enveloped in the sounds of a moving yacht, I thought more about Denise and other women who had influenced my life. Denise is the right decision. She's the total package—tough, determined, considerate, beautiful, and a great lover.

Though my port lights I saw distant lightning.

The midnight's log entry noted building and confusing seas, messengers probably, of the lightning—now considerably closer. I fell back to sleep.

We had been making seven knots with the mizzen, jib, and main winged opposite one another, wind steady at 20 knots with bursts to 25 knots, and confused 10-foot seas coming from different directions, making us roll uncomfortably. We had Pilot Charts aboard. They give a summary of relative conditions for wind, current, rain (or snow), and wave height, based on nearly a century of observation. The charts are broken into five-degree sections of all of the world's oceans. That night the Pilot Charts indicated sea conditions were unusual for these latitudes, but not worrisome.

About 0200 Tony stuck his head through the hatch: "Problem on deck, Pops. You better come topsides. Wind is piping up too."

On deck I found that Jim, on the helm, had decided to reef the main, but we were running free (wind behind us) and the huge sail was all the way out portside, pressing heavily on the lower shrouds and spreaders (rigging). Our reefing system was a sophisticated Hood roller boom system, where the mainsail rolls around a bar on the inside of the boom as it is lowered, allowing infinite reefing positions, and by lowering weight from aloft to maintain a better 'righting moment' should capsizing become a threat. It was cutting-edge technology and I was proud to have it. Jim had foolishly attempted to lower the main while it pressed against the rigging, an impossible job because of pressure and friction. He should have sheeted in the main to free it of the rigging. Why he didn't I will never know. By the time I was on deck, the mainsail was badly torn along the luff, the luff wire had jumped the track and a batten was jammed behind the upper portside shroud of our rigging. In other words . . . high up the mast.

"Shit, are you crazy, Jim?" I both asked and asserted. This man had a captain's license and supposedly years of experience. I went after Jim, "No one with your credentials should let this happen. Damn it Jim—were your sleeping?"

I was seriously angry and with each word to Jim or command I gave to others, the Amazon would challenge it or question it. I was in no mood for her defiance.

"Shut the fuck up, Denise!" rolled from my lips with no regret. She turned to Jim, saying, "Stop what you're doing now, Jim.

Whatever we do to help this man—he will try to sue us for it!" I couldn't believe what I was hearing, and got really pissed.

"Tell you what, Denise," I shouted over the wind and agonizing sound of ripping sailcloth, "You didn't want to be cook so you booked as an able-bodied seaman. Start acting like one or get your ass below and stay there."

This quieted her, but damage both ways had been done. There would never again be a comfortable relationship. I would handle the trust issue later. First we had a torn sail to get clear of the mast so we could begin repairs.

Tony and Kyle were ahead of me. Kyle, working a mast winch, hoisted aloft Tony, already in the bosun's chair. Going aloft is risky business any time, but safer close to shore, where one could be plucked from the ocean by a rescue vessel or helicopter. In this situation it was far different. With *Endymion* pitching in a choppy sea it took real guts. Tony had the guts—and the bruises to prove it for many following days.

With Tony safely on deck again the sail was shoved below for repair and we set a temporary storm mainsail. We managed a surprisingly good patch job before sunrise, and set the main again. All in a night's work—so to speak.

During the repairs, Jim sulked, and Denise was over the top hostile. I wasn't handling it well but gritted my teeth and tried to be civil. That ended when I found only Tony had worn a harness during the torn sail event. Truthfully, it wasn't a notably nasty night, but it should have been conspicuously evident that being harnessed, regardless of sea state, was important. I hit the roof again, demanding adherence to the harness rule—"simply put, wear the damn thing."

More quietly, I suggested Jim and the Amazon speak with me privately the next day. Waiting served as punishment anticipating what was to come, and provided a calming period so we might speak rationally. Their attitudes had shaken me. The one most needing a cooling down was I. In the seclusion of my cabin I started the mood altering process.

Being in charge is often a lonely position. Occasionally the intent of orders, like those about the harness, wasn't fully comprehended by everybody. Things said in general often were taken too personally. Certainly the motivation and responsibility of crew are different than that of skipper/owner. I was lucky—most of the time my crew thought clearly and acted responsibly.

The Amazon didn't show at all on Easter, except for her watch, and it was just as well. Jim grumpily pretended to enjoy the eggs Kyle, as our bunny, passed out as treats.

According to Tony, "Kyle makes a good bunny rabbit because he has enormous ears." In reality, Tony does. Kyle and Tony, with their good cheer and continuous bright attitudes, made up for a heap of negatives. The day turned into a splendid one. Reverend Chuck provided inspiration through his recording, and I again felt at peace and in harmony with my universe. It all set me to wondering what people all around the world were doing at that exact moment. I gave thanks to God and thought of loved ones far away.

By April 22nd we figured we were only a couple of days from the Equator. We were deeply tanned and wore only enough to cover privates and prevent painful sunburns. The heat and humidity were downright unbearable—and we hadn't caught a fish in days, probably because the ocean was too deep to support the food chain. Last time "fish on the line" graced our ears was off Mexico where the monster sailfish had taken everything we had, and snapped a sturdy fishing pole for spite. And guess what—the spinnaker was up again, the competition was keen and the insults were flying.

The repaired mainsail didn't look any the worse for wear, and my morning rigging inspection turned up no apparent weaknesses, so I was satisfied. We had a perfect wind and were turning in good daily runs. Log entries demonstrated individual moods. Jim wrote, "Wind up," not much enthusiasm. The Amazon contributed "fine conditions continue." The spark came from Tony, who wrote "Pacific Cup in Progress, King of the helm." Kyle retorted, "Very moving watch" (he logged 9.2 nm) and also wrote "Goodbye Tony's Late Night Bar & Grill."

The competition would close when we cross the fast-approaching Equator. Kyle would be noisy in victory should his 9.2 km run be the winner, but it was close—all five of us were within a half knot of each other's best hourly run.

145

By the 23rd we altered course more southerly to keep the 15-knot wind we had enjoyed almost the whole crossing. Luckily, we found a slot in the Intertropical Convergence Zone (ITCZ), which was normally doldrums flat calm and miserably hot, yet we blasted through the normally windless area and were now only two degrees (120 miles) north of the Equator. There had been no rain since Manzanillo. Only lightning—likely heat lightning. What we seriously needed was a fresh water wash down, to say nothing of serious showers. A little squall would be nice.

We set a lottery for the exact time we would cross the Equator. To understand what a big deal this was, consider we were in the middle of the Pacific Ocean, with references to nothing really except the imaginary line called the Equator. Calculations for the crossing moment were based on sextant, readings from a primitive sat-nav if we could get them, but mostly on scientific-wild-assed-guessing (SWAG). The next day rain squalls gave us our first real washing in 11 days.

We looked nutty, all lathered up, running around deck nearly naked. It felt wonderful, and provided a needed routine break as a continual line of squalls pelted us with a good rinse. None packed a wind punch, so no danger, just slower sailing. The spinnaker, now named 'the bitch,' was retired when the breeze moved forward.

Kyle whiffed Tony: "You don't smell like a sewer anymore."

A crossing celebration has been traditional aboard sailing vessels for centuries. King Neptune arises from the sea, crawls over the transom, demanding first-time crossers to shed their Pollywog designation and become true Shellbacks (A person who has crossed the equator at sea). A certificate is given to each person aboard, signed by the Captain—and everyone MUST be in costume for the affair. It's also time to break out that one bottle of booze and party.

Just the thought of this event brought renewed unity to our small group. Because she was the only one aboard to have crossed before, Denise was to be Neptune. She took well to this brief period of superiority. Crossing jokes found their way into our conversations. Tony, for instance, was putting aside some change for the tollbooth he knew would be present. Kyle painted a red stripe across a T-shirt to match the long faded stripe allegedly painted around the Equator, so he might slip across incognito, and I had prepared crossing certificates for all, stated as follows:

On _____ (date), at _____ hours Zulu time, _____ US Passport # _____ did cross the earth's Equator aboard the US Flag sailing vessel *ENDYMION*.

By accomplishing this feat in such desolate waters, and having been duly introduced to the Southern Hemisphere by King Neptune himself, _____ is now elevated to the lofty position of "Shellback" and is bound through eternity to the fraternity of Mariners who have challenged God's restless, peaceful sea.

Sworn by my hand _____ (signed and dated)

Captain, US Yacht *Endymion* USCG License #

CHAPTER 22

CROSSING GUARD
AT THE EQUATOR

By midnight, Endymion rolled and slapped sails on a windless slate-gray sea with the helm almost impossible to control. It wasn't dangerous, just annoying, hot, sticky, and miserable.

Sailors call this wallowing in the doldrums 'doing doughnuts.' At least frequent rainsqualls provided fragmentary relief. And for joy—regardless the battery problem, we fired up both engine and icemaker. Hurrah! Cold drinks on the Equator, nothing sounded better.

We lived on deck. Endymion's sweltering, stagnant air below invited seasickness. Tension-free blocks banging on deck magnified the bedlam below.

In the cockpit, sweat-drenched Kyle leaned across the combo backgammon/coffee table.

"Hey Tony, remember you told me about your dad's class with Capt. Swede, where he said you can always feel the wind by moving your head in a circle—if your eyes are wide open?"

"Yeah . . . what about it?"

A smirk appeared and Kyle plunged forward. "You said there is always air movement and your eyes feel it first because they are so sensitive. Right?"

"Yeah—something like that, and it tells the direction of the wind," Tony added, happy he had remembered and delighted to add the wind direction tidbit.

"Well, here's what I think," said Kyle, slowly turning to expose his eyeballs to the faintest of drafts. "It's got nothing to do with eyes, but you got horrible B.O., Tony and it's stinkin' me out across the cockpit." "Stick your nose up my ass then, and see if dem eyes can tell you where this fart starts," Tony replied.

I joined Jim for the 0200 watch, once more fascinated by the billions of stars in the sky, many of which were already dead, still beaming light across space to enchant us. I also kept an eye on a half-moon that rose slowly from an ink-black mass of clouds building on the distant horizon. We shut down the Perkins to welcome silence and ghosted along on whispers of a new gentle warm breeze. There's something special about those first moments when blocks tighten and sails fill with early cat's paws of a new wind. Mantovani's "To Amadeus with Love" drifted from the deck speakers. I felt intensely close that moment, to my dad, whose spirit I felt beside me in the cockpit. I pictured Grandpa, aboard the original Endymion years ago with wind and sea the same as for me this night.

I have another treasured 1905 photo of Grandpa on deck with his helmsman, one hand gripping the rigging on a windy day. He's wearing a gentleman's suit, as successful men did in those days. I have Grandpa's stem-winder watch on a fob with a medal engraved providing details of the Kaiser Cup race. It hangs on a bulkhead right below me in the salon of my Endymion. Those moments reminded me of a poem I have slightly modified from an unknown author:

Today, I love the wind as it blows

Across the Pacific, stretching for land.

Today I love the warmth of the sun

As I love the touch of Denise's hand.

Today I love the smell of the sea,

The rush of waves rolling under me.

The sea, the wind, birds and sky,

I want them all and I know just why.

Today I'm touched by all of God's things

That cover the sea or grow on the land.

I'm happy today. I'm in God's hand.

Deck scene Grandpa's Endymion. *Circa 1905*

Much as God and I have been having an awesome affair out here, He sadly was not pushing us to the crossing. The wall of rising black clouds dissolved and another day passed with temps over 100 cooling to 90 degrees beyond sunset. The bunk sheets were damp straight through—and stank! Even the foam rubber mattress emitted an offensive fragrance. The dull, tiresome routine had us on edge. The wind came—and died. We fired the engine up—and shut it down. But we were harvesting ice cubes, heaps of them!

Equatorial doldrums can be cruel. In dead calm seas with crushing humidity, rainsqualls skirted us, some only feet away. Swimming was out. Lurking sharks and fear of the unknown kept our bravery in check. We were close to the Equator—"E" as we called it. Chef Kyle had prepared a one-pot pasta so fiery we had to eat it with bananas to stave off its bowel-numbing potency. As we thanked Kyle with gestures, the wind suddenly piped to 25 knots, blowing directly from "E." All night we made only 27 nm forward progress. We were close though and in revenge, Kyle shouted "There it is!" and, like dopes, we all looked.

Combining sextant skills with dead reckoning we figured at 1659, on our 12th day at sea we entered the Southern Hemisphere. King Neptune presided with dignity over our small group, advancing us from our lowly pollywog status to shellbacks by anointing each with a few drops of red wine. Straight to the lips it went. We toasted by clicking paper cups laced with a fermented Amazon concoction that struck a narrow margin between our getting drunk or going blind. Our official crossing was at 00.00'00 north and 127.32'20 west, essentially the middle of the pond.

And we had a contest winner! Kyle, the cheerful kid with a big smile and outstanding work ethic had narrowly won the spinnaker completion. His 9.2 nautical miles in a one-hour run beat the Amazon's 9.1. Kyle showed no humility accepting his $40.00 prize money.

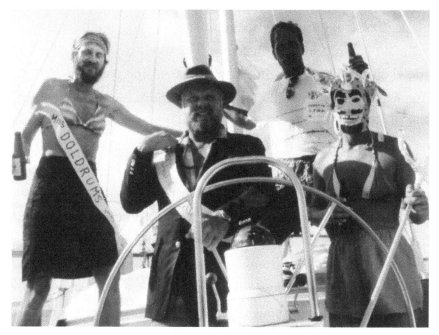

Crossing the Equator—L-R-Jim, Skip, Kyle & the Amazon. Tony took picture.

We had not seen another vessel since the freighter many days ago, confirming my belief mid-ocean is one of the safest places to sail. There is nothing to hit.

My adrenalin was pumping that night. I couldn't sleep so I took Tony's 2200 watch. He didn't care. I slipped into heavy weather gear and harness because the weather looked dismal. No moon, no stars, and sticky as usual. As soon as Tony went below, hard tropical rain—the most forceful of the trip—hit suddenly. Wind velocity leapt from 7 to 30 knots in moments. It was manageable so I saw no point in disturbing the others.

Between rain drilling my eyes like pellets and the wind, I could hardly see the instruments, or that defining line between sea and sky we often refer to romantically as the horizon. The fickle wind shifted 60 degrees, from southeast to southwest, making it challenging to maintain sail trim to keep on course. The waves were again confused and choppy with significant white water. At one point the horizon simply disappeared. I could see only black from the deck to heaven, with flashes of now-breaking waves moving in pandemonium. Alone on deck, I became disoriented. I couldn't line the compass up with the swinging wind guide. I was certain the white smear of waves were going in the wrong direction. I labored mentally to pull everything together, but couldn't. Not knowing and without bearings I headed off the wind instead of into it, straining to find the horizon, my heart pumping and eyes crying for relief from the salty spray; a wave caught us on the quarter, throwing me awkwardly and painfully into the leeward rail.

Damn—that hurt, I thought, knowing I'd have bruises, but making me conscious everything was working from my brain to harness, carefully clipped to a through hull fitting beside the cockpit.

It was over in ten minutes, and no other crew had come topside for a look-see. *It's amazing*, I thought, *how much punishment we can absorb and adjust to—how we live in a different rhythm, where it takes legions of resolve to stay alert and focus for weeks at a time.*

My stamina, in fact all of our stamina, had been tested by breakage, doldrums, storms, and tense moments. I wondered, what would Denise, my friends, and family be doing at this moment? Are they sleeping, at work, stuck at a stoplight, or walking the dog? Would they understand this life—comprehend these situations?

Sunday, April 26th, we broke free of the remaining doldrums. An easterly 15–20 knot wind was perfect. Up went the bitch (spinnaker) and up went our speed. Tony's log entry read, "Freight train . . . Yea!" That night our minds were blown again by a breathtaking assortment of shooting stars. They were everywhere. For over an hour, set against the blackness of night at sea, hundreds of shooting stars cascaded to earth rendering me again speechless and thanking God for the privilege of witnessing his universe in action.

We were 700 nm from Nuka Hiva and had sailed 2405 nm since departing Mexico when Jim, in better spirits, added the words "Rapid Transit" to his log entry.

Later that day I took sick, even way out beyond everything, sailing where there are no germs or viruses. My symptoms of fever, headache, nausea, and chills indicated flu. I slept for two semi-delirious days, awakening to wonder how single-handed sailors cope with such problems?

I recovered with a new respect for the comprehensive medical kit Denise had gifted to us back in Newport Beach, and though he wasn't licensed, I began teaching Tony to use the ham radio.

On April 28th, the subdued Amazon blurted, "I would kill for a Good Humor toasted almond ice cream."

Rain pestered us, mostly quick squalls like the one that threw me into the lifelines a few nights back. Ordinarily, we could see them coming—small storms filling only a portion of horizon and packing a punch for only a few minutes. Worse than rain was the dampness below deck and resulting unwelcome smells likely emanating from strange cultures.

Tony hovered over the charts for a good bit on this day, boasting with brimming bravado, "We will be at anchor in Hiva Oa by 1630 on May 1st—a Pacific crossing in 19 days, not too shabby for this granola bowl collection of nuts and fruit characters."

155

He could be close. We had been working *Endymion* hard. That's part of the game. The faster we cross, the less our exposure to the whimsy of the sea.

The color of the ocean had changed to a lavish aquamarine, and the whitecaps whipped up by the steady, less humid wind had become pure white. Following seas had been building and averaged 10 to 12 feet, making them a blast to surf the yacht on. We had averaged 8.6 knots the past 24 hours with the high riding 'bitch' making surfing possible. It was outrageously fun to be on the wheel, feel a big wave come from behind, lift *Endymion's* stern, and with intensity, fling the entire yacht forward into the trough, until another wave picked us up and started it all over again. I'll never get enough of it.

Also different were the flying fish in the Southern Hemisphere, a larger species, more blue in color and, being cheeky perhaps, more intelligent than their northern cousins, because they didn't land as frequently on the boat.

"Strange," Kyle commented, "I have never seen one of these critters along the West Coast. Lots of them out here though, so whadda we call em, roaches of the sea?"

CHAPTER 23

FLARE

S unrise this morning was remarkable; looking astern, the sky
gradually lightened as the ball of the sun, hauntingly large, pushed
above the ocean mist to become the sun we avoid with our eyes. We
had logged 197.9 nm the previous 24 hours, spinnaker up, riding
a gentle sea pushed by slowly strengthening warm tropical breezes.

We were two days and ten hours from Tony's predicted landfall
in the Maldives Islands, and only twenty hours from an event that
would influence our lives forever. All of us.

The Amazon delivered a tasty scramble for breakfast. We savored
hot coffee, the last of our once fresh cherries, and, being in a good
mood, she rewarded us with cinnamon biscuits.

Routines this day, like most, were simple. We checked fittings
on deck and aloft, entered creative log comments, played some
backgammon on deck, listened to the helmsman's choice of music,
dreamt about Polynesian beauties, and grabbed a few zzzz's.

Nearing dusk the wind was down a bit, as was our guard.

We were seven hours and fourteen minutes from the event when the sun slumbered to the west. In the cockpit conversation was light, varied, and occasionally serious.

The Amazon: "It's been days since we landed fish; why keep dragging the stupid lines?"

"You think it slows us down?" Kyle's voice carried mild irritation.

No answer. Tony chimed in: "Who cares? First of all, no fishing line is stupid, second we're in the middle of the ocean over 1,000 miles from any land in any direction. My burning question is—has any boat ever crossed this exact spot in the ocean?"

"Atta boy, Tony! Show us there is something between your ears," I said.

"I'm curious what's under us," Jim remarked. "It's deep, like your mind isn't," offered Kyle.

"All of you . . . fuck off!" said the Amazon, falling into one of her moods.

And so it went, serious, not so serious, until the event that changed us.

Tony was surrendering the wheel to Kyle for the 0200 watch, when he suddenly shouted, "Flare! Over there! Flare!" He pointed forward. We all saw it.

Bone-tingling shivers throttled down my spine, raising chicken skin bumps. A flare in mid-ocean, late at night can only mean serious trouble for someone.

"Grab a bearing. OK?" Tony told Kyle. "Got it!"

I got one too," I said, "with the hand bearing compass."

Kyle altered course. Ten eyes looked into darkness for another flare. Tony dove below to plot our best-known position.

"Eight degrees 15 minutes and 27 seconds South Latitude, 136 degrees, 30 minutes and one second West Longitude" he said. "We are 505.25 miles south of the Equator and 2132.3 miles off the coast of Ecuador."

And someone desperately needed help.

We tuned our VHF and high seas radios to distress channels and fired up the ham set. Tony put the radar on twenty-mile outer band limit.

I flipped on our thousand-candle strobe light, broadcasting our presence to a vast empty ocean.

Minutes passed.

Nothing. Not a sound, radar return, or eyeball burning sighting. "Or, was it really a flare?" Kyle asked.

"I saw it clearly," said Tony. "It lasted three or four seconds. I'm sure it arched. Yeah, it did! I saw it arch. It had to be a flare."

I agreed.

Tony, with binoculars trained on Kyle's bearing, said he had checked and estimated the elevation and then checked the luminous scale, finding nothing to relate what he had seen to any star or planet. "If it's a distress flare they have to be closer than twenty miles or we wouldn't have seen it over the earth's curve."

Our radios and radar remained mute. Not a sound.

We sailed, engine assisting, in the direction of the flare, intensely watching the sky and monitoring radios. We shared deep concern this night for another mariner, in distress, on a vast sea. After two frustrating, intense hours we concluded it thankfully was a false alarm. But, we had all seen at least a portion of it. I still had the willies.

Our final conclusion, never unanimous, was that it had been an extra-bright shooting star behind a thin veil of cloud giving the illusion of a flare.

Unquestionably, the calls "Flare, Man Overboard, and Fire," are frightening words at sea. Though we hadn't heard of any other vessel in this area, we had been honor bound to assist had it been a flare. We may never know the answer. It was interesting, however, that on the next ham net roll call, both Renaissance (now 200 miles distant) and a base in Hawaii reported last night's flash in the sky. Being seen from such diverse distances signaled to us that it must have come from the heavens.

Though this frightening fraction of our sea time is etched forever in our collective memories, it's comforting to believe this was likely a meteor, reminding us once more of our finite place in the scheme of life and the universe.

We sailed on and at 0800 on the last day of April, we positioned ourselves 100 nm from Traitors Bay, Isle of Hiva Oa in the Marquesas Island chain fringing French Polynesia. Soon we would touch land, visit Poste Restante for mail, eat ice cream, and possibly see some legendary Polynesian goddesses. Stifling the mood, I told my mob it was time we began thinking about "slow sailing."

"What the hell is that?" asked Kyle.

"Well, Kyle, let's estimate we are able to make out the island by mid-afternoon, meaning arrival after dusk. It's just my rule, Kyle, but I won't sail into a strange, small South Pacific harbor at night with no moon and no navigation aids. I'd like to break the rule, but no dice. We've been sailing fast—we need to slow down to make our entry in daylight."

"Aw shit," said Kyle with a grin and a chuckle.

The following midday we dropped the mainsail and took a small reef in the jib. Endymion slowed to a crawl in the beefy, steady wind. Out came the fishing poles and along came—no fish. We didn't care.

Jim and the Amazon, standing on the bow, were first to see the island and define the mountains' ragged edges as separate from the clouds. The Amazon let fly a whoop. Jim drew her into a hug and a kiss. The rest of us settled for handshakes and fist bumps. Drawing closer we brought the charts to the cockpit table, where hunching over them we could identify each peak. They were exciting moments. It was the first port in a long, well-done journey. Arriving today would put us in port after eighteen days at sea, and in time for an evening cocktail at anchor. Pleasing thoughts.

May 1st. 1745 hours. Tony is at the foredeck windless: "Let er rip, Pops!" I put my finger to the remote, and our anchor slips into Traitors Bay, headed for the bottom. We'd sailed over 3,000 nm in eighteen days and ten hours, averaging nearly seven knots around the clock. Standing in the cockpit, I was struck by the tropical splendor of our first landfall, mentally patting my crew on the back—yet taking a moment to remind myself, that if we had been off even a fraction of a degree, we could have missed the island by thirty or more nautical miles.

It felt odd, standing on a motionless deck, no sails above me, no sound of rushing water. Endymion was firmly anchored in thirty feet of crystal-blue water covering a slightly visible firm sandy bottom. Here we were, in Michener's paradise. More palm trees than I had previously imagined lined the nearly five-mile bay. Ambush Point jutted out at one end and Alligator Point contained us from the other. Colorful names no doubt denoting history, and somewhere in the lush green hills, with rain clouds hovering over rugged peaks, lay the grave of the French Impressionist Paul Gauguin. All in due time, we would visit. For now, I just wanted to forget the ocean's emptiness and focus on the beauty of this island.

Anchored in Traitors Bay—Nuka Hiva Island

It was so quiet and so serene before me, except for a heavy woman in bulky clothing doing laundry on a rock. Were she here, my Denise would say, "Now, that's crapola."

CHAPTER 24

POOF GOES THE GENERATOR

Before any serious work, we first needed and deserved a day's break. We piled into the Avon. The Amazon was first ashore. Taking a half-dozen steps on the sand, she dropped to the ground to make sand angels with her arms. Tony, Kyle, and I followed suit. Jim collected shells. We broke into groups with Tony, Kyle, and me following a flower-lined dirt path we hoped would take us to Poste Restante and the clearing officials, if there were any. The Amazon and Jim searched for ice cream and hopefully went trolling for a new boat to call home.

No one we encountered spoke English. It didn't matter. Life wasn't complicated and hand signals worked. The people were hospitable, but we noticed, not overly cordial. We wondered why?

Missing town center, we wandered aimlessly, taking in unusual sights like horses in car ports with no cars, gravestones in front yards telling their own stories, and houses so choked in fragrance-laden vines it appeared buildings had been reclaimed by the original inhabitant, the jungle.

We hiked to Paul Gauguin's grave and agreed with the master painter—it's a wonderful view. There were no golden arches or whirling buckets of chicken in the sky on this island. In fact, there were no restaurants, so we purchased our first wild range chicken (meaning from a backyard), with somber directions to pluck it before you eat it.

We took vendor assistance for the crucial first step. The chicken was alive when we chose it and dead when we paid for it.

At Poste Restante, a damp dark wooden structure offering paltry relief from the sweltering heat, a folded piece of paper, palmed by the person opposite Tony, was slid across the counter to Tony with a whispered, "See me first!"

"What's that about?" asked Kyle.

"Nothing good, if you ask me," said I, who hadn't been asked.

Tony took (and probably flunked), French in school, but we elected him spokesman. Following backroom negotiations, Tony found what the note-passing mail guy wanted was guns, but more than that—bullets. If we had them, they would pay top dollar.

"No guns, no bullets, no dollars, we got nuthin'," Kyle adamantly proclaimed. He did not know about the $60.00 revolver secreted aboard long ago, and used so far only to frighten birds. We huddled, and since we had seen no officials, we could probably sell it without getting a free ride to the slammer. Tony presented the buyers situation: "The guy told me there isn't enough meat in paradise, so they go to the hills hunting goats, but they don't have enough ammo because the gendarmes restrict the sale of bullets hoping to reduce crime—simple as that."

We helped cure the economy and food shortage by parting with our pistol and two boxes of bullets for a criminally unreasonable

NO RETURN TICKET – LEG ONE

$750.00. Yankee money. That left us only a flare pistol to fend off birds or bad men.

The following morning we got to work. Jim headed for the engine room to service the Perkins diesel and the small diesel generator. The Amazon happily shined the galley and scraped away mysterious oddities lost from forks or mouths during assorted moments of bashing seas or panic caused by humans. Kyle and Tony, in the inflatable, scrubbed the hull removing a nasty coating of algae clinging to fiberglass above the waterline—it happens to all vessels on long crossings and looked wretchedly horrible. I tore down and lubricated winches, and, like jigsaw puzzles, put them back together. I hadn't expected so many picayune pieces so precisely fitted. Days were intensely hot and we felt it more because we were not moving. For Jim and the Amazon working below, it had to be torture, so they took lots of breaks. We consumed gallons of liquid compensating for sweat.

Shortly after noon our second working day, Jim appeared on deck: "Well, that's it, Skipper. The Perkins and the Ferryman (our small generator) are serviced and ready for action!"

"Really, Jim, including the complete 200-hour service on the Perkins?"

"Yup, even zincs, filters, belts, and oil change!"

"And the generator, Jim, you changed oil and filters?"

"Sure did, Skipper," Jim reported. " I just need to find a place ashore for the old oil and waste parts, and it's a done day for me."

"Good stuff," I said to Jim. "That was fast. Have a beer to cool down, and on your way below, how about firing up the generator; be nice to have ice. OK?"

"Right on it," said Jim as he disappeared down the companionway. I continued working—a small cloud of doubt hovering above me. The generator was only 3 kilowatt, but mounted on steel brackets that held it above the Perkins diesel. The engine room was tighter than the skin on a grape. To compensate for the inaccessibility, bulkheads to the engine room were removable on all four sides. Even checking the generator oil level, much less changing it, is difficult work. That Jim finished so quickly seemed a little off.

"She's purring like a kitten," Jim boasted as he emerged from below, beer in hand. The Amazon, also with a beer, was taking another breather.

I don't know why I asked, but I did. "Jim, the generator oil cap. It's a bitch to reach. It's on tight?" "All's well that's done well."

The Amazon tersely added, "Jim's a top mechanic. If he says something, he means it, so you don't need to harass him, Skip."

I didn't acknowledge her jab and continued my winch work while they sat quietly sipping beer in the beanbag chairs.

Maybe everything is fine, I thought, *I'm probably pushing too hard*.

Then I smelled smoke—faint at first. I couldn't quite get a handle on the source, but I knew something was wrong.

"Holy shit," said Jim, looking toward the hatch. Inky dark smoke billowed from the companionway.

"Looks like—smells like engine fire," I screamed and raced toward it, Jim a step in front of me. Below decks Endymion was filled with smoke and the wretched stench of burning oil.

"Hold this," Jim shouted, removing an oil-soaked engine room panel, allowing more acrid smoke to pour out. Big drops of oil showered in all directions like sparks from a flare, targeting everything from our clothes and faces to the galley and our comfortable salon upholstery. "Shut 'er down quick!" Jim spoke with urgency. I was already choking off the fuel, causing the generator to sputter. It stopped with an unnatural grinding sound.

166

"You damned idiot," I screamed. "I specifically asked about the friggen oil cap! It wasn't on the generator—look—it's on the galley counter. What's the matter with you, you dope!"

I couldn't stop—didn't want to. "This is a fucking mess! You did this, Jim—to a brand new boat and new generator. What kind of crazy asshole are you? Get the fuck outta my way." I pushed Jim roughly aside. Anger welled in me.

"Dickhead!"

Oil was everywhere. I was pissed, and Jim knew it. He cowered in the companionway, unable to speak.

Tony and Kyle had rushed below, each with a pile of rags. We all started wiping, while I continued attacking Jim in front of everyone. It wasn't how I'd been taught to behave. I didn't care! This was a grade school mistake that should not have happened.

"Christ Jim, how could you be so stupid! The generator's toast. You're an idiot!"

I spun on the Amazon. " And don't you say anything, Goldilocks."

She looked at me with open hostility and disbelief, her eyes glazed, color drained. But she wisely held her tongue.

Very slowly my enormous rage gave way to reality. The whole of *Endymion's* engine room, workshop, companionway, galley, chart table and salon were oil drenched, including insulation and headliner—covered with ugly dripping slippery black stuff! It was an impossible situation that would take weeks, or months, to make right again. I was also worried about the generator.

"OK, Jim, you're the proclaimed expert, dipstick the damn thing, and let's see what we have."

Jim didn't want to. With others looking on, however, he couldn't say no. We watched. The stick came up dry.

167

For the rest of the afternoon everyone worked in the confined engine room. Removing hatches gave access, but the hatches themselves were oil soaked. This was our toughest, nastiest, most grimy job since the birth of *Endymion,* and we worked without breaks. Even the reluctant Amazon lent a hand, later volunteering a nice dinner, a 'peace offering,' she shyly said.

There comes a time, after a satisfying meal, when we wander to a favored spot, to retire with private thoughts. I chose that time to make my way slowly to the aft deck beanbag cushions, for an overdue private discussion with Jim and the Amazon. I dove right in: "Denise, Jim—I want you off the boat by noon tomorrow. I'll see that your bond is forwarded to local officials before you leave."

"And just where do you expect us to go?" asked the now more humble Amazon.

"I'm sorry to say, Denise, but I really don't know or care—just get away from the boat, and take a wide berth around me! And one other thing—don't expect a referral!"

"You're the dickhead," she nastily replied, tiny beads of sweat breaking out, and she was about to spit at me—almost getting booted from Endymion that moment. Our hearts beat rapidly. I mentally worked through the increasing issues and knew I was right. Only the late hour and unavailability of an official to post their bond prevented me from having them 'walk the plank' that night..

Jim and his moody partner departed Endymion at 1130 the following day. I had taken care of the paperwork ashore. Before boarding the inflatable, with their belongings, Jim agreed in writing, to pay for all parts necessary in the repairs. But how? Where would this drifter find even a fraction of the required money?

I wondered also, what boat might take them aboard?

CHAPTER 25

NUKA HIVA—WE MADE IT!

Late afternoon, May 15th, we crawled carefully through coral heads into Taiohae Bay, our last anchorage before pushing on to the Tuamotus en route to Tahiti. It was time for some reflection.

In my California business career I was caught up, like a lot of guys, in winning the corporate battle, rewarded by the hedonistic self-indulgence that followed. It took years of fermentation to adjust to and accommodate the distant goal of drifting and blending. I knew I could find a better life, with more wholesome values, where money plus power were not the guiding purpose of life—as I felt it had become in America. I can't say for 100% certainty I've discovered utopia by cruising, though it's a different world.

Compared to America's affluence, we have seen a lot of poverty. What amazed me was how happy people were living in those conditions. True enough, they hadn't seen the other side and didn't know greed, jealousy, rage, or the lack of confidence that results. The unit I'd come to admire was a strong family—much stronger than the majority of American households. I've observed a good balance between work and recreation, family and church.

Other cruisers are interesting. Mostly couples in their thirties through early fifties who've broken free of jobs for extended 'rest' periods or just plain sold out, as I had. Powerful medicine if you had the guts to take a swig. There are also pocket cruisers, folks who lack the substantial financing for an undertaking like this, but had marketable talent. Most in demand were mechanics, sail makers, or carpenters. The best tradesman sailor was a refrigeration mechanic. Ice cubes have massive value in the tropics.

Nine yachts shared Taihoae Bay, none of them mega yachts. For owner's pride, by the way, we call any vessel capable of coming this far, a yacht—be it big, small, lavish, or fundamental. Looking around, there was one from Brazil, one from the Grand Caymans, another from France (wonder if he posted a bond), one from Mexico, and even one from Japan. The others were US flag. In common we shared a serious desire to survive, the wish to see the world, and most of us to make a positive difference in the world. It wasn't corporate collateral, and I, for sure, wanted to be a part of that legacy. Cruising folks I met, were self-sufficient, rugged, and compassionate people who didn't take well to being controlled.

We enjoyed sharing knowledge and resources, which earned coveted mutual respect. We shared charts, plans, dreams, fears, and experiences and somehow managed to arrive here—a long way from the boardroom conference table. Adventurers I've shared company with were different than people at home, who too often ignore the plight of others as they scramble for survival in a greed-cluttered world. Because of our lifestyle, cruisers were relaxed and different—yet alike in pursuing a romantic lifestyle. OK, enough pontificating. Not surprisingly, the cost of cruising was a favorite discussion topic. None of us anticipated Pacific Franc pricing. Try $6.00 a (small) jar for peanut butter possibly past its 'good until' date stamp. Eggs at $10.00 a dozen were a crowd pleaser, and I loved corn flakes for $7.50 a box.

Endymion was well stocked with staples before leaving US waters, and Mexico was a bargain. We used much of our frozen foods and canned goods on the crossing and had spent only $52.00 in the Marquesas. Three fifty a can for beer was the deal breaker. We simply gave it up. Liquor became a distant memory. Ahhh, the sacrifices we make! The three-egg omelet became one egg, and we used rice, noodles, or beans to extend almost everything. A pleasing result of those sacrifices was a more appealing body, requiring a shorter belt. We caught plenty of fish. Mostly dorado, wahoo, and tuna.

We never fished if we already had fish aboard from the same day. Except for Las Hadas, we had spent around $600.00 a month. Crew paid me a stipend of $10.00 a day for chow and *Endymion's* comforts, commensurate with what other vessels charged. Tony paid nothing, but he's blood.

All yachts attempt to avoid expensive repairs, and we had done well. That would probably end when parts arrived for the generator Jim so carelessly destroyed.

Another reflection regarding boat size and condition; *Endymion* was new, and at 43 feet one of the larger yachts in this anchorage, or any anchorage we had dropped our hook in. Were I to start from scratch again, I would choose a well-equipped used vessel, a few feet shorter, less expensive to maintain and easier to handle. It may take longer getting point to point, but when you're drifting—who cares?

Cruising brings unexpected challenges and uncertainties. Today's challenge was finding a bothersome tiny leak in the Avon inflatable, and developing a safe method to transfer butane from a French-built tank into a U.S.-built receptor. We always somehow managed.

Would I continue to cruise? Interesting question. One thing I've learned can ruin a cruise quickly is sailing under pressure. We've seen everything from financial worries to weather creating time-line problems, to health issues at home, or a partner who isn't into the cruising lifestyle. Any pressure can be a real drag.

Storms and damage create havoc, affecting decisions, pocketbooks, or planning. Up to this point we had coasted along, mostly stress free, content with our surroundings in our two-foot zones, and proud of our abilities to master the challenges that regularly confront us.

The highest of many rewards was knowing someone at home cared, simply because they loved us. And speaking of love, Denise checked in yesterday on the high seas radio, joyfully reporting the cast was off her leg! Her right ankle, however, was frozen in place from so long in a cast, requiring therapy before she could strut like a cheerleader. Regardless, we picked July 9th as her arrival date in Papeete, Tahiti. As a couple, we are more than the sum of our parts, so that works well.

Tony's been a remarkable mate but a bit lazy when hard work is lurking about. This was understandable considering his age and the meager wages I paid. Tony became a master at barter, recently swapping five beat-up cassette tapes for $50 Pacific Francs. He bought fruit and veggies for the boat, and a few brews for some native guys he'd been surfing with. His generosity was impressive.

Small things played a heavy role here. To get groceries we must land our inflatable Avon on a sandy beach, hopefully with little surf. Next came a hike, often over a mile, fending off horses, chickens, pigs, numerous dogs, and countless curious children. It was often amusing.

Once in the store selections were miserable and prices astronomical. We would fill the ship's bag, hike back to the inflatable and pray we could paddle through the surf without losing our purchases. If you were new to the game, it was about a fifty/fifty risk. Good chuckles for those observing—and of course we all watched.

CHAPTER 26

BEVERLY HILLS GREG

Man—Nuka Hiva was hot! *Endymion* below decks was pure inferno. Sleep was impossible before midnight, so I slept on deck, often interrupted by sudden, cooling squalls.

One evening Kyle and Tony heard tell of a 'dance night in Taiohae. They spiffed themselves up, went ashore, found they had mistaken 'dance' for words meaning 'movie shown on a bed sheet' and returned to the boat unhappy. The solitude during their absence allowed me to linger on deck with music I enjoyed. I pegged the volume on Streisand and Sinatra cassettes enough to deafen anyone within a half mile. But there wasn't anyone within a half mile. Could you picture that in a U.S. population center?

Back in Las Hadas, Greg, an attorney from Beverly Hills visiting another yacht, had expressed interest in joining us along the way. Greg, at around age thirty, had already established himself as a spokesmen for numerous rich and famous clients. Tall, thin, scholarly in appearance, Greg had an easy disposition, a thirst for travel, and an inquiring mind that I enjoyed sparring with. My only reluctance was a mental flag that he may not take direction well.

By high seas radio we agreed to meet in Nuka Hiva. I had no idea how difficult that would be for Greg. He first had to fly to Papeete and then take a small, once-a-week prop-driven puddle jumper to Nuka Hiva. "By the way, Greg," I had asked, "would you mind bringing along a few parts for our generator?"

The Monday flight, postponed 'til Wednesday, delivered a tired, unhappy, grumbling Greg on Thursday evening. He toted nearly 200 pounds in parts, was exhausted from delays, the load, the heat, and the inconvenience of forking over the amount of cash demanded for the bond he hadn't expected. But he did.

Greg, with his higher IQ, was enlisted to help on the generator problem.

"Here's the deal," I explained to the weary soul. "We've attempted to rebuild it ourselves. Collectively we have zero experience, don't have the right tools or patience, so we have done nothing."

Greg was unimpressed. He wanted to sleep. So we let him and pushed on in the morning, "The generator is 'gone,' Greg. The main bearing has to be pulled and replaced!"

"And you know that how, if you have neither skills nor tools?"

"Because another guy on another boat told me, and that, my friend, is why your luggage was so heavy."

He got the picture, and explained to Tony, Kyle, and me, that to pull this bearing, the generator must first be removed from the yacht and taken ashore to a mechanic possessing a bearing puller tool. Unbelievably, such a person existed on this tiny island. At least he claimed to be Mr. Right.

Now it became challenging! To remove the generator from the engine room we first had to remove every possible part to reduce weight and space. Next we stripped the wiring, unbolted the generator, and braced it with two by fours, before torqueing it into a position to somehow lift it. The generator, unfortunately, was located under the cockpit area, meaning the cockpit sole (floor) had to be removed, which also required disconnecting the wheel and steering quadrant. It was a huge project on a scorcher of a day.

"Now I really dislike that sleaze ball prick Jim," I said to no one in particular.

"Yeah, but you took him aboard, Dad," chuckled Tony, wrench in one hand, banana in the other.

For this maneuver to work, Tony and I squeezed inside the engine room against the aft bulkhead, Tony to port and me to starboard. Sweating and cursing profusely, we managed to move the useless generator a few inches. It was heavy work.

Then Kyle yelled, "Awww – shit!" as he slipped on the oily decking losing his grip. The generator slid back on the two by fours, squarely pinning me thigh to chest against the bulkhead. Tony was also stuck, but wriggled free. "This sucks! You OK, Dad?"

"I'm OK, nothin' broken, I don't think, but it's a crappy place to spend lunch hour. Get me out, you guys!"

Greg took charge, the three pushed, shoved, grunted, and gradually built enough leverage to budge the heavy machinery sufficiently for me to squeeze free, physically shaking, and still cursing—but free. We wrestled until sunset before getting it settled on the aft deck. The workday ended near midnight when we had the cockpit floor temporarily back in place, with steering working enough to maneuver the boat if necessary to relocate.

Moving the generator to shore required creative thinking and some time away from the problem. Tony's higher-than-a-kite surfing friends devised a unique solution to protect the machinery against salt water. Somehow they "acquired" a body-bag-size, waterproof French postal bag, big enough to stuff in the whole generator. Lowering it from *Endymion* into the Avon, required painstakingly rigging a pulley system to our dinghy davits. We waited three days for calm-enough conditions to get it ashore without flipping the inflatable. Then we made a run for it. Dominick, the island's chief mechanic, a Chinese man with an Italian name, met us with his dilapidated, exhaust-burping, rattling truck. We hefted the mailbag onto his truck bed and bounced our way to his shop. Long into the evening we watched as Dominick worked his magic on our machine. Finally, in broken English he proclaimed,

"Not bearing. Bearing OK. Problem different. Leave here. I see."

The man of many words had just told us how much we had done for nothing.

"This is a shitty vacation," Greg let us know his position.

For the next three days Dominick pondered our dilemma while we took in the island's beauty. One morning following a torrential, bug-killing, pounding rainsquall we counted twenty-two waterfalls in the hills surrounding our anchorage. More awesome beauty would be hard to find.

When the rain abated, Greg and I decided to hike those hills. Local surfers advised Tony, with a big laugh, to have fun but "stay in the creeks, so you don't get lost in the jungle and be eaten by wild pigs or snakes."

We didn't believe them.

Setting out early the following morning, hoping to beat the heat, we hiked the creek bed for several hours. Gaining altitude we occasionally glimpsed the sea, shimmering in the sunlight, and Endymion riding at anchor in the turquoise bay. At one point we surprised a local bare-footed, brown-skinned, Polynesian gathering coconuts from which he would make hemp lines, who demonstrated his ability to walk barefooted up the slender trunk of a tall palm tree, machete in hand to cut free a barrage of coconuts, causing us to scatter and from which we had to duck or run.

A half hour and ample sweat later we were at the trailhead. Before us lay a pond, almost big enough to call a lake. The pond edges were laden with lily pads with honeysuckle-scented flowers poking from them. A twenty-foot vertical drop waterfall fed the pond. We were under it in seconds.

"Hell with this," Tony said. "I'm taking me a swim in this here paradise pond," and he climbed onto a large rock, preparing to jump. "Whoa there boy! I just saw a bright yellow flash of something dart past," cautioned Greg.

"I'm stickin." It was Tony again.

"I saw it too . . . went over there," said Kyle, pointing to marsh-like weeds. Frogs looked up from beneath a fold, eyeing air that was thick with hungry bugs.

Greg lobbed rocks at them. "Take that, and these too."

The yellow flash appeared again, darting rapidly in front of us, close enough none could mistake a six-foot-long sea snake not about to yield its territory.

"That's it . . . I'm outta here." Tony led our still unbathed mob on our descent.

Dominick was waiting, face as long as the snake. "Found problem. No oil. Injector pump fried." He seemed totally defeated. I felt likewise and cursed Jim with another volley. Now we had plenty of expensive extra parts, but not the ones we needed. What we did have was a generator we needed to return to *Endymion* through the surf. It hadn't needed to come ashore in the first place.

Smiling, Dominick said a pump would be waiting for us in Papeete. What a guy! He wouldn't accept payment because he had not fixed it but was accepting when we offered a sixer of Yankee beer, and coveted contraband on the island, a recent issue of Playboy, compliments of our legal advisor, Greg. We also gave Dominick a practical gift—Visine for an eye ailment.

We were ready to sail again. One more trip ashore for the still stuffed mailbag, and who should I see on the beach but Jim. I gave him a bill I'd been carrying for the parts purchased so far. Jim had agreed to this. He stuttered, said he had changed his mind and gave me a check for half the true amount. I wanted to suggest paying in full would help to keep his teeth, but I figured some payment is better than none. I would forward the check to Denise in California. If it didn't clear, and I see Jim again . . . I'll just pop him one. Pacific justice.

Aboard again, with all secure, we were ready to move to our last Nuka Hiva anchorage on the island's south side.

"Up anchor," I called from my position at the wheel, and I pushed the button on the remote. Slowly, 200 feet of 5/8 chain rolled noisily across the windless, clanking into the forepeak chain locker. With all but a few feet remaining, and just as the anchor cleared the water, the windless clutch slipped and 200 feet of chain roared out of the locker, raced around the windless, and settled again on the bottom.

"Shit!"

Out came the tools. Three hours later we left this lovely anchorage.

CHAPTER 27

TUAMOTUS— THE DANGER ISLANDS

Next stop, hardly a pinprick on a global map, was the low-lying Tuamotus Islands.

Outward bound from the tip of Nuka Hiva, Kyle scored a great game fish, a wahoo, whose weight we guessed at fifty pounds. Thumping it fatally on the head with our aluminum fish bat, we filleted the handsome fish, enjoying tasty sweet white fish meat for multiple delicious dinners and probably a few lunches to boot. Life was good again!

The word Tuamotus means distant in native Polynesian lore. Sailors know these as the dangerous islands. Scattered throughout the Pacific in an area as big as Western Europe, these islands, though not intended, became the final destination of the Norwegian adventurer, Thor Heyerdahl, and his raft Kon-Tiki. Some outer fringe islands were subject to French nuclear tests and are "off limits." (Thank you, we didn't want to go there anyway.) Others contain ancient sacrificial burial mounds from a forgotten civilization, and all atolls are part of the infamous Ring of Fire

Most Tuamotu islands in the five distinct archipelagos, were circular shaped and towered six feet above sea level—add maybe twenty feet if you climb a palm tree. The surface was mostly coral, and, where able to support plant life, we found surprisingly rich soil. We believed the fringing reefs were the remains of volcano rims that spurted and roared millions of years ago, and that the channel to the interior lagoon was where lava once flowed. Tidewater could rip through these narrow slits with dangerous intensity. The lagoons were sometimes deep, but usually neck-high shallow.

The difficulty for mariners approaching a Tuamotu atoll was being able to see the islands at all because they were so low. And, since not all mariners are vigilant, the fringing reefs are dotted with remains of wrecks—monuments to near-miss navigation.

Sailing was superb as we neared Manihi, our first landfall since leaving the Marquesas 470 nautical miles astern. Log entries included: "Close spinnaker reach. FUN!"—"Steady trades once again"—"Smoothest night since L.A."—"Shooting stars fall like rain," and—"Best sunrise ever."

When we calculated ourselves inside twenty nautical miles of Manihi, we still couldn't see it with our eyes or radar. Night was falling, so we slow sailed to avoid the coral responsible for aforementioned wrecks.

It was light by 0430. We stayed offshore until the sun was well over our shoulders. Tony then went up the mast in the bosun's chair to the first spreaders, with Polaroid sunglasses, to guide us through the coral heads, as we cautiously approached the only channel through the reef. We missed slack tide. Coral formations, accurately named 'bommies,' lay just below the surface, and were capable of ripping a good-size hole in a moving vessel, such as us. Tony picked a path through the coral by shouting, "Bommie at 1:00 o'clock,"—"Large bommie at 12:00 o'clock"—"Sixty yards distant," and so forth.

Greg and Kyle checking for bommies

An abundance of reef sharks, as many as ten in a minute, fascinated us—their sullen dark eyes patrolling the inlet. Equally fascinating were the native youth who, in the midst of the sharks, zipped past us on a fast inner tube ride, dashing out of the narrow channel.

"Ahhh," sighed Tony, "this will be good on my board!"

To which Kyle went one up with, "No sissy board for me; I'm swimming naked with the sharks."

Neither did either because we unknowingly dropped anchor close to a native shark pen, an underwater cage where sharks were lured into a chamber through a one-way opening, by placing baitfish inside.

When the cage filled with sharks, and the baitfish had been devoured, the native fishermen harvested the sharks by gaffing the shark from above—while balancing themselves in rickety outrigger canoes.

We watched. Tony and Kyle, curiosity driving them, examined the cage by taking the inflatable around the perimeter. Their vivid descriptions of seven-and eight-foot frenzied sharks, attacking smaller ones in ferocious fight to the finish blood baths, depleted their boastful desire to swim with the beasts. Instead they went ashore, leaving "Pops" to enjoy the solace aboard Endymion.

I made a close inspection of the yacht. Cosmetically, she was showing early strains of multiple-person crews for extended periods. Varnish needed work, fabrics were soiled, and there was an assortment of scratches and dents, so-called battle scars from dropped items during sudden movements, something that should be expected.

I quit complaining to myself, and thought again how incredible this journey had been. Here we were, drifting and blending—anchored inside the rim of an extinct volcano. No waves, peaceful, warm sun, and not a bug in sight.

The boys returned, reporting a seawall a couple of miles away where we could tie alongside and resupply from Turipaoa, the island's one small village. We moved over at dawn.

A group of islanders took us on tour. There was one beat-up video player on the island, no television or radio, and no phones. Natives with gaping holes where teeth once lived, or browned-out teeth from munching betel nut, smiled broadly without embarrassment. They'd never seen a football game, paid taxes, or heard of the Academy Awards, and were amazed, maybe even slightly frightened, by my Polaroid camera. What they did have was a twelve-foot-high skateboard ramp. "A damned good one," according to Tony.

Close quarters at Turipaoa

Women performed pick and shovel labor to build walls and gardens, while the men folk fished—and, I believe, drank. A single generator powered the village until curfew at 9:00 pm.

Island fresh water comes from rain catchment systems built into buildings. I never saw a hose except for our ten-footer for the anchor wash-down system. Greg powered it up, showering unsuspecting children, who shouted with glee racing back and forth through it. Shortly every kid in the village was in line.

After a few days relaxing, we sailed to Rangiroa. Serious rain enabled us to fill our water tanks using our own catchment system, where rain runs down the mainsail, travels inside the Hood boom to a hose connected to the fill cap for our tanks.

Rangiroa is a larger island. The lagoon is over forty miles wide. All of the water in the two-foot tide rushes through two openings from the center. We timed our arrival and zipped into the lagoon on slack tide.

"Whoa! What's this?" asked Kyle.

To our surprise, Kia ora, a classic small resort, appeared close by. Intrigued by the thatched roofs, long wooden dock stretching into the lagoon, and brilliantly white sand beaches, we chose to anchor in hopes we could take advantage of whatever they offered. It turned out to be a hamburger of questionable ingredients at $15.00 Pacific Francs.

In hurricanes, these islands can go completely under water with everything lost. In a 1983 storm one hundred and thirty souls disappeared forever, all from one small motu (island). They now have the island's only solid structure, a hurricane center where, in a storm, the whole island will seek refuge with newlyweds ranked next to children in importance for survival. This motivated my crew to scout for potential brides in case of a storm.

Of the many wrecks on Rangiroa's rugged coral, we found the wreckage of actor Sterling Hayden's yacht Wanderer. It was aboard Wanderer that Mr. Hayden regained his sanity, after falsely being branded a communist by the McCarthy hearings in the 1950s. Those fiercely argued hearings also wrecked his movie career. He wrote a book about it called *Wanderer*, and it's from that book we borrowed the christening poem for *Endymion*, that reads in part;

   "Noble vessel built strong and true,
   We have gathered here to christen you.
   Brightly decked with flags so fine,
   We entrust you now to nature's brine.
   May you avoid the sunken rock,
   The hidden bar, with its sudden shock,
   The iceberg vast, the fog so dense,
   All dangers of the sea immense.

I can safely say, I am one of few ever to have seen the twisted remains of *Wanderer*, hard up on the coral, reduced almost beyond recognition by seas and storms. The sight was sad. I had always, in a vagabond's sense, related to Sterling Hayden.

It amazed me how the christening poem so accurately described this voyaging and my moods, and my heart cried in silence for the man whose own adventure had ended here. In those emotional moments I felt the romantic kinship sailors feel for the life we live, be they rich, famous or ordinary people—drifting and blending.

CHAPTER 28

INTO A STORM

Our time in Rangiroa dragged, compliments of an intensive southerly depression. Waves inside the shallow lagoon were short and choppy, pulling hard on Endymion, even though we had an extra 'snubber' (device to prevent chafing) on the anchor chain, to reduce the jerking motion.

"What's with these nasty harbor waves?" Kyle asked no one in particular. "I can't read my damn magazine we're being bumped around so much!"

"Let out some more chain," advised the lawyer who had never been to sea.

Tony set them all straight: "Listen jerkos—we've got two hundred feet of chain out in fifteen feet of water. That's lucky thirteen times scope (length vs. depth)! More won't stop the bouncing. These waves, in case ya didn't know it, they get steep because it's shallow and the underside of the wave has no room to gradually drag across the bottom to make the wave fall over itself and break like on Huntington Beach sand. You're not surfers, so you don't get it!"

"Screw you, weasel face!" Kyle had spoken.

Personally, I thought Tony gave a good explanation, and while it's true friendships develop between those who sail boats, we were getting on each other's nerves a bit.

I'd been lamenting some crew goofs. One night Greg had relieved me on watch. I was nearly asleep on my sweat-drenched sheets, when Greg called down, "Captain, we have lightning to the northeast."

"How distant?" I groggily asked.

"Quite distant. No danger, I'm sure," he replied.

At least he had given me a rough bearing. Going off watch, I had found conditions clear through 360 degrees. *Oh well*, I thought, *not to worry*, and I drifted into dreamless slumber.

An hour later it was Greg again. "Skip," he shouted through the port into my cabin, "I suspect a short circuit electrical problem."

Now he had my immediate attention. "Where?"

"The trailing generator. It's sparking, and I don't want to touch it." It was 0400. I was dead tired and couldn't understand how a 12-volt generator that tows a line with a propeller just below the surface, could send flashes of light up the rigging and into the air—mostly because it lay in a heap on deck.

Reluctantly, I crawled from my rest to discover a 'man overboard' light had landed on deck after falling from its perch on a life ring and was emitting a strobe flash every two seconds. False alarm, but at least the strobe worked.

Another considerably more dangerous problem also involved Greg. We were coming through the single pass on Ahe Island mid-morning in twenty-knot winds. Tony had improved his system of reporting

190

bommies, by using clearly understandable hand signals from his position in the rigging. We miscalculated slack tide in Ahe Pass and it was flowing at wickedly strong eight to nine knot ebb, pushing tons of water from the lagoon. Tides after strong onshore winds can ebb for days, in spite of moon, planets, our personal schedule, or witches. Navigating in these conditions takes absolute concentration and crew teamwork. It's a nerve-racking, stomach come to visit mouth occurrence.

We conquered the pass without incident and decided to anchor in the picturesque lagoon close to where we believed we would find the gendarmerie. It was a lee shore on a blustery day. I wasn't thrilled with the lee shore situation but saw no alternative.

Kyle went forward and got the anchor ready. "Any time, Skipper," he shouted.

From the rigging, Tony added, "Looks good to me Pops, any time you want to drop."

Greg was aft. His simple job was to bring in the cursed trailing generator as we slowed approaching the anchor drop point.

Tony said, "Drop!"

I hit the remote switch and the anchor noisily started down. I put Endymion into reverse to set the anchor. At that very instant, the windless clutch again slipped, sending all three hundred feet of chain racing to the bottom. Greg had not pulled in the trailing generator, choosing instead to gawk at the scenery, and, hearing the calamity, abandoned his position and ran forward, wanting, innocently enough, to help. Endymion, still in reverse, ran over the neglected trailing generator line, solidly wrapping it around our propeller, immediately stopping our engine, and the anchor was not set.

"What the hell's happening here?" came from me. "Aw shit, I bet we caught the taffrail."

191

"You didn't get it up?" I asked Greg in disbelief.

"No, I let go when I heard the chain running."

"Jesus . . . Doesn't anyone think around here?" I asked the world within earshot.

We were in a bad situation rapidly getting worse, and we were only two hundred meters from a lee shore, dragging our anchor toward it—with no engine. But, we didn't panic, at least not completely.

"I'll grab the tools," shouted Greg, dropping below deck. Greg wasn't long in the teeth for experience at sea, but he was eager and had strong mechanical ability.

"Gimme a hand stripping the windlass." Greg was looking to Tony for help.

"See ya on the bottom," shouted Kyle, diving over the side into the clear water. I watched Kyle pull chain from the bottom of the lagoon and wrap it around a nearby giant coral head. That action stopped our steady march toward shore. I heaved an audible sigh of relief and scurried aft to free the taffrail generator at deck level, so we could later unwind it from the propeller below the surface.

"Good stuff, Kyle!" Tony shouted over the bow to Kyle when he surfaced. "You and the bommie saved us!"

In reality, luck was present as well. The net loss was the trailing generator line Kyle later cut from our prop. It took six hours of splicing and whipping to put it together, but we could not make it work.

The last judgment error put gentle Greg on the beach. It involved the same generator, only set up in the rigging this time with an airplane type propeller we carefully fashioned from extra Avon paddles. Once in place, a lanyard was pulled to put the propeller in motion. Lawyer Greg of Beverly Hills pulled the wrong line, releasing the whole contraption to fly wildly, yanking the electrical cord out of the generator and splitting the propeller.

"Not bad, Greg. You coulda killed one of us!" said Tony sourly.

Truly, he or it could have. Things happen unexpectedly, and that's why we call them accidents. These, however, were too many mistakes, both expensive and serious enough to require I mitigate potential tragedy. Greg had paid a moderate sum to sail with us. The money, while welcome, was not as important as safety. Greg didn't know yet, but he would leave *Endymion* in Tahiti. It wasn't working that well, and I suspected he felt the same and there would be no hard feelings. I would return his money.

There were positives though. As we got closer to Tahiti, the price of beer inched lower, $2.00 a bottle, though we didn't carry any. Another plus was our acquired skill provisioning from the land, such as fruits and native breads. The ocean was also a heavy and consistent purveyor to our meal plan as there were no restaurants. We consumed no junk food, save for some popcorn. We used all leftovers for some purpose, *if* we could get to them before Kyle targeted them for bait. He never caught much, and I doubt the fish had any attraction to the bait. Net result, we each shed weight and appeared healthier.

For a full six days, while we tugged and yawed at anchor, the winds had been edging gale force, but dry. These storms originated somewhere deep in Antarctica and were amply warmed before fetching Polynesia. Aside from wind, I was concerned with the relentless march of big seas that missioned themselves toward us almost 5,000 miles ago, and had developed strength and personality that took few prisoners. We had wisely stayed in reasonable shelter at this bumpy anchorage.

Finally, on Saturday, June 13th the wind stalled to a mere whisper. We felt safe making the pass and heading for Tahiti 200 miles beyond the horizon.

Even at slack tide the Atuona Pass ran a powerful six knots. I spent an hour walking the pass to study its safest route. Big dolphins jumping waves kept pace with me. Against the current, they would punch out of the water and land in the apparent same spot, proving the current's strength.

We timed our exit perfectly, bidding goodbye to Rangiroa at 1230 on a brilliant afternoon. We powered around the southern tip of the island and set sail for Tahiti's capital city, Papeete. By 1800 a dark brooding sky had clouded over completely. Big rolling seas, fifteen to eighteen feet trough to tip, were steadily marching beneath us.

"Can't be another storm," commented Kyle as if reading my thoughts.

"Hope not," I said, wondering if the swell would remain through dinnertime.

"Yeah," chirped Tony. "Well, maybe it is. Some o' them native kids say don't be fooled by a couple days of good weather—these blows come one right after another this time of year."

An hour later the wind Gods lived up to their evil reputation, throwing us into headwinds at twenty-five knots with a wicked jarring fifteen-foot cross sea. The motion was uncomfortable, damn near punishing. I gave serious thought to turning back, and said so to the crew.

"We're gonna be catching some fury pretty quick, I suspect.

Might be smart to reverse course and give it another day or two to flatten out."

"Chicken!" was my unanimous reply.

Tony added, "Sail er over or sail er under . . . that's what I say!" Greg was silent. He didn't look well.

I seldom went against my intuition. I knew the crew was restless and wanted to get to Tahiti, and we'd been in howlers before. I relented. "OK. We'll be bone tired, but Tahiti it is." But I wasn't comfortable.

All my life I had avoided intentionally going to sea in rough weather. It's one thing to get stuck out there, but going willingly into bad weather while entrusted with others' lives didn't sit right. Greg, Kyle, and Tony had put their faith in me and I now put mine in *Endymion*. By 2000 the wind was thirty knots—force 7 and we were committed. When the wind builds above thirty knots it begins to scream in the rigging. By midnight it was howling.

Tony's log entry was brief: "Bitch. High wind—high waves."

Seas were hitting from two directions, possibly indicating separate storm cells. Being a small yacht taking a battering in stormy seas on a pitch-black night caused me to question my sanity. To reduce punishment we bore off to a course that would take us well east of Tahiti. At least the seething high seas with crests breaking into windblown spindrift with spray akin to shotgun blasts were hitting us at sixty degrees instead of head on. Wave swells approached twenty feet high. With a cubic foot of seawater weighing 60 pounds these waves could hurl 20,000 pounds of water at us at any given moment. We had to claw and crawl our way around the cockpit. At least our course was more accommodating for our rest-seeking bodies.

Greg, poor guy, was soon seasick, miserable, and wondering what the hell he was doing so far from suits and Ferraris in Beverly Hills. Huddled in the cockpit's corner, taking shelter under the dodger, he also took valuable space for one of us still able to work the yacht, if needed. Conditions were deteriorating and I wasn't happy, but I sympathized with his misery.

If ever a boat was capable of magic, *Endymion* could deliver. Silently though, I asked God for some help: "*Just enough to get us through this,*" I asked and though it hurt my pride, I admitted to God that forty-three feet of yacht felt pretty darned small compared to His storm.

Kyle answered my question, "How ya doin?" with one word, "Shitty." There wasn't much conversation.

Tony covered for Greg's watch on the helm. Kyle stood his, as I did mine. Tony was best at the helm, I suspect because his surfing talents aided his understanding of wave dynamics. He made me proud in those wicked conditions, standing at the wheel, harness plastered against him by the wind, his hair drenched, and a big smile as he coaxed us through heavy seas, a soggy microwave burrito stuffed in his mouth. It was our nastiest night since leaving coastal America. Kyle wrote shakily in the log: "Decks awash . . . storm control."

But control wasn't easy. We had reduced sail to a tiny jib (forward sail) and a rag of a mainsail. *Endymion* would plunge her bow three feet beneath the surface of huge oncoming waves. When the bow broke free, three feet of solid water would sweep across the decks, flood the cockpit, and bury us in wash to our necks before disappearing astern. I was on the verge of abandoning our course to turn and run downwind, with the seas, and away from the battering we were experiencing. We were forereaching, which is remaining under very shortened sail while still maintaining control to make forward headway in full storm conditions. What I like is being under control. If I were to put the wind at our back, we would increase the danger of broaching as we surfed down a giant wave—and these were twenty-plus feet. This was raw nature showing fury and it had both my attention and respect. I wasn't frightened—and I surely wasn't a hero. I didn't have time for fear—the shaking would come when the storm passed. Besides, I had confidence. *Endymion* was a well-balanced, high freeboard vessel that had never faltered. We stayed the course.

The problem, even when forereaching, was to keep from falling off monster wave backsides as we drove through and over the tops. When we actually became airborne, 45,000 pounds of yacht pummeled to the trough in free fall with a thundering, bone-jarring crash that could pump fear into anyone and damage a boat.

"She's a strong yacht," I yelled, trying to keep the crew engaged and build confidence with the wind shrieking and screaming in pitches I thought came only from movie theatres.

It was a tough sell with everything thrown into shambles below deck. Pots, pans, books, personal gear, small equipment was scattered everywhere. Salt spray and mist had even wet the below deck bulkhead speakers.

At 0200 I entered into the log: "Storm—log suspended."

We slugged it out all night with only a storm jib and main reefed to postage stamp size, yet we still made six knots forereaching, but well away from our destination.

Spirits tanked.

Retreating to my cabin, I checked Adlard Cole's classic book on survival tactics, *Heavy Weather Sailing.* Holding it unsteadily in the bucking aft cabin and fighting nausea from stale air, I confirmed we were doing what's best in a raging storm, but it wasn't a big confidence builder.

With daylight, Kyle managed some pancakes before tossing his cookies over the side. I fired up the engine to charge batteries. That proved a mistake.

Endymion, with her boom slapping the waves, was heeled (tipped) and rolling so much, the raw water intake cooling the Perkins was occasionally above the wandering waterline a few seconds too many. The impeller froze—overheating the engine we so needed to charge batteries. I had to shut it down.

Tony, still stuffing soggy food into his human intake opening, volunteered. "I'll go below and replace the damn impeller—anything for you sorry asses."

"No, Tony. It's a big job in a tight space. We can't risk you getting hurt. You're needed on deck."

My words were punctuated by an enormous breaking wave barreling across the length of Endymion, burying us in several feet of swirling, turbulent, rushing water. "Hang on," yelled Tony.

We came up sputtering—realizing our situations severity. This was a doozy of a storm. We had no engine, and a non-functioning generator. The howling gale would likely get worse and we had zero way to make power.

By mid-day our batteries were toast. We barely had power for me to radio a report to a NOAA weather ship stationed in Papeete. "We haven't enough juice for navigation lights, or compass. We'll stay clear of shipping lanes through the night, and come in tomorrow."

Before dusk I used our last ounce of precious power reporting our dead reckoning position to NOAA, who pledged to look out for us.

There's a fine line between giving up and being weary. As darkness again covered us we were exhausted, cold, soaked, with two of us wretchedly sick. Plus, we had no instruments to guide us to Papeete except the sextant, impossible to use due to clouds and sea conditions. Privately, I had creeping doubts about our precarious situation.

We had been sailing way off course without making log entries—and I had only a vague idea where we were. Without navigation aids, we had to rely 100% on my ability to 'dead recon' navigate, working compass bearings, wind, boat speed, drift, and current. Although physically whipped, my brain was in turbo. I checked, rechecked, and triple checked my calculations. My crew counted on me—and I had promised God to deliver them safely.

Kyle, done in, excused himself and stumbled below. Tony and I sailed *Endymion* through total darkness of the savagely stormy night, seeing only turbulent white water without a horizon, a night without stars or any onboard lighting. Total darkness.

"Whadda ya think, Pops?" Tony asked as another wave engulfed the cockpit, trying to rip him from his harness.

"I think we're gonna make it!"

Throwing the wheel over to avoid another dousing, Tony summed up his feelings, "I'm acutely uncomfortable, and I'll heartily welcome a hot breakfast."

I couldn't picture any of us whipping up omelets, but my gut felt our heading was more on the money, though I couldn't be sure. Four lives counted on me, and I accepted that weighty responsibility. I felt pressure and apprehension I couldn't share, so in the depths of the dark night, though drenched, cold, and shivering, I resolved to stay in my two foot zone, collected, calm and showing confidence—and again I prayed.

Around 0300 the shrieking wind began to die and the seas to settle. When the bells struck 0400, Tony and I remained the only two on deck, switching positions frequently to stay alert. I sensed something was different. It's a sense sailors have. I thought I could smell land.

Looking directly into his salt-encrusted eyes, I asked Tony, "Smell land?"

"You're joking of course, great Father of mine." "No, I'm not Tony—I really think I smell it."

"Well I can't!" said Tony, and there followed an awkward silence, as if I was ordering him to smell what I hoped I was sensing.

"I still can't smell it, Pops—but I think I see it. Look there!" he said, pointing over the port bow.

A faint glow was in the sky. The glow that comes from distant city lights refracted from overhead clouds.

"Yes, Yes, Tony, that's it!"

We were instantly invigorated, discarding a giant burden, replacing it with glee. It was a feeling so intensely relieving, seeing the glow on the horizon—knowing we would now make it. I could feel the relief flooding my body. I felt warm. My confidence returned. Maybe Tony would get his hot breakfast!

Gradually we began to identify the lights of Papeete, though figuring distance was difficult. We also saw lights from passing ships. We were secure now. We had passed the test.

I went below for a clean fresh water washcloth. It felt so good I could have married it. Instead I brought it to Tony. "Here, take a break, son, wash the salt from your eyes and face. You look like a ghost."

Life slowly improved. We took fewer waves aboard, and Greg even reached the lee rail to hurl. I don't think anyone, except maybe Tony, ever knew I feared we could have become statistics that night. As dark gave favor to light, we became energized. A group of weary guys on a small sailing yacht, feeling good because we had decided to 'go for it,' and it had worked.

"Your honors, Dad." Tony stepped aside and offered me the wheel. Under sail alone, in a wind almost gone, and seas still rolling, we short tacked our way between the fringing reefs of Papeete. As morning commuters were edging their way to work, and still under full sail, we dropped anchor and heaved a collective sigh of relief. The wind was gone. The sails flapped idly. The four of us stood on the foredeck of *Endymion,* from Newport Beach, California, now fifty feet from city traffic in Papeete, Tahiti—doing a football fist bump.

Was I proud, pleased, and satisfied? You bet! The storm was over. It would not be our last.

CHAPTER 29

REUNION IN TAHITI

Practically every person on the globe has heard of Tahiti. Most yearn to see it at least once. Mission accomplished. Tied along the concrete quay, the high-five fist bump had given way to pure uninterrupted slumber amidst the clamor of the Tahitian Islands' largest city.

Bathed and freshly dressed, we later crossed the busy waterfront and raced for the first restaurant and our first table service meal since leaving Mexico nearly two months ago.

"Whoa!" said Tony, grabbing Kyle's shirt with one hand while restraining me with the other. "No way: $15.00 Pacific Francs for a lousy hamburger?"

"What's that in Yankee dollars?" questioned Kyle.

"Dunnow, dumb shit. We just got here."

"Outta my way, jerko," said Kyle, pushing forward to order what became one of many delicious burgers devoured during the next couple of months.

Papeete sits at latitude 17 degrees south, about the same as Acapulco is north of the equator. In other words, stifling hot with high humidity.

Shortly after the burger fest, Greg said, "Thanks for the ride, see ya in California," and left. It wasn't unexpected and it was on good terms.

Kyle and Tony, once rid of initial Hinano beer hangovers, became resolute, returning *Endymion* to her pristine condition, including a polish of her hull, until interrupted by a stranger watching them work. He struck up a conversation with Tony and Kyle, came aboard for cocktails, introduced himself as "Bob," and claimed mutual friends in the Huntington Beach surfing community. Bob was a pleasant fellow, long blonde hair and striking blue eyes like a poster board model for Billabong.

"Mr. Skip," he addressed me over wine and beer batter shrimp at our cockpit table, "the boys here and me have been talkin'."

"Go ahead," I encouraged.

"I skipper a hundred-foot offshore repair and supply boat for the commercial fishing fleet out here . . ."

"Sounds like good work," I interrupted.

"It is, it sure is," he said, leaning forward as if sharing a military secret. "But I need some help, and wonder if I could borrow your crew for a while?"

"Explain 'a while' and explain 'borrow' while you're at it."

"I'm headed to the States for two weeks. I'll pay these bandits," he pointed to Kyle and Tony, "$100 a day each, if they will move aboard and keep my systems running while I'm away. They can also use my inflatable. It's fast."

"Please, Dad," said Tony. Kyle held his hands like in prayer, adding, "Yeah, please, Pops."

I saw no problems. They were caught up with work, and it would allow me privacy with Denise when she arrived, plus be good for them to have some serious jingle in their pockets. The deal was sealed. Tony and Kyle moved to the supply ship a half-mile across the harbor the next day. I never saw Bob again.

It didn't take long to tire of the Quay in Papeete. It was dirty. The water was polluted. Cars sped by fifty feet away leaving continuous diesel vapor to fill my nose by day, and lay across the decks at night. Only the rats were impervious—and there were many.

It's no small wonder I was interested when Mike, a fellow yachtsmen, thumped on the hull. The Australians, he had learned, were planning a gala celebration for their Bicentennial and were inviting foreign flag private yachts to race from Hobart, Tasmania to Sydney, New South Wales, along with the world's true Tall Ships—the first race ever of its kind in the southern hemisphere.

"Will you go, Skip?" he asked.

"Doubt it. It's across the dreaded Bass Straits. That's way too much punishment for me. I'll pass."

"But it's summer in Australia. Better weather," he said in inviting tones.

We pulled out my pilot charts. Mike was half right. It would be summer. The charts showed only a 40% chance of gales compared to 48% during winter.

Mike's enthusiasm was infectious. "Look," he said excitedly, "it's a once in a lifetime opportunity. Come on, Skip, let's sign up!"

We did, posting our applications to the Australian Race Committee that afternoon. The Aussie press had given the event considerable coverage. Mike had me keen on the idea. I should hear from Australia about visas when we arrive in Fiji, hopefully in August.

I enjoyed being alone. It was my first time alone aboard *Endymion* in almost six months. I wrote a stack of letters and postcards to my folks and friends. A few cards pictured topless, brown-skinned native women in a tropical setting paying too much attention to a bearded white guy. It may have been in poor taste, but it was my humor. Each card carried a simple message: "How's work?"

Tomfoolery aside, Denise was soon to arrive and I faced a major decision—go ahead with this union or not? Sitting alone in the cockpit I thought about the storms we had encountered, the knockdown where I almost lost *Endymion* and the seemingly endless shipboard repairs. This was a profound moment for me. Was I about to drag Denise, the lady I love, into something more than she wanted, or more than she could handle? Was I putting her life on the line? Could she take it? Most people can't.

I made a list a list of pros and cons: positives of love and enjoyment vs. potential loss and conflict. In my twenties I made many more mistakes than now, and working problems with pros and cons has served me well both making decisions and having the conviction to see them through.

I made my decision by nightfall. I wanted Denise to come. There was no one I would rather take life's journey with.

I had but one more letter to write—to Denise.

My Dearest Denise,

> *We came together, fell in love, joined our souls in a dream and were separated by the dream itself and your unfortunate accident.*
>
> *Now we are to reunite, to continue our dream, to live our lives as one. I want this.*
>
> *But I must caution you.*

I have found this sea-going vagabond's life to be harder than expected. Nature takes pride in her strength, turning a quiet ocean into menacing tumbling water, attempting to frighten me or break me. I've been lucky so far, but there are no guarantees.

You're a strong woman, Denise. You can handle both the moods of nature and Skip.

The question is—Do you want to?

Is this really the life you choose, fanciful and adventurous, but without a white picket fence and church full of friends—at least for now.

Think about it. Think hard, long, and carefully. Then come to me!

Love always,

Skip

The letter was posted. I hoped Denise would be up to the challenges. She'd earned the right to try. I had to wait.

As the days passed another doubt crept unhurriedly into my mind. I visited Kyle and Tony on the big boat. Motoring back to *Endymion*, I wondered about the all too-knowing grin Kyle wore while showing me around their new digs. Why didn't I see any tools on this 100-foot working supply boat—Why wasn't there heavy equipment anywhere on the massive open decks—or was it something else? Why would this big complicated boat hire Tony and Kyle to look after it, since neither had a license or mechanical experience? Or maybe I was bothered by the $100.00 a day offered to each just to lie in the sun, eat lobster, and drink someone else's booze. Getting by financially in this loony bin French town wasn't cheap, but even so, that was a lot of pay. There was a fox in this woodshed somewhere. I could smell it.

Putting the thought aside, I dove into my daily chores, and when completed, I sat in the cockpit, sipping a Hinano and answering endless questions from passing tourists who wondered how we got here from Newport Beach. I didn't mind. It made me feel important. Tuning in the ham net that evening, a chap I had met in radio school years ago had linked me by radio with Denise. With her words bouncing off the clouds and heard around the world, Denise said, "Yes! I love you. I'm up to the challenge. I'm coming."

I had heard the music and placed an expensive international call to Denise. We developed an itinerary for her arrival at 0500 on July 9th. Denise was to pick up a $2,000 cashiers' check from my bank to be used toward our security bond in Tahiti.

The owner/skipper deposits a bond with the authorities, enough to cover expenses if the crew gets in trouble or the yacht is abandoned in country. I fought with the gendarmerie over the absurd $2,320 fee, because I was confident in my crew, and I would never leave Tahiti without my boat. They argued the boat could sink. I said they were nuts, and I didn't have that much money. They said—get it. We were at a standoff I likely wouldn't win. When they learned Denise was arriving with money, they offered a police escort from the airport. What's this? They didn't trust me?

I was lucky not to have been booted from the country right then. For Denise's arrival I had *Endymion* looking as sharp as the day Denise first saw her. Fresh flowers, baguettes of savory bread, and iced champagne had been carefully placed by 0330 when I hoofed it to the gendarmerie and met the policeman who would escort me picking up Denise. He was a relaxed, likeable young fellow with a clean-shaven face, dark complexion, and inky black hair. He was impressive in his tailored blue uniform and seemed intent to please, so I started coaxing him to help carry what I knew would be a colossal amount of luggage. 'Denise Dearest' and 'pack lightly' were oxymoron's .

An advantage of a police escort was Denise not having to wait with the mob to clear customs. From a police viewing room I was asked to pick out Denise as she deplaned—real high tech stuff. Denise was nearly last off, accompanied by her close friend Marcia Delano. I had no idea—nothing had been said to me . . . surprise . . . surprise! Denise was eye candy and looked radiant, though tired, in a pretty red sundress and deep California tan—an angel. Marcia was also stunning in a snow-white outfit complemented by deep black striping that accentuated another superb tan. Compared to the other exhausted, overweight, shabbily dressed deplaning tourists, these two were stars, with an entrance made more noticeable because Denise, a head turner, checked in at five foot one inch while Marcia, a former Frederick's of Hollywood model, towered over six feet.

So, here they came, Mutt and Jeff of the beauty world, into the hands of the wide-eyed gendarmerie. The girls thought it exciting, having a police escort.

Denise had the bond money, but in travelers checks, and we needed a bank. Gendarme Pierre assisted, passing Immigration and we started gathering the ladies' luggage . . . one, two, four, seven, nine—ten pieces!

"How in hell did you get this all checked?" I asked Denise.

"Cried a lot. It always works!"

"Do you know how much extra this coulda cost?"

"Plenty," said Marcia. "Now be a good boy—we want a champagne breakfast."

"OK, my pleasure—business first though so Pierre here doesn't throw us in the slammer."

Pierre wanted in on the breakfast. He located a bank, oversaw exchanging checks for the monster bond—and we left the airport.

Our transport was two squad cars with trunks so full they had to be tied in place. We were in the first car, and luggage followed with a junior officer. We went by private escort to a pleasing breakfast, followed by continued police escort right to the stern of *Endymion* where our escorts loaded the unwieldy luggage into the inflatable, but thankfully declined my insincere offer of coffee.

Settled in the salon, up popped Bernard from a neighboring yacht, with a bottle of champagne—in each hand. He followed with a silver tray of fruits and nuts including pomplamouse, a sweet, tangy grapefruit cousin treat. Denise and I wanted to be alone, but Bernard wasn't budging. Then Bernard's wife came aboard, and the girls got a whiff of why we bathe in the tropics. This lady needed to visit a shower and bring some soap.

The girls were tired. It was insufferably hot and our guests eventually left. Denise could hardly hold her huge eyes open and commented as she laid her weary head to pillow, "I love you, Skip. This is better than Manzinillo. It may take me a week to adjust, but I'm here for the duration."

Good!

Tony and Kyle showed up for breakfast the next morning in a spiffy new high power speedboat supplied by their employer Bob, a jet-black two-seat model that looked like it had been rocketed from a powerful sling shot.

"Crapola! Will ya look at that," wide-eyed Denise exclaimed, as they tied alongside and she threw her arms around Tony, hugging him tightly. "I missed you so much, Tony."

"My talent and charming ways. Lady, I'm glad to see you too; old Captain Bligh Skip has been on a tear. You're lookin' good, Denise"

"Yup, Tony, and feeling better. What's with the 'E Ticket' ride?" Denise pointed to the speedboat, adding, "I know you didn't buy it—you and your friend here swipe it from Disneyland?"

"Naw," Tony laughed nervously, "we got lucky. It's just for a couple of weeks."

"And this," I broke in, "is where it gets suspicious. These clowns can barely tie a bowline, and some fat cat pays ten times going wages for them to protect his boat from a wind storm or thieves. Tell ya what! I'm not buyin' it."

Kyle and Tony all but fell over each other explaining the legitimacy of the offer, and invited Denise to visit and check it out.

The boys sped away in their new toy, and the ladies went back to unpacking while *Endymion* rocked and bounced in the wakes of commercial traffic in the highly congested harbor. Papeete may be tropical, but it wasn't paradise.

Having two stunning ladies aboard motivated Bernard to escalate his visits from occasional to constant. He proved his value. Bastille Day neared, and he scored front row seats for the festivals of kickboxing and hula dancing. I could think of nothing better than whiling away hours in Tahiti, sipping a Hinano, and watching hula dancers.

The girls enjoyed laying in the bean bags on the aft deck watching muscular Tahitian men practice for the "war canoe" competition. On Bastille Day, athletic endurance would be tested, with big, two to twenty man canoes paddling sixty nautical miles around the island of Moorea and back, regardless of weather or sea conditions.

Bernard and his ancient Peugeot provided entertainment too. It required a push start unless facing downhill. Bernard had long ago mastered jumping into a moving vehicle and popping the clutch. Denise and Marcia became the 'push' people because the girls, in bikinis, drew crowds of Tahitian men wanting to assist. Bernard, a small man, would yell, "poosh . . . poosh" and these native men would fling his aging Peugeot forward. Bernard once treated us to a magical tour of the island with a picnic under fragrant flowering trees, beside a lazy stream. The views toward Moorea and Cook's Bay were inspiring. I wanted to be sailing again.

A Bastille Day festival is akin to Carnival in Rio or Mardi Gras in New Orleans. Preparations had been underway for months, with participants building stages, training for races, and practicing hula moves. Denise savored the music and intoxicating scent of Polynesian gardenias, worn in the hair or behind an ear, and the waxy frangipani blossoms found everywhere, with a rich sweet scent.

King Tāufaʻāhau Tupou IV, ruler of Tonga, was to review the largest parade. We wanted to see this man, reputed to weigh 450 pounds—supposedly fashionable for Tongan royalty. The parade route was so crowded we climbed a tall tree and watched a hovering helicopter lower the monarch in a giant padded sling, bang on, right into his custom-built doublewide chair. He was the biggest man I had ever seen, who we later learned dieted to motivate fellow citizens to lose weight for a more healthy life. (King Tupou died in 2006. He was eighty-eight.)

Bastille Day was the Tahiti we had waited for. Denise loved it. Tired of crowds I wanted to move along.

Kyle and Tony swung by, raving about their jobs protecting the big boat. They'd been asked to stay on but Tony, duffel in hand, was rejoining *Endymion*. I was pleased in spite of his grousing about the money he would lose. He looked thin, like he could fall between the slats on the dock, but Tony swore, "Dad, it's a working boat for the fishing fleet. They had enough frozen lobster to feed this Island. Me and Kyle ate well."

It didn't ring true. I felt a piece of the picture was being withheld, but I couldn't put my finger on it. Kyle decided to stay aboard the big boat, saying he would "catch us later." I cleared his paperwork with authorities. We said our farewells.

We never saw Kyle again.

CHAPTER 30

MARCIA—THE NOT SO MERRY MERMAID

Californians know that Catalina Island, as the song says, is "twenty-six miles across the sea." Early morning mist across the sea can magnify objects, making them appear closer. Moorea, from the Papeete harbor entrance, appeared a good bit closer than its actual twenty-one sea miles, which, how about that, equated to Catalina's twenty-six statute miles.

"Distance agrees with me!" said Marcia before we'd untied from the quay. "Bring that island closer. The shorter the ride—the better."

Any distance in a boat is for Marcia an endless journey of agony because she gets seasick, leading to a personal hell few can understand. It happens to Marcia in cars, planes, and even at the dock on a windy day. No pill, armband, prayer, or whisky had ever helped.

For Marcia's benefit we planned our short passage to Moorea on a morning of calm waters and gentle breezes. As insurance, we pumped her full of Dramamine, slapped a couple of patches on her wrists, and prepared a cozy, comfortable spot for her in the leeward cockpit. We waved to Bernard, who sadly cast off our lines, crying out, "I will meese you . . . no poosh anymore my car—be careful and don get seek, Miss Marcia." The precise reminder she needed to drive her over the edge.

I swung the bow to port and aimed for the harbor entrance. We were abeam the public washrooms where we hoped Bernard's wife had made an appearance when Marcia let fly her first missile. I've never understood what attracts a sick person to the high side of a yacht, but Marcia jumped across the cockpit, and grabbing the rail, held her head to windward and gave the world her last meal. The freshening breeze returned bits and pieces to our instruments and me. I screamed. Denise howled, Tony ducked—Marcia threw up again.

Motion sickness is a miserable experience. Tony had the presence to grab a bucket and give the area a salt-water wash down. Marcia, so wanting to be a trooper, was beyond miserable for the entire four-hour slow sail passage. We made her as comfortable as possible.

Sick as Marcia was, and though the weather was perfect, I had to pay attention. The Avaroa Channel into Cook's Bay wasn't a straight shot. To the inattentive, sparkling azure waters could shortly become troubled waters. Coral heads were plentiful. We used our Tuamotu technique, sending Tony aloft to the spreaders to point out bommies and guide us by hand signals, through the twisting narrow channel.

Clearing those dangers, we motored casually through twenty or so anchored yachts hailing from ports as wide flung as Iceland and Japan. They, too, had been lured from Papeete to astonishingly seductive Moorea. Marcia began a slow return to health with color returning to her cheeks. We swapped greetings with anchored boats as we passed, a fun part of cruising. It's people watching people, and yes, we all put on at least a bit of a show.

This had also been Denise's first passage in many months. Like riding a bike, she had impeccable harmony with the yacht and her shipboard mates. Had the crossing been tough?

Denise wrote home:

Skip was proud of the way I "took charge" when the jib line got caught and I went forward on my own to free it.

Indeed I was!

Tony, quick to seize an opportunity, had spotted an attractive blonde Viking on a yacht from Sweden. Once anchored, he swam over to say "Hi."

We didn't see him for weeks.

CHAPTER 31

MOOREA CLUB MED

At one tenth the size of Tahiti, the beauty of Moorea by comparison is amazing. Riding modern golf carts or ancient scooters around the island's one narrow road exposed us to views better than the best doctored-up postcards. Even Marcia romped with us, enjoying solid earth beneath her feet, though we did nearly lose her once when passing a commercial dock where a roadside hawker said she could book passage on a steady tramp freighter for the frightening trip back to Papeete.

"It will be quick," he had said.

"I'll be back," promised Marcia.

With spirit replenished, Marcia decided bravery was her forte and stuck with us exploring the island's fringing reefs—slowly under power.

Five o'clock always arrived on time with mystic power drawing cruisers to their VHF radios at cocktail hour, where, with drink in hand, we jabbered with our kind about what we had seen that day. The radio net around Cook Bay convinced us to head northwest inside the fringing reefs to Club Med, a facility too commercial for we who deeply love this laid-back lifestyle, but yachts were welcome as long as we paid for our beads.

Thus on a bright sunny morning with the sun at half-mast, we nosed out of Cook Bay and turned left along the reef. The pure blue water felt cleansing. Elegant full-bodied palms hung over the skinny channel's edge, the kind people dream of lying beneath, with book in hand—because people don't know about ugly land crabs that scare the crap out of you, or ants that could carry you home.

The stunning blue water was crystal clear, loaded with curious brightly colored fish dashing about as they checked us out, strangers in their private pond. We hugged the shore picking our way slowly among the bommies. Native kids waved and yelled out, some perched high in coconut trees. Two preteen boys came to greet us in a rickety dugout canoe, their smiles and chatter encouraging souvenirs. Their eyes light up when we tossed them bubble gum.

Islands, too small for even a hut, were to seaward. We watched seagulls quarrel over scraps with the mighty Pacific beyond them. Denise was discovering new happiness every day, and I was delighted. Along our narrow, winding channel we discovered anchorages inviting us to put life in slow gear, anchor for a spell, take our time, maybe play cards and always sip fruit drinks (laced, of course). One tiny lagoon wasn't more than three times the size of *Endymion*, and we found ourselves whispering in the solitude. It appeared people had been there before, but that day it was ours alone.

"Do you suppose," I asked Denise, "we will ever see another place like this?"

"Not in this lifetime," Denise said quietly, taking my hand—we lived a year in that hour.

Denise and Marcia created a warm weather salad of seafood and local greens while I pretended to fish off the bow. I didn't really want to catch anything, just admire the rainbow of fish and creatures investigating our anchor and chain. This had to be Michener's paradise.

We slept in the cockpit, for there wasn't a breath of air, and running the generator to cool *Endymion's* interior would be a sin. In subdued voices we talked of family and friends, wishing we could share moments of this utopian night. And in our own moments, we each drifted to sleep.

One weaves an uneasy relationship with the sun that rises to catch you unaware, sleeping in the cockpit. Old Sol could quickly eliminate morning dew, but its brightness stung my eyes. Tropical temperatures didn't just go up, they shot up.

So there we were, still wiping sleepy stuff from our eyes, welcoming the day and thinking about our first cuppa, when . . .

"What the—what's that?" asked Marcia.

We fell silent, coaxing our ears to hear more than birds and crickets singing from the jungle.

"It's a motor, I think," said Denise.

It was. Moments later it became the intruding roar of a large approaching overcrowded tour boat jammed gunnel to gunnel with tourists as colorfully clothed as a Jimmy Buffet outing, and they had diving gear, tanks, compressors, and bullhorns. An enormous Club Med flag flew from the bow.

What happened next was true—so help me God!

This intruder passed slowly to land against the beach. All aboard were looking at us standing barefooted and barely clothed on *Endymion's* deck, coffee mugs in hand. Suddenly one fellow yelled out, "Skip—Skip Rowland—is that you?"

There in the Club Med dive boat was one of my former clients from the Manufacturer's Rep business. Al Barker, Executive VP of Bionaire, had been at my going-away party, and was one of those who had cut off my necktie, symbolic of departure from the business world. He was the first living soul from my past to see us in our natural environment—half a world away from home. We screamed out a tentative meeting at Club Med for that evening.

"Now you're hitting my stride," Marcia remarked, knowing Club Med must be close. She was painting her nails and decorating her face long before we set anchor at Club Med.

Club Med had Marcia in her niche, popular with the yuppie lawyers and doctors playing the Club Med game. We had dinner with Al and joked about friends still working. It was hollow joking, as Al would re-enter the grind next week while we might make it to Australia by Christmas. Club Med enthusiasts' energy-packed vacations reminded Denise and me why we wanted to turn tail and sail away. They reminded Marcia it was time to get back to her old ways. So she stayed at the club, and we bade farewell to our beautiful, statuesque, dark-haired friend.

Denise and I were alone on our yacht—our first time, just the two of us since leaving Newport Beach. We slipped into another of those hidden quiet anchorages for a couple of days just to enjoy each other. We made love, tender and tempestuous. In the aura of Denise I felt safe and loved. "May this be forever please? Thank you, God." With the sea calling, I contacted Tony and his Swedish toy by radio. Locals agreed to deliver Tony the next morning. He didn't seem the worse for wear, or prepping for a quick wedding, so we made ready to sail again. Shortly afterward we reluctantly weighed anchor and carefully worked our way through Tareau Pass, on a course for Raiatea, a long night's sail away.

CHAPTER 32

ANCIENT SHRINES
AND OVERPRICED WINE

Raiatea-Tahaa – In a lifetime of sailing, I've never had such perfect, harmonious conditions, or enjoyed a sail as much as from Moorea to Raiatea. Once outside Tareau Pass, the ocean was crystal blue, a hue so rich it challenged the imagination. Light winds, no sea, and pleasant temperatures added to ideal sailing conditions. I snatched the beanbag from the aft deck, carried it forward, and sank into it, allowing myself to become one with everything beautiful on God's big ocean. Again, I wished every person on earth could be where I was, even if for a moment.

It was still a good twelve hours to the spot we had picked to land on Tahaa. The starry night was again perfection. What surprised me was the amount of ocean traffic.

"Gotta be island supply boats," remarked Tony, tending a luckless fishing line trailing us.

From the wheel, Denise commented, "They don't look very safe."

She was right. The supply ships were ants on the sea—low in the water with boxy cabins towering above the deck. Most were loaded beyond any conceivable legal parameter. All had generations of chattering people.

Tahaa and Raiatea is really one island, with a mountain at each end, connected by a reef and thin middle lowland. It is the largest of the "Leeward Islands" and closest in size to Bora Bora further to the west.

Throughout the day we, meaning Tony, caught a barracuda. They're a lousy fish for eating. Tony somehow released them without suffering bites or gashes from their razor-sharp teeth. As the sun dipped out of sight, a lovely forty-six inch Wahoo decided to tempt fate, taking a chunk of our still trailing lure. Denise, with a passion for fishing, was on the rod and reel for this one. It was a battle. Denise won.

There could not have been a better ending to a South Seas day. Denise, taking salad duty, and Tony manning the deck BBQ in calm seas, created a fine fresh fruit and seafood meal. Neil Diamond serenaded us through our soft drink cocktail hour, and the Boston Pops Orchestra played the classics from deck speakers for our sit-down, cockpit-style dinner, served on the coveted backgammon table, covered with real linens, courtesy of Lady Denise.

It was a "be in love with life" evening. And we all knew it.

The night, aside from a myriad of stars, was dark, but not pitch dark like nights shrouded in clouds. With nightfall came the realization that the 'ants of the sea' vessel traffic was still out there, but few had navigation lights, if any lights. I recalled my Marine Corps training, learning how to determine rough distance in darkness from something as small as a glowing cigarette. People on the ant boats were smokers.

Denise, on her pre-midnight watch, said, "I'm watching a light 60 degrees off starboard bow. Can you see it?"

"Negative." Tony tried to sound nautical.

"Something's there; got to be a boat, and I can't figure its course." Denise sounded concerned.

Tony and I thought we could make out the shape of a small boat close by, on about the same course we were on and closely matching our speed. Tony checked the radar.

"He paints a reasonable radar picture; but then he should at half a mile from us. No problem!" he said to Denise.

"OK, but the smaller wooden boats all over the place, Tony? Can you see them?" Denise asked.

"It's a problem. Some I see—some don't show at all."

"Damn radar," said Denise

"Not really." I got into it. "It's the best Furuno makes today. We should be glad we have it. Soon we'll have even better radar that shows the rain—and probably clouds."

"I can't wait," Denise said sarcastically. She was listening to the ship's clock chiming midnight and the end of her watch.

We kept an eye on the clunker boat Denise had warned of for another hour. It eventually pulled far enough ahead we no longer feared it.

Once, close to 0200, an out of tune diesel thumped by close at hand, forcing us to change course to avoid a collision with a bizarre-looking boat loaded with happy people. It also resembled a box-shaped boat, and we surmised the laughing people had no idea where they were, probably didn't care, and wouldn't care in the morning either. Just like all nights, we made it through this one. There was a lesson here, I believe, in vigilance. Our practice has always been, even on autopilot, to have someone at the wheel, hopefully alert and listening, because autopilot, for all of its virtues, does not have the collision avoidance warning system of human eyes or ears.

According to our charts, Tahaa offered two safe places to anchor. The one we chose required sailing around the island's northern tip and then a slide south for a few nautical miles to a safe entrance into a lagoon reasonably protected by fringing reef.

We made our entrance almost precisely twenty-four hours after leaving Moorea. Several yachts bobbed at anchor. Ahead we saw a small town dock with a rusted hulk of a tramp supply ship lying aside and forgotten, and a white sandy beach, with a small sailing yacht firmly aground.

We anchored and did important things, like adjusting our sun awning, setting out the hammock, enjoying a tasty wahoo sandwich, and lowering the inflatable to explore ashore.

A couple in a small rowing dingy came alongside to welcome us 'to paradise.' First they warned us, "There's two strange boats anchored at the far end. Castoffs. See em'?" inquired a bronzed heavyset lady of middle age, looking up from the dinghy. "Surely they're druggies."

"Ya think so?" Tony asked.

"Yeah. They're skinny . . . and unsocial!"

Tony found that unfair. I found it a sign of the times that drugs were virtually in every niche of the globe.

Our welcoming lady also warned prices in stores were twice the average Papeete prices. The couple meant well, but didn't come off well, more like busybody people we had left ashore long ago. A German man asleep, we were told, had stranded the boat we saw on the beach during an exceptionally high tide. The tide went out. The boat did not. It will be there until the next moon tide "unless he gets a change of attitude," informed the lady.

Skip in our foredeck hammock

"Think I'll go see if the druggies need some milk." Tony was destined to visit the source of the woman's scorn.

Going ashore, Denise and I experienced sticker shock. A tube of lip balm was over $10.00, a six-pack of warm canned soft drinks, with tinges of rust gaining a foothold on the rims cost $12.00, and my favorite mid-quality Chablis, a mere $23.00. All Pacific Francs. As expected, Chinese merchants, who came to the islands like locusts, controlled the merchandise, while descendants of Polynesians royalty worked the plantations or one of three small resorts in our newest paradise.

Anyway, we had a good look around, savored a $10.00 cup of vanilla ice cream, and made arrangements for rental bikes. Tony opted out. He felt a big lazy coming on, and I wondered, maybe a short 'howdy' to the two strange boats with the skinny crew. Denise, who loves all living creatures, played with free-range animals of every sort, motivating her to write home:

> "Animals seem to speak my language. Pigs, dogs, cats, goats, and even horses follow me everywhere. I take food scraps in my bag. Skip's expecting them to swim out to the boat."

Denise plopped a line in the water, hooking three ugly "triggerfish" in minutes. She tossed them back, explaining, "Some reef fish are poisonous, so why take a chance? They're probably mutations from the French, Commie (Russian), and US nuclear testing right after World War Two."

Denise and I rode bikes the next day till our bums were sore and legs ready to part from our hips. Being ashore required different muscles.

The peaceful little retreats we found made the effort worthwhile. At one spot, we met a young man and his German Shepherd, thriving on and living for each other's company. There was a seawall with a small landing ramp next to it. The man would throw a stick and his powerful Shepherd would leap from the wall, plunge into the water with feet spread, retrieve the stick, and bring it to his best friend. He was an American from Redondo Beach, Ca. cruising the Pacific in his Cal 25 (25ft. sloop) and Cheyenne, the Shepherd, was his crew and companion. The couple, so to speak, were two years into their voyage—a remarkable story of love and adventure.

While on Tahaa we saw remains Denise and I first thought were ancient sacrificial sites, where maidens were possibly offered to the

Gods during fiery, lust-filled gatherings of warring chiefs. We learned later, from a respected Hawaiian scholar, that we had been mistaken. The crumbled remains were likely temples for learning called maraes (meeting places). We inspected one close to the shore of Raiatea that allegedly had been a place of learning for priests and navigators from all over the Pacific. The eerie shapes left us still believing there had been sacrifices by the shore where once temples may have stood. The unforgettable site so close to water's edge caused us to wonder if there was more to learn, because centuries of rising water may have swallowed the evidence.

Denise at unknown ruins on Raitea

Denise offered a thought: "You could be in trouble here, Skip."

"Yeah . . . why?"

"Your reddish hair. Long ago, redheads from Peru, like your idol Thor Heyerdahl, came here from South America, mingled with the natives, had babies, and devastated the stronger natives because they carried some ill-gotten recessive gene. Maybe they burned redheads to get rid of them. So, Skippy—you better watch out for what peeks at you from yonder palm trees."

"Geeze, Denise, where in dickens did you come up with that one?" "Nursing school. We studied about what happened on Easter Island. If it happened there, why not here?"

It made sense. I agreed. We saw several more such maraes during our stay. Homes with tombstones in the front yard were another unusual sight.

"Nothing like being laid to rest at home so friends passing by may wave or whistle a tune," I said to Denise, "though it could be a hurdle for a real estate broker."

"It's not so funny, Skip." Denise didn't care for my frivolity: "Some cultures wanted their ancestors close by. It showed respect, and you should get some."

I apologized to Denise—and the deceased.

Before leaving for Bora Bora, we needed to replenish our dwindling wine and beer supplies. Price labels on the wine bottles in local stores were astronomical. "Robbery is one thing . . . rape another," I said to Denise as we scoured the isles of Won Ton's Wonder Store, a colossal trap for outdated trinkets and unsalable merchandise. It pissed me off to be robbed so blatantly. The price labels were old style, not the break-apart ones used to deter thieves in the USA. I couldn't resist. The robbed became the robber. I switched labels on several bottles. Advantage—mine. But would it come back to haunt me?

There was one more thoughtful chore before leaving the island. The German had hired a small bulldozer to push his grounded yacht back into the sea. The steel jaws and teeth of the machine, operated by the island's finest bumbling unskilled labor, would certainly chew holes in or mar this gracious little twenty-eight-foot yacht. So a group of us, sans the skinny suspected druggies, spent a morning placing pieces of timber over the leading edge of the machine to soften the jaws' contact. Additionally, we dug a shallow moat from behind the yacht to the water and lined it with wood so the boat would have a smoother ride to the sea.

A crowd gathered as we made final preparations and the German yelled, "Fire her up." Even with our prep work, it took ten additional full-muscled men to guide the small vessel to its relaunch. It worked though—and we felt the comforting inner glow one gets from helping another person. The German must have felt it too. He offered warm beer to anyone who wanted it, which was everyone.

We could feel the lure of Bora Bora pulling us. It was said to be the world's most beautiful island.

CHAPTER 33

BORA BORA

There are hundreds of Pacific islands teeming with rainbow-colored birds, waterfalls carving paths in mountains—and enough snakes to keep one from getting too comfortable.

Bora Bora was one of them—beautiful and seductive.

Through the wind-swept mist of a late South Pacific afternoon, the shape and dominance of Mount Otemanu, Bora Bora's most-photographed peak, raised goose bumps. Once a towering volcano, it was visible from every motu for miles, as the island's centerpiece. Had this volcano never erupted there would be no Bora Bora, no fabled song, no soft moonlight nights at quiet anchorages, or reefs to explore with moray eels lurking in the shadows. So, thank you Otemanu, mountain with the rugged black face—center of the island. You have beckoned us, and we have answered your call and touched your shores.

It was, excuse me please, another description-defying paradise afternoon, as we poked our way slowly along the western fringing

233

reef of the world's most thought-of island. It was time to go slow, let it all sink in, make forever deposits in our memory banks. In many places the reef barely touched the surface, rendering it dangerously non-apparent. Were it not for the occasional wave falling over itself, we could have found it the hard way—going aground. Reefs like this with precious little exposed surface, potentially lead to rough seas in anchorages, as we would later learn. August, however, is generally a quiet month, and the amount of water crossing the reefs is minimal and sparkling. The breeze was light and caressing as we sailed comfortably within fifty feet of the reef. We felt safe. Our depth indicator confirmed it.

A few isolated sections of reef poked slightly higher than the main portion. Dirt managed to somehow hang on. Picture-perfect palm trees arching toward the water, coconuts clustering below the tops, managed to cling to the Spartan soil. You've seen them in postcards. I can say with authority, the glossiest, most touched-up, New York agency postcard doesn't stack up to the staggering real-life beauty of Bora Bora.

There was one navigable pass through the reef. Big, wide and obvious, it also invited problems because it was shallow.

As Tony put it, "Well Pops, if you don't believe the charts or fathometer, take a look at that guy swinging the net."

A couple hundred feet from us, waist high in rich blue water, stood a native fisherman with a casting net. Beside him, tethered to his flowery shorts, a wicker basket held tonight's colorful reef fish dinner. Seeing us, the tall stranger with a wide sun-shielding hat and designer sunglasses, raised a rugged brown arm and waved hello, while also signaling the water around him was two feet less than our required depth.

We understood his universal sign language: "Go where I point-n stay safe." Our instruments agreed, so we reduced sail and turned to starboard—no problem, but the current was unexpectedly strong, causing Denise, on watch, to brace as she struggled with the wheel to keep us on course. Minutes later we were safely inside the reef, in deep water.

A cluster of anchored yachts lay a mile distant, their masts and hulls glimmering in the tropical sunlight with the mighty mountain as backdrop. A single dark cloud floated above the island, giving it a surreal, magical appearance. Like a fly to the web, we headed for the anchored yachts, finding several French yachts, as might be expected, a couple from Canada, a half-dozen US flag yachts and others from Greece, the UK, Italy, Sweden (though not Tony's dream girl), and even one flying colors from South Africa.

We carefully chose a spot north of a village called Viatape, and dropped our chain and the heaviest of our three anchors in about twenty feet, with a potential three foot influencing tide. Within minutes our radio chattered with welcomes from other yachts.

Several small inflatables from anchored yachts came alongside offering fruit, drinks, and friendship. One was a couple we had met previously, from a lovely older wooden yawl with beautiful overhangs. We called them 'value people,' capable, self-sufficient individuals, constantly offering to lend a hand. All sorts of people cruised—millionaires with nannies and paid hands, shoestring budget folks, and those who had put money away and earned the right to enjoy their future however they chose.

A surprise visitor was Ted and best mate German Shepherd Cheyenne. I couldn't wrap my head around how they arrived before us, but never mind; Cheyenne was putting on a show diving from the dingy for his stick. What energy. It was tricky, one 180-pound man rowing a plastic dinghy with a 100-pound dog lunging from the unsteady platform to fetch a piece of wood. Ted and Tony hadn't met but had a common interest that created friendships. They both surfed. Bora Bora had the flavor of a party place. It was a relatively safe anchorage, holding was good unless you were really stupid, and there was a favorable mix of interesting people comprising all ages, families, couples, singles, rich folks, poor people, and working stiffs. Yup, a party in the making for boats anchored in front of a small waterfront hotel, the "Oa Oa" (meaning friendship), and it had a bar. We would come to know it well. First order for pleasure was a hot shower with pressure water. It was free for 'the boat people.' We weren't to linger however, as fresh water was in short supply.

Oa Oa hotel on a peaceful morning.

For a sailor, the Oa Oa had a dream bar. At the entrance hung an enormous bulletin board for anything you wished to post, from parts for sale, to crew needed. Games were available to while away lazy days. A large covered dining area with huge, slow-moving fans faced the anchored yachts. It was a wondrous place to sit and watch, or just sit, if you so chose. Two of the island's most charismatic people, Greg and Elaine Clayton, owned the place. Originally Californians, they sought distant horizons and became fixtures on the world's most enchanted island. We didn't know or care how they managed to do it as Americans, being a French island, but we were pleased they wrangled the slot and we're not asking questions.

The Oa Oa's eleven rooms were not bragging material but were always occupied. A selling point for Greg and Elaine, we later learned, was encouraging room guests to mingle with the 'courageous adventurers who had sailed to this island'—and to ask us questions. They did, and we reveled in giving exaggerated answers, making everyone happy at the Oa Oa.

Greg and Elaine were laid so far back they could get porch splinters. "There are no rules," Greg explained, "except two, and you better listen up! First—Water is in constant shortage. You can have twenty gallons of fresh every day but you must carry it to your boat. Never come alongside (his dock) to fill up. Never! Two—You may use any of my shore side BBQs, utensils, even plates, but every last one of you in turn, must buy your drinks from our bar. We gotta live too!"

"Sounds fair to us," announced Denise.

To which generous Greg added, "Hey guys, I'm not that mean. You're welcome to the twenty gallons of fresh water a day I mentioned, that's per vessel, not per person. We just don't have it. I'm serious about no yachts tied to the dock. It won't hold them in a wind. Dinghies are OK. pile 'em on for all I care—and enjoy your visit."

Greg's bar rules worked for bigger budget yachts, but at $10 to $12 Pacific Franc per drink it was tough for pocket cruisers like Ted. Cheyenne drank free, a reward for entertainment value, and that pup could guzzle a brew PDQ.

All yachties eventually discuss weather phenomena. Denise, though new to offshore life, had put many stateside recovery hours into armchair exploration of weather patterns and how to read them.

I felt it a worthy contribution, considering two minds are better than one, especially when weather threatens.

"You know, Skip," Denise confided as we cuddled back in the sweet evening air flooding the cockpit, "one reason I'm interested in weather is because I'm afraid of being knocked overboard when weather is bad."

"Seriously? Your afraid?"

"Well, when I was a kid we had a pool, but I wasn't a good swimmer. In truth, I'm afraid of drowning."

"Coulda fooled me," I chirped.

"Well, I'm not fooling. I'm feeling like—well—like impending doom—that we, well like—this is still storm season. I don't feel comfortable and I don't like it."

Holding her closer I encouraged her to go on. "Tell me more." "I dreamt I was drowning once, well actually, a few times. I'm afraid of falling overboard, and you said we have long passages coming. I would feel more comfortable if we had more than Tony, you, and me. I'm not saying something will happen, but creepers, Skip, can we at least think about extra crew, maybe just one person—please?" There was no problem. I believed Denise was right, and I loved her. We decided to find another crew member, not necessarily an experienced sailor, although that would have been nice. We wanted someone fun, who liked to laugh, had a good spirit, and could lend a hand staying focused if things went sour. We headed to the Oa Oa and one of our best decisions ever.

Pinned to the bulletin board was a business card, picturing a handsome young man, hands folded and leaning into the portrait camera. It introduced Tom Peek. Minnesota born and raised, Tom was a writer-photographer-musician-world traveler. He wanted a ride.

"We need to meet this hayseed," hooted Tony.

"Quiet, Tony." Denise got on Tony like she had me about the family graveyards. "He looks like a nice man. Maybe some culture will rub off on Skip."

"Yeah, and he worked for Senator Humphrey. He must have smarts," I concluded.

We interviewed Tom, and breezed through our ritual of Tom sizing up the boat while we sized up Tom.

"I like this guy. He's smart." Tony had spoken.

Tom, a six-foot four-inch Scandinavian farm boy from Minnesota, joined our motley band the following day. We were to learn, as advertised, Tom was everything his card claimed. It started when Tom cooked breakfast, to which Tony commented, "Great meal, Tom, another day we don't get poisoned by Dad."

We got lucky. A heavy-duty mooring became available directly in front of the Oa Oa. We snared it. Our neighbors on other moorings were a Swan 65 from London and a classic double-ended wooden ketch from Iceland. This was the most secure I had felt anyplace—since January.

CHAPTER 34

UNLEASED FURY
AT THE OA OA

The Maramu winds of Bora Bora have many cousins with equally enchanting names—Chinooks in the Rocky Mountains, the Chubascos of Mexico, the Wily Wily from Australia, and Santa Anas in California. All are devil winds. Maramus rip down from the shadows of Mount Otemanu during July and August unleashing torrents of rain amidst howling winds of thirty plus knots, gusting suddenly to fifty knots.

There would be no more snorkeling or strumming ukuleles on this day. Milliseconds after we had entered the hotel, a maramu hit with deafening vengeance, ripping apart awnings, scattering lawn furniture, even tearing board games and cards from the grips of guests. Tony, I was told, dropped his burger, and that, if anything, should give relevance to the size of the calamity. Everyone dashed immediately—tourists for cover, and yachties for their shore boats.

"Let's go, Tom!" I shouted as we bolted to our Avon, which was tangled in a jungle of lines with a half dozen others secured to the same cleat on the Oa Oa dock.

"Get the line, Tom, and get in." I shouted, moving unsteadily from one bouncing dinghy to another, attempting to reach ours. Playing hopscotch during an earthquake would be easier, and I watched Tom, who had never done this before, hesitate, and plunge recklessly forward, landing eventually alongside me, unharmed.

Wind-whipped waves were breaking over the dinghy dock as we left it. Families, couples, and singles were nearly submerged as they clamored to get back to their endangered floating homes.

Pulling alongside *Endymion*, I was again thankful for our powerful Honda four-stroke outboard engine. We could not have rowed against this wind and sharp, steep waves sweeping the lagoon. Climbing the boarding ladder, I saw Tony waving frantically from shore, saying, "Dad—come get me!"

But we couldn't and I had a nerve-tingling moment of regret. Why hadn't I found Tony first? Was I stupid? I needed him! I found myself willing Tony to get out here; Denise will be OK on shore, and these things do blow out, or so we'd been told.

Tom handed me the painter, which I secured as Tom climbed up the boarding ladder. I knew the importance of lines, knots, and how to use them. A good line with a proper knot can be your best mate, but if the knot on a strong line can't be broken and it takes you or your yacht with it—well, not so charming. I could (and still can) tie a bowline behind my back with my eyes closed. In fact, given two ends of a line, I could throw them in front of me, tying a bowline in mid-air. It's a skill best used for winning bar bets.

On deck I saw only a broken batten in our large sun awning and a heap of backgammon chips hugging the cockpit sole. Not big damage considering the wind.

"Hang on, Captain!" Tom yelled. A forty-foot French sloop, out of control and with no one aboard careened toward us, dragging a broken mooring line. Its oversize long boom swung wildly as the boat, pushed by the waves, barreled toward us.

"Pillows, Tom, pillows . . . grab the biggest . . . don't tie it, just hold it where he hits us."

Pillows were really semi-inflated boat fenders used to keep piers and boats from mutual damage. Denise had renamed them 'pillows,' perhaps to keep a reminder of home and all that was once comfortable. Thinking it cute, Tony and I had adopted the word. It confused Tom.

"OK, Captain," said Tom, suddenly getting it and holding two of our largest. He was poised to do as told. I was impressed.

I had grabbed a boat hook, intending to catch the rigging and push the approaching yacht away from us. But a puff of wind caused the French boat to miss us by a couple of feet. One down.

Over the radio a concerned voice was calling: "*Cool Change, Cool Change, Cool Change* . . . Captain Gary . . . listen up! One of your mooring lines has chaffed through."

We could see Gary ashore with his wife and kids, all trying to get into his pitching dinghy. Would they get to *Cool Change* in time? We watched a diver from another yacht hoist himself aboard *Cool Change* and thread his way slowly forward on the unfamiliar yacht. He was looking for ways to further secure it. Back at the dock Gary had left the family and was speeding toward *Cool Change* in his powerful inflatable, waves trying to flip him at every pounding opportunity.

Once aboard his yacht, even with the diver's help, Gary was unable to attach another line to the bouncing mooring, so he decided to cast off and seek shelter in the lee of a nearby small motu.

With *Endymion* secure, I felt Tom and I should help others return to their vessels, so we climbed again into the thrashing Avon and sped to shore with Tom hanging dearly to the painter and me with one hand on the outboard handle and the other clutching an inflatable fitting. Something to the right caught my eye. *Hare Maru*, with Cheyenne still aboard, was loose and driving toward a nasty reef. Tony and I knew the owner was hiking the island, likely unaware of what was taking place here.

Rain and spray had penetrated every crevice of foul weather gear Tom and I had climbed into. It was getting dark. We were chilled in the tropics. Tom turned to me, "We should go after it, Skip!"

I spun the Avon to put the wind and waves at our back, our most secure position, and shut the motor to idle. The Avon lurched to a clumsy stop.

"Tom—quickly—change places with me. Move, Tom! You steer and I'll jump aboard *Hare Maru*."

"I'll do my best."

"Stay focused, Tom, and whatever . . . don't get tossed onto the reef."

Hare Maru was dangerously close to the reef, where a couple of abandoned boats, including a classic wooden sloop, already in pieces, were taking a pounding.

Hare Maru was a scant fifty feet from the reef, backwash waves mixing with wind-driven seas made it difficult for Tom to maneuver or for me to stand and leap onto the distressed yacht. I was crouched, prepared to leap, when *Hare Maru* hit the reef, stopped suddenly and snapped off the lower half of her rudder. Our forward motion, impossible to stop, carried us into the yacht, launching me painfully into the port side rail. I grabbed for the boat's lifelines and managed to hold on, dragging my left leg and climbing aboard as Tom backed the inflatable to a safe distance. My knee and left forefinger were bleeding and my head ached. What hurt most was seeing Cheyenne, the Pacific's best loved dog, tied to the mast, cowering in fear. Seeing me, heck seeing anyone, sent Cheyenne's tail into overdrive. He was held in place with a bowline, easy for me to break, and Cheyenne, already with sea legs, dashed for the cabin.

Coral reefs crumble easily. *Hare Maru* lurched and pushed further across the reef every minute. The stomach-turning crunch of coral devouring fiberglass was painful to hear, adding to the nightmarish event.

Searching for a line to affix to the mast and heave to another boat, I looked below long enough to see Cheyenne plant himself into a settee while books, pots, pans, and fittings flew and clattered in every direction as the boat thunderously bashed its way further onto the reef. Seawater mixed with sand and jagged coral edges, cascaded into the cabin through a broken navigation station port. (window)

I found a hefty line, tied it around the mast and led it forward to toss to a couple of small inflatables standing by—all the while grabbing another handhold as I inched forward on deck, now tilted to 70 degrees. Somehow I was able to heave the line to the inflatables standing by. They had good intentions but they lacked the power to pull *Hare Maru* from the coral's death grip. *Cool Change* had returned to help and was circling nearby. The line was affixed to winches and the 44-foot yacht from Chicago pulled like a mighty pit bull, but to little avail.

It had become pitch dark. The relentless wind and seas gave up nothing. A crowd had gathered ashore, many with flashlights. The Oa

Oa contributed a powerful light, similar to a sealed beam headlight. Alone on the stranded boat, I heard a voice calling for Cheyenne.

Ted, with tears in his eyes and heart, was making his way across the reef to rescue his mate, Cheyenne. Hearing Ted's voice, Cheyenne's ears went up, and he scrambled from below and practically flew into the water in a simple display of pure unfiltered love.

Cool Change, still with towline, was having problems. Her engine was overheating. Gary had to hold back on the throttle, being careful he too didn't get dragged onto the reef. Meanwhile Tom, still a rookie and driving our Avon inflatable, came too close to *Cool Change's* stern as it came off a wave. *Cool Change* slammed into our Avon, rupturing the fuel line, nearly knocking out Tom, and almost sinking the inflatable. I saw the strobe signal light and powerful deck lights of *Endymion* through the pelting rain, maybe 100 yards distant. I figured Tony must be aboard analyzing what he was seeing and planning his next move. Moments later *Endymion's* powerful, hand-held searchlight provided enough light for another small inflatable to take Tom in tow, returning him safely to *Endymion*.

By this time Ted had waded back from shore to Hare Maru and used a spinnaker pole to pry *Hare Maru*, assisting *Cool Change* and Gary, who continued pulling *Hare Maru* in spite of his overheated engine. Two beefy tourists managed to cross the reef to lend broad shoulders to the effort. After two more passes with weight properly deployed, a rising tide and slightly abated wind, *Cool Change* managed to pull *Hare Maru* free of the reef, but she had no steerage because she had only half a rudder. And it was bent.

Three inflatables joined *Cool Change* in towing the stricken small yacht. Everyone shouted encouragement. Gary, a corporate head-hunter in his previous life, was stalwart, leading the tow procession through driving rain, back to *Hare Maru's* original mooring, where two additional inflatables waited with lines, already threaded through the mooring thimble, to secure the stricken yacht, at least for the night.

The wind was down to a manageable 25 knots when I realized for the first time Denise was still ashore. The whole event had taken place directly in front of the Oa Oa. There were 100 or more spectators, a mixture of tourists, hotel guests, and crew unable to return to their yachts. Denise had not been idle.

Seeing Cheyenne leap onto the reef to find Ted, Denise, who loved all creatures, went to help. Cheyenne had cut his paws and back on the coral. The dog was bleeding, in pain, and could have been nasty. Denise wasn't bothered. She carried her four-legged patient through the water and sand, falling herself at one point. With assistance from Greg, while soaked and covered in sand, she was able to peroxide the wounds and stop the bleeding.

Most yachties came ashore again close to midnight for post-storm quarterbacking. No lives lost. A few bandages and sprains, however, three inflatables and one pristine wooden sloop destroyed beyond hope of repair

A long night was not yet over.

While Tony and our Avon remained for the quarterbacking, Denise and I hitched a ride back to *Endymion*. I climbed aboard first. Denise was putting her foot on the first ladder step when a wave pitched the inflatable, sending Denise into the coal-black water. I reached for her but missed. I couldn't see or feel her! Denise, who said she wasn't a strong swimmer, managed to grab the ladder moments later while calling for help. I pulled her aboard. Thank God she hadn't been crushed between the hulls or run over by a propeller. She did lose an earring.

Eventually, Tony and Tom tired of rehashing events, pulled alongside in our Avon. Tom stepped onto the ladder and Tony, as he should have, shut down the engine with the taped-together fuel line. But novice Tom had not taken the painter line with him when he climbed the ladder. Tony was now adrift, and headed toward the same reef that had claimed *Hare Maru*.

Tom, somewhat frantic, aroused me. It didn't take long to find Tony in the beam of our spotlight. Still attempting to start the engine, he was only a few feet from the reef. While we watched, Tony, with great presence of mind and superb timing, lifted the engine's prop to avoid it hitting bottom, and laid prone in the inflatable as the waves swept it over the reef. With nothing lost but pride and a slipper, he waded ashore with minor coral cuts, to later be attended by Nurse Denise.

The Oa Oa gave Tony coffee . . . and a free room.

CHAPTER 35

YACHTS THROW A PARTY

Unexpected storms create chaos among anchored yachts. They make a mess of everything; people get angry at each other (especially captains and crew), but storms also bring people together post wind and rain to PARTY!

After this storm, VHF (short range) radios were a-buzz with normal banter, cussing, and laughter. Everyone had a theory of what might have happened if? The air was freshly ionized and everyone knew we needed a good party.

Three of us from larger boats in the anchorage were chosen to get the ball rolling. Truth is, we appointed each other, quoting 'spirit and ignorance of disorder' as justification for a visit to the Oa Oa cocktail lounge for negotiations with Greg and Elaine.

Not to be blasphemous, but it should be noted Greg had elevated himself to the position of the Island's God. Be it noted, no such respect was given, or even considered. It was a salubrious mid-day luncheon, one where little was eaten but decisions were crafted.

The Oa Oa would supply everything from tables, BBQs, utensils, and condiments, to bath facilities. In return they asked only—you got it—that ALL alcoholic drinks be purchased at their bar at (their) regular prices.

The date selected was five days hence. We could not wait longer for there was no telling how long conditions would be favorable for departing Bora Bora. I would be the organizer, probably because I had no other visible talents. My first duty was to capture the fleet's interest in having a party. I jumped on the VHF every hour for a full day, advising interested persons to tune in the following morning for an important announcement about what promised to be the best party ever in all their God-given days on earth. Almost forty boats were at anchor. Five would abstain because they were either French or Mormons. The remaining yachts averaged lazy crews of three and a half . . . not counting pets, one hundred and twenty-five people plus a few hotel guests wanting to horn in, and that was fine too. Sailors love to meet new people.

One such character was Tom Peek who had joined us aboard *Endymion*. He fit in so well some folks on party night thought Tom owned *Endymion* and had financed Denise and me on this voyage to nowhere.

Anyway, my morning broadcast was a success. Every yacht wanted to volunteer a main, side, surprise dish, or even a 'dish' the captain once thought beautiful until she got too much sun, and too much of him. We had volunteers bumping over each other. It was the talk of the anchorage and why not, nothing else was happening.

Then, two days before our event, a lavish sailing cruise ship of 150 feet, with several masts and aluminum furling sails, slipped quietly past our anchorage. *Windsong* hailed from a tax-free haven, of course. We dropped our jaws, radios, breakfast, or beer, watching in awe as her sails rolled silently into the mast as the ship ghosted past, dropping anchor a mile upwind. Shore boats were lowered to take the mega-rich passengers to the sights we saw for nothing.

The ship gave me an idea, so I went to the radio for our standard 0830 event meeting.

"All hands, all hands, all vessels, all vessels, this is party headquarters *Endymion* with an important announcement. Last night at Bloody Mary's (restaurant) the chief steward and several crew from *Windsong* got wind of our party plans. Here is the BIG news. *Windsong* will supply desserts—for free. So, if you planned a fluffy pastry, please fiddle with something else."

The radio crackled. Several crews were well into their culinary creations and were not happy making a change at this late date, though they appreciated *Windsong*'s generosity.

The following morning I cemented event attendance by announcing, "All hands, all Yachts, morning party meeting is in order. Surprise! Surprise! Surprise! One of *Windsong*'s passengers is Willie Nelson, himself, and Willie has agreed, free of charge, to sing at our BBQ. What a party this will be and what fun we will have at the Oa Oa just nine hours from now."

Willie probably was nowhere in the Southern Hemisphere and Skip Rowland, as will shortly be apparent, was headed for big problems.

The party started with a bang. Every boat was represented and everyone in high spirits. I saw no evidence of wine smuggling and the smile plastered across Greg's radiant face told me the bar was doing record-breaking business. Some ladies had dressed as if attending a coronation at a real yacht club—likely to impress Mr. Nelson.

Halfway through the third Mai Tai and salads wilted in the heat, one of the *Canowie* crew pointed toward the anchorage and sang out, "What the hell is this?"

Windsong was outward bound on an evening tide. The conversational buzz withered like the salads, and a gaggle of eyes locked on me. It wasn't that my fraudulent antics to attract a crowd were truly harmful, but ladies who had abandoned special dessert projects were peeved, and Willie fans sensed something off-key.

"Let's see you get your way out of this one, Dad," Tony chided.

A light fired in my mind. I shouted out, "Hey, it's not all bad, folks . . . I'm sponsoring a cocktail for anyone who has a birthday today . . . How about that?"

The buzz was back. I was backslapped; thanked, kissed a few times, and even told I was a nice guy.

"Drinks are expensive here," Denise argued. "And there are too damn many birthdays."

When the party died, Greg handed me my bar bill. Denise almost died. She grabbed it from me. "Holy cow, Skip, one thousand one hundred and fifty US dollars! Are you nuts?"

Over one hundred souls present that night shared the same birthdate and Denise had a major 'mad on.'

My problems were not over. It was time to be heading west. Still hung-over, I gathered my ship's papers and passports and headed for the Gendarme's office in Vaitape, the island's small town a mile away.

"Good Morning Sir," I said, approaching the desk.

"Step back," I was told in crisp English.

"OK—sorry," I said, reaching across to present my papers and politely requesting return of my over two-thousand-dollar bond put up in Papeete.

252

Silence.

An eternity later, with no words spoken, the officer put his chop (stamp) on my papers and told me, "You are free to leave Bora Bora and return to Papeete for the refund of your bond. This pass is good for thirty-six hours. You must sail soon."

"You're kidding me!" was all I could say. "We pay a bond to visit your country, and when I'm leaving you want me to sail hundreds of miles backwards, to get money that doesn't belong to you in the first place?" I probably said it wrong.

"It is the rule!"

"It isn't right." I was losing it. "Dial your boss, OK, and have him wire the money here."

"You call him; here's the number," he barked and, never looking up, wrote it on the smallest scrap of paper he could find.

"Use that pay phone," he said and pointed to a pay phone on a street corner pole.

Fuming, I stormed from the office, muttering obscenities. It didn't sit well and I was in a mood no man should be in while in another man's country.

The phone took coins I didn't possess. A nearby market made change. Back at the phone I jammed in the equivalent of ten dollars US and dialed. The phone went bzzzzzzz. I tried again. Same result. Now I had an audience. Another captain wanting to leave had received the same don't give a hoot treatment from the Gendarme. He, too, was pissed.

In anger I ripped the phone from the pole and threw it on the ground—my brain signaling, *You're a jerk, Skip. Jail is next. Calm down!* I stormed the Gendarme office, charged the officer's desk and he backed up. Two big Frenchmen ushered me into a seat. The big shot slowly regained his composure. I don't suppose this happened often. "I called Papeete. I have permission to return your funds." His eyes glared into mine. "You must leave Bora Bora by midnight tonight or I will have you arrested."

Impossible—we hadn't provisioned and needed water and fuel. I had not seen a patrol boat, and a little-used law of the sea states no vessel may be *ordered* to sea from a safe harbor if the weather conditions are dangerous. I counted on there being no accurate forecast for Bora Bora.

We stayed another week in Bora Bora, without incident before sailing under ideal conditions for our next destination, Rarotonga.

CHAPTER 36

RAROTONGA—ANGUISH AND DELIGHT

Rarotonga provided unique challenges, moments of both anguish and delight, but an ending with profound personal sorrow.

As difficult as accurate weather forecasts were to receive, every yacht in mid-Pacific was well informed of conditions in general, and what to expect ahead. Ham radio nets provided most of the data and a few (very few) of the mega yachts had a new contraption called a weather fax, which beamed in the same semi-reliable pictures seen on TV weather reports. Even having one, the operator needed to be "spot on" to obtain a readable printout, by perfectly catching a specific satellite signal as it ripped across the sky, so we mostly just listened in to hams.

It was August 25th. We had logged 6423.7 nm since departing Newport Beach on January 10th. My superb mathematical skills equated that to sailing a blazing 28.44 nautical miles per day, so we were truly "drifting and blending."

What was important was being on the back end of the Pacific typhoon season, and we were. Rarotonga had been hit recently by winds topping 125 miles per hour, and the harbor was seriously damaged. We would be among the first to enter since the typhoon. Portions of Fiji (well to the west) had also experienced a bad typhoon season.

For now, all was sunny, bright, and slightly breezy as we left Bora Bora in our wake.

Somewhere, about six hundred nautical miles ahead, lay Rarotonga. It felt good to be at sea. Tony's first log entry expressed it well: "getting the hang of the helm again." Tom Peek was proving an affable mate. By early afternoon we gave him his first trick at the wheel. The wind promptly died to nothing, making steering truly impossible for a novice, so Tom switched on the engine to use our autopilot for better control.

The night was one more never-ending orchestra of stars. Being below the Equator, most constellations were unfamiliar to us. Even Hemingway would have difficulty describing how that particular night, with only four of us so far at sea, so deeply engraved itself in our memories and our souls. We shared improbable moments of serenity, all of us in the cockpit, comforted by the lingering warmth of the day, in a motionless boat on a windless sea—the sky ablaze with celestial wonder. Experiences such as that one develop friendships that survive the ages. I could sense this with young Tom . . . although we would eventually clash.

When morning broke, still with paltry wind, we had logged a sluggish one hundred thirty-six nautical miles, a little under six knots an hour. At mid-morning the breeze freshened and we zipped along at trolling speed, so out came the poles, lines, and bragging rights. Bingo—first crack and Denise had a fifteen-pound barracuda.

256

Tony went to work on the fish while Denise and I set the spinnaker. Tom became more accustomed to the wheel, even casually one handing it for short durations. How Tony made a meal, a tasty one at that, from a scavenger fish was beyond me. It was good. Tony had no problem rewarding himself with multiple pats on the back before retiring for an afternoon nap.

The clock struck seven bells marking 1530 hours (3:30 pm). Denise had been on the wheel for about a half hour. Tom had shared space in the cockpit. They both enjoyed talking, but Tom gave new meaning to the word 'chatterbox.' I went below to a chart exercise and could hear them both competing for the last word.

There dwells, in this part of the world, a small powerful phenomena called a "line squall." These are tiny independent storms that breed in warm water. The clouds they quickly form are densely black and the rain is piercing, as is the accompanying wind that often slams across the water at forty knots or so.

Coming topsides for a moment I scanned the horizon.

Not three minutes away and bearing down on us like a runaway freight train was the mother of all line squalls. I calmly looked to Denise, our momentary captain by virtue of the fact she was at the helm, and said, with my hand pointing abeam, "Pardon the interruption you two. Denise, what do you plan to do about *that*?"

"Here Tom," she said without missing a beat, "take the wheel. I have to get my rain hat."

Thus, the least experienced took the helm while Denise protected her precious hair from approaching elements, now 30 seconds away, and I yelled, "All hands, all hands."

Tony helped me douse the spinnaker, which was almost down when the first rain and wind swept over us. Struck broadside, *Endymion* tipped dangerously before gaining her senses. Tony, clutching an armful of spinnaker, lost his balance and slid into the lifelines, cursing loudly. I was able to grab him by the bathing suit and with my other hand opened the forward hatch to stuff the spinnaker below. Denise had set a world record for getting into wet weather gear and replacing herself at the helm.

Denise did not see the approaching line squall.

This had been another of those unexpected close encounters. Denise was correct taking the helm instead of coming forward to wrestle the mammoth sail in a big wind. At just over one hundred pounds she was no match for a wind-filled spinnaker. Besides—we all cared about Denise and the whiff of perfume announcing her presence for her next watch. And I wasn't certain how I would explain a missing body from my crew list at the next port had she gone overboard. Better she stayed in the cockpit.

Tom, who claimed to be a budding young writer, developed an idea for a story. "A yacht such as *Endymion* is sailing peacefully on a starry night when a crusty, barnacle-laden hand comes slowly from the ocean and grips the vessel's rail with tenacious strength."

"Shut up . . . shut up," Denise exclaimed, "That's horrible, Tom."

At end of day three, Rarotonga was in sight but we couldn't make harbor before nightfall. Clouds protesting a rising moon would make the night a dark one and we didn't want to hit anything entering the storm-ravaged harbor. Tony and I developed a plan. We knew the harbor entrance navigation lights were gone—swept away by the typhoon. The guest docks along the quay were gone, and a sunken powerboat was reported to lay just off mid-channel. Range lights were also out except for one. The good news was having ample deep water. We studied the chart and picked our entry route into Avarua Harbor (cum marina). Next we took a break and slow sailed, feasting on fresh queen fish for dinner, compliments of Minnesota farm boy Tom. Our chatter focused on how much beer we could/would consume once we were tied up, and how quickly we could get to it.

Approaching from the south we switched on the radar, sighting the island on the twenty-mile ring. It just fit. The radar placed the harbor just dead center of the island. Working together, Tony and I took range and bearings every few minutes, occasionally calling for Denise, at the wheel, to slightly correct course to compensate for drift and current.

By 2100 daylight had slipped away and we stood two nautical miles off what we reasonably believed to be the narrow entrance to the harbor. We moved with only engine energy. I had the helm, Tom was lookout, and Denise was beside me feeding me constant speed and compass information. Tony was at the radar. It was he, with skill and concentration, who really guided *Endymion*.

The ocean that night had a fair chop to it, so we moved slowly. We needed to enter the damaged harbor as if we were in dense fog, able to stop in half the distance we could see.

"Radar says one half mile," Tony called out.

Straining, Tom said he thought he saw something—so we all strained. Tony, his voice edgy, reported the radar indicated rocks close at hand. "Twenty feet to starboard." shouted Tom, positioned in the bow pulpit, signaling to turn five degrees to port. Down to less than two knots forward speed, we ghosted past a pile of rocks partially leveled by nature's enormous forces. Cemented to one rock, a metal post, bent sideways, had once held a harbor entrance light, testimony to the power of the sea.

"That was close!" Denise said quietly.

"How we doing on the sunken boat," I yelled to Tony.

"Stupid question, Dad," he shot back. "Under water—off screen. Can't tell you nuttin'. Come port another ten degrees," Tony added.

"Aye aye, dickhead."

Denise, now looking to port, said, "That looks strangely like a seawall to me."

It was, or was part of what had been one before the storm. "Watch it!" Tom shouted, jerking his hand, signaling to turn quickly to starboard. I took *Endymion* starboard five degrees, barely avoiding a cluster of newly sunken rocks.

"What are you doing, Pops?" Tony had noticed the move on radar.

"Fine tuning," I said. "Tom spotted rocks underwater that you couldn't see on radar."

We moved even more slowly in the direction where Denise thought she saw a seawall.

Then, from dead ahead, there bellowed a hearty masculine voice, "Welcome to Rarotonga and Avarau. You are the first boat to arrive since the storm. Congratulations! Let me help with your lines."

A rugged, handsome, dark-skinned native man stood atop a seawall directing us with a torch (flashlight). We were nearly at a standstill.

"You'll like it best," he said, "if you turn your stern to the wall I'm on, throw out a bow anchor, and back down to me. It's good holding, all mud and a few new rocks. Docks have been washed away."

We did as requested, tossing him lines he skillfully crossed and made fast.

"Come aboard?" I asked, looking up to him.

"No can do. You have to fly a Q f lag. Health Officials will fumigate your vessel for ants and mice," he said and promptly turned, disappearing into the dark.

"That's a bummer!" Tony muttered. I knew he could just taste a beer. "What's a Q flag?" Tom inquired.

Tony explained clearing customs, immigration, police, and other authorities in every port before leaving the vessel. "Until we do we are 'in quarantine,' so to speak, and must fly the orange 'Q' signal flag—but I never heard anything about fumigating for critters. It's a new to me. You too, Dad?"

"Beats me," I said. "Guess it won't hurt."

We could hear a rock band. It wasn't far away. There would be beer—probably cold beer. We were salivating. Even Denise was up for a taste, though she agreed to remain aboard while the rest of us hoisted each other up the seawall to find the music, beer, and our eternal fantasy . . . native dancing girls. I took one glace back at *Endymion*, the only yacht, in a harbor littered with destruction. I saw Denise touching her fingers to her lips, then the wheel, and I heard her softly say, "Thank you God—Thank you *Endymion*."

Walking toward the laughter and beer we were halted by the same man who had helped us tie up. He was big.

"Sorry sir, you're quarantined. No one may leave the vessel until you clear in the morning."

"Oh come on, only a couple of beers. Have a heart. What are you—the police?"

"Double sorry sir. I *am* the immigration officer. I don't want to but I must request you return to your vessel."

We were upset, angry, and about to cry, but we reversed direction boarding *Endymion* and cracking a couple of warm diet cokes.

"Shitty substitute," Tony murmured. We could hear the music so clearly.

"Hey . . . I need a hand here," came a familiar voice from the quay.

Atop the wall, like a mud god idol, stood our immigration officer with a case of beer—under each arm. We whooped and hollered like school kids passing a math test.

He would accept no payment. The beer was lip-smacking icy cold and our new friend came aboard this time.

There wasn't enough aspirin on the island to fend off the next morning. Before the sun was fully awake we heard a thump on deck. I was sleeping (recovering) in the cockpit and heard a new voice:

"Welcome to Rarotonga. I'm the Postmaster and have a letter from the Bicentennial Committee of Australia. You must be important."

"Toss it down. Let's see," I invited.

Inside was official acceptance of our application to compete in the first ever Tall Ships Race in the Southern Hemisphere. The race packet, including visas for Denise, Tony, and me would await us in Suva, Fiji at the office of Frank Johnston, First Secretary of the Australian High Commission.

"How about dem apples!" Tony exclaimed, watching Denise and me in a long hug. All we had to do, per race instructions, was arrive in Australia by mid-December.

Tony, Denise, and I headed for the village of Avarua, fighting off herds of scrawny chickens, to clear our papers. Tom stayed aboard. Denise wandered off to convert money to Cook Island dollars, enabling her to exercise her favorite sport—shopping. I wouldn't stop her. This was the place to do it and she soon had an armful of unique wooden carvings and colorful batiks. We stopped at the Hibiscus Restaurant, a charming spot with outside patio seating where locals regaled us about things to do and places to go. Rarotongans related to New Zealand as Tahitians related to France, except these folks were truly friendly, and spoke English.

We discovered church was a 'must do,' and there were plenty of bars and discos where Tom could play piano. "This—I gotta see," chuckled Tony.

Back aboard *Endymion*, Tom bubbled over with excitement. "There was a reporter here," he said, "who wanted to interview Skip, for being first in the harbor after the storm. She wanted your opinions and all."

My juices flowed. Every skipper fashioned himself, in some way an adventurer, explorer, and risk taker and relished the thought of momentary fame through a print interview.

"Hot damn! Great news Tom. You told her we were checking in? When will she be back? I'm up for this!"

"I don't think she'll be back, Skip—at least not until the paper comes out on Friday," Tom glumly reported.

"Why not? We're making news here. I can give a superb interview."

"Well, it's too late," replied Tom. "I gave her the interview because you were gone."

"You *WHAT*?" I went ballistic! "You gotta be kidding me, Tom. This is *my* yacht, I'm the captain, you're crew, and rookie crew at that. What gave you the right to speak for me, besides that little business card claiming you're a writer and all that other bullshit?"

I was fuming. I'd lost it. Tom knew it, as did anyone within one hundred yards. Tom had actually been proud to give the interview, but became ever so humble in the shadows of his monster skipper who was furious.

"Damn you Tom." I couldn't stop. "How the hell can you speak for me? You have no idea what I would have said. Not a clue! The skipper is *always* the spokesman for the yacht –not some three-day wonder crew. What the hell did you tell her anyway?"

I didn't wait for an answer. I was pacing (if that is possible) in the cockpit. Tony and Denise kept their distance stowing supplies or doing some other crap work that kept them in hearing distance. Tom just stood there, taking it all in and looking sheepish.

He tried to apologize. "But Skip, I know you're the captain. I told her that. She wanted the interview right then so it could make the paper, so I tried to say what I thought you would say."

"Oh yeah? Well Mr. Navigator, pretend I'm the reporter now, tell me what skills and tools you used to navigate to the island in the dark, big boy!"

"She didn't ask that kind of question, Skip. I can't answer that."

"Damn right you can't!"

I was cooling, beginning to feel guilty. I'd shouted enough—a lifelong fault. So I added, "When that paper comes out I want a copy, and you'd be wise to be on the other side of this island, or off it completely, if you misquoted me!"

Tom was genuinely hurt. He had done his best. He liked us. Truth is, we all liked him—a lot, but it would take a while for me to calm down. Angry as I was, I respected Tom's honesty explaining how it happened and how he stood firm under my anger and insults.

Denise had an idea. "Here, *captain*," she said with excessive special emphasis on the word captain. "Have a cold beer and a fresh green salad. I made it just for you, everything picked fresh from the island this morning."

She had me. She asked Tom to join us. She had us both. This had been the best four-person crew ever. The skipper shouldn't screw it up.

That night we found a small restaurant and bar with a rare treat for us—fresh meat! The manager invited Tom to play piano. We didn't expect much as we watched Tom adjust the bench for his six-foot plus frame, but when his talon fingers touched the keys, my God—that man could play! It was soft, soothing, whispering music. Tom's hands, shaking under my reproach just hours ago, gently caressed the ivories. In my heart I folded back any doubts about Tom. This was as good as Streisand at anchor in Nuku Hiva or the wood flutes at Las Hadas.

After dinner we went to Porky's, the hottest of the island's many nightclubs. Among the night people was one outrageously popular entertainer who was everything except cute, lovely, or sexy. Kia Orna (meaning welcome) owned the stage when she picked up the mike in one hand, and a coconut in the other.

"Put the damn clock on me," she commanded—and plowed her face into the coconut, husking it with her teeth, by the clock, in fifty-seven seconds. She possessed the crowd who roared with approval and applause.

"Cripes, I never seen nuttin' like that," said Tony.

When the cheering subsided she requested a volunteer from the audience. Many fingers and eyes pointed to me. Why, I will never know, but maybe being a big white guy in the front row had something to do with it. Kia Orna tugged me by the beard and dragged me to the dance floor. In my ear, she whispered instructions on coconut husking, and then announced I would try to break her speed of fifty-seven seconds. This was insane! The music went up, the crowd roared, the bets were on, a bell rang—and God will confirm I chomped down as hard as I could.

No good. I could not tear even a fiber from that husk, though I tried and tried. With my time up Kia announced it was 'slow dance time' and she would be dancing with me. She was a large woman, shaped like the coconut, and I knew her teeth were sharp. So we danced. She moved like a butterfly.

Sunday we all attended a 150-year-old Christian church and were escorted to visitor pews in the balcony. The church, a massive structure, was covered in vines and surrounded by graves of past parishioners including two celebrities. The former premier was buried near the front door. His eyeglasses adorned a sculpture of his head, along with beaded necklaces signifying his previous prominence. A more interesting marker was a wooden carving of a girl sitting against a tree, reading her bible. It was the tombstone of the first person known to have died from a bonk to the skull by a falling coconut. She passed at age twelve.

The church was stiflingly hot. Islanders in their best whites sat below, their kids sequestered to balcony pews with us visitors. The faithful praised the Lord in song and a tall preacher, elegantly dressed in black, welcomed us warmly in perfect English. His podium resembled a helmsman's station from an old clipper ship. In time I thought I recognized the old podium from photos I'd once seen of Irving Johnson's well-known schooner, *Yankee*. It had gone to permanent rest, aground somewhere in the South Pacific. I knew then, what island had beached her.

The service was long. Children grew restless. Out came peashooters and spitballs. Worshippers in the cavernous interior below us were under attack until the kids spotted a hornet's nest in the rafters. Take twenty children, with plenty of practice and ample ammo, and it's time to leave. The targeted angry hornets caused near panic. The wise preacher ended the service.

While on Rarotonga Denise wrote home:

My first real test of "crossings." We were four days and almost four nights because we were slow. And although Skip says I can handle the boat well, and I do, after two and a half hours on "watch," keeping the boat on a specific course you tend to tire and the waves and wind can throw you every which way. But, as Skip says, he's "real proud of me so far." Cool, isn't it?

The newspaper with Tom's interview arrived Friday. Page one featured a quarter page picture of Tom, broadly beaming aboard *Endymion*, as if he owned it. The article wasn't all that bad and Tom had correctly quoted me as saying we "are fond of Rarotonga and its people," although we'd been on the island possibly four daylight hours when the interview was conducted, so it was a quick but accurate observation.

At the start of this chapter I referred to profound sorrow—deep personal sorrow. Allow me please to add the words *heart breaking*. The following Monday Tony and I played a round of golf. Tony played poorly. Something bothered him and he resented my asking. I felt he was uncomfortable about a discussion we had the previous night regarding responsibilities. I decided to let it be.

When we returned to *Endymion* after too long in the nineteenth hole, a brooding Tony went below with hardly a 'hello' to Tom or Denise. At that moment an unexpected squall hit us. Fighting to hold our awning in place I called, "Hey Tony. Some help here . . . OK?"

"Screw you!" Tony yelled back from blow. "I'm not helping and I don't give a shit. I'm leaving."

"Come on, get yourself up here. We gotta get this thing tied down!" I hollered to Tony over the rain pelting the yacht.

"Hey!" Tony shouted back. "Get this clear, Dad—I'm leaving. Tonight!"

Shockwave!

Somewhere in the preceding days Tony had made a private decision. With a few beers warming his innards he announced his intentions, which he'd solidified by purchasing an airline ticket two days ago. He was flying to New Zealand, where he would seek a work visa and employment. His announcement was as unexpected as the attack on Pearl Harbor. I was stunned, but there was no changing his mind.

Denise comforted Tony as he packed his belongings. I sat alone in the cockpit. Tom made himself scarce. I was in despair. I dearly loved this kid. My kid. What had happened? Why didn't I sense it? Why didn't he say something? Why could we not even speak to each other? "He's really going," Denise said coming up the companionway, tears in her eyes. "He's pretty broken up, Skip—be kind with him, let him know you love him." Denise cried openly. I did too.

"Tony's in a hard place," Denise continued. "He's missing friends and afraid he won't fit in again at home. He's homesick, Skip, and frightened about your disapproval. You need to let him go, Skip, and now of all times, Tony needs your blessings."

I made every effort to comfort my son as we shared our last meal aboard—one of my life's most difficult moments. We walked together to the taxi that would take him to his flight, my arm around Tony's shoulder. "I love you, Son. I always will."

As if punishment, *Endymion* was anchored where we could see the lights of departing planes. I stood on the bow, my eyes flooded, watching Tony dissolve into the night.

CHAPTER 37

DESERTED "SAVAGE ISLAND"

The loss of Tony left me bewildered and lonely. Tony's huge contributions, his uncompromising companionship and engaging sense of humor would be missed. His absence hurt deeply. When we left Newport Beach I didn't believe Tony would sail further than Mexico. I felt the lure of friends at home would draw him back and yet we sailed together for eight months and eight thousand slow motion miles. We shared meals, laughter, times of drama, moments of fear, a few unplanned calamities, and mostly a dream—but doubt is the enemy of dreams. I came to believe Tony doubted his future, longed for what he missed in America, especially a woman to care for—and to care for him.

I hoped Tony took with him a high degree of confidence. He had proven himself to me. Like dads everywhere though, I worried about him, and prayed for him. Simply put, Tony was the son any dad would want.

Tom understood. Seated on the cockpit combing behind me, he placed his hands on my shoulders and recalled a moment from the big blow at Bora Bora. "I saw your love for Tony so exposed that night, Skip, when I didn't tie up the Avon correctly and Tony went drifting off. Do you remember?"

"Sure Tom. I also remember how badly you felt," I responded.

"I thought you blamed me."

"Naw, Tom, you did your best. Those were nasty conditions. We all get tested." The Minnesota musician with his words had unknowingly helped to calm a heart in turmoil. Mine.

Sailing south to Niue with only Denise and Tom presented a challenge. Still inexperienced at passage making, both agreed to up their contribution, however, it's impossible to instinctively or absolutely be prepared for what can suddenly arise at sea—and they understood.

Denise said, "There's always a way, and we will find it."

"We'll pull together," Tom staunchly added, and I believed them.

And so we sailed on to Niue, which lay six hundred miles west of Rarotonga and six hundred miles east of Fiji, rendering it difficult to date the girl from the cheering squad of the next island's team. Aside from Andorra, tucked in the mountains between France and Spain, Nuie was one of the smallest nations on earth, about the size of Washington, DC, making it a truly tiny speck on a huge ocean chart. We'd become pretty good at finding 'specks' and I wanted particularly to see this island, previously known as Savage Island, for the reception awarded Captain James Cook long ago.

Niue means, "Behold the coconut" and there are reportedly gazillions of them. The islanders are said to be big but gentle, some perhaps descendants of Cook himself.

It was an easy six hundred miles over several days and nights, with perfect weather. Tom wrote in the log: "Slow beautiful sailing."

"Perfect sailing under full moon, only I need to sleep more."

Denise entered, grabbing two slots on the page for her plaintive expression.

On one of my watches Denise wandered topside to console and comfort me. I had been despondent about Tony.

"If I may say so," Denise opened the conversation, "what you have done with your life takes daring and resolve. You're not a bad guy, Skip, but you need to relocate your self-esteem."

"Meaning what?"

"Meaning get back on course with your challenges. Open your face to a smile and accept that Tony had a personal crisis—that it was his personal crossroad and he needed to make his own decisions for his future and his own self-esteem."

"Makes sense I guess," I said weakly, knowing Denise was correct. "Tony will always love you, Skip. And in time he'll appreciate all that you've done to guide and mentor him. Now he needs his individuality and self-recognition. What's more important to you, I would think, than the event with Tony, is how you handle its consequences over time. So smile, Skippy, you have broad shoulders. Let me see the power and spirit in your personality!"

"Thanks Honey." I did feel better, and was grateful for Denise's understanding. I thought back to something Tony had once mentioned when talking about Denise.

"Dad," he had said, "Denise is incredible. She puts on perfume, fixes her face, and looks great every single time she comes on watch no matter the weather, hour, or mood. I bet there isn't another person like her on this or any ocean, anywhere."

On my watch our primitive Magnavox satellite navigation instrument took a dump and needed reprogramming. For an electrical genius such as me, it was a two-day affair littered with creative vocabulary.

Then the forward head plugged up. In both a perfect world, and the opposite, toilet repairs were the captain's duty. Damned if I knew why. It just was.

Our last night out from Niue our autopilot, "Harvey," started sending us on errant courses, inspiring Denise to write home:

Sailing with Skip's great sound system is beautiful but nowhere near
as entertaining as negotiations between Harvey and management.

That last night at sea we spotted navigation lights behind us. In the dark a lightweight racing yacht slowly ghosted past us. By VHF radio we met Ray Martin, from Vancouver, Canada, his yacht *Tantivy lll*, and charming mate Margot, also headed for Niue.

Looming into sight the following day Niue appeared as a huge granite rock with huge waves assaulting it's shore. Through binoculars we could find no beach, harbor, or charted anchorage. We headed for the lee of the island and village of Alofi where we were to check in.

We soon saw *Tantivy lll*, rolling uncomfortably at anchor. We chose a spot close to them in an uncomfortable swell and dropped our hook in seventy feet of ocean water. To put out proper scope took all of our three hundred feet of chain. I was surprised at the depth. Anchorages since Mexico had been in water no deeper than fifteen feet. The water around Nuie was remarkably clear because there was no harbor to create pollution, no commercial traffic by sea, and no rivers on the raised coral island to carry silt and dirt into the pristine ocean. Lucky us. We could see bottom.

Tantivy lll Ray hailed on the VHF. "Suggest you folks wait till shadows are low, or tomorrow to go ashore. Waves have been pounding that bulkhead—look about eleven o'clock—it looks like a stone wharf. It's the only place to land, and it's been splashy in there."

Ray was bang on. "Thanks, Ray. I won't attempt it today. We're a bit beat anyway. Want to row over for a cocktail?"

"Watch us." I looked toward *Tantivy lll.* He and Margot were on the rail in swimsuits. He put the mike down, saying "Coming atcha," and they dove overboard.

We were soon exchanging stories of how and why we got there. Ray was a risk taker and person of little caution. He had been an Air Canada pilot. Not particularly interesting, many cruisers are former airline people familiar with navigation. Ray was different. Prior to his airline experience, he had been a Canadian Air Force fighter pilot, and the *only* person in the world to survive a mid-air collision with another fighter plane.

"God is my co-pilot," he explained. "I take risks I like . . . have no fear and when it's over—it's over. Simple."

"Remarkable. I salute you," was all I could muster. But it made me think—we cross oceans for the adventure, knowing the potential for danger not found in ordinary life experiences. We were sitting with a man, as regular a guy as found in any boardroom or sales meeting—yet Ray had lived on the edge, cheated the grim reaper, and was living life to the fullest.

The following morning Denise and I headed ashore in the inflatable, first removing the engine so it wouldn't get bashed if we made a bad landing. We were careful rowing in. A particularly precocious wave practically lifted us onto the huge concrete berm, and set us down hard enough for me to bruise my bum. We jumped smartly though, hauled the Avon to a secure position, and scampered off toward the village.

"Golly, this place would make Deadwood City seem like a metropolis," Denise said as her eyes roamed the horizon looking for buildings where she could exercise her black belt in shopping.

We saw only two aged structures. One said "POLICE" in worn letters on weather-beaten siding, and though not advertised, we sensed by the old gas tank outside, two rusted scooters, some empty milk cartons, fruit rotting in a basket and a jungle of discarded candy wrappers, that the second building was a general store.

We chose the Police Station.

We expected a laid-back operation on such a remote island. Heck, everything in the South Pacific moves like it's in another time zone. But we found the police chief, the sole officer on the island, in a crisp uniform with a tidy office and friendly nature. He said we could go where we wanted on his island, warned that cliffs to the water are steep and dangerous, and spoke of a 'secret' cove where maidens were once sacrificed after being tied to rocks in a rising tide. There was a devilish glint in his eye as he placed his heavy finger on a map's imaginary X where the cove was located, and spoke directly to Denise, "Spirits are present. Some are not friendly—so *if* you venture there, go in the brightest daylight."

"Chief," Denise questioned, "it is such a beautiful place, and there are so few people. Why?"

Denise was radiant in a tight but classy little sundress complimenting her curvaceous body. I guessed the Chief had never whiffed delicate perfume and had seen only box-shaped bodies and betel nut teeth for several years. Denise had his attention.

"Alas," the Chief explained, "our island was once home to fourteen thousand people in fifteen villages. We had schools, hotels—we had everything, but New Zealand had bigger paying jobs. The young began to leave for the music, dancing, and freedom in New Zealand. Soon our villages became ghost towns. The young were not replaced. Now we are less than fourteen hundred people island-wide, and only twenty hotel rooms. We make a paltry living from farming—and raising our special lemons (his voice rose in a moment of enthusiasm), but it does not take care of us." The chief held a lemon in his hand that looked more the size of a grapefruit. "Now," he continued, "we must even bring animals from New Zealand to feed our people and we, sadly, are on a subsidy from the Commonwealth."

He seemed an unhappy man as he explained the island's national debt is close to nearly three hundred dollars per remaining person. "We get small fees where we can," he told us, pushing twenty-dollars driver's license applications in front of us, saying, "You will need them for scooters, and you will need scooters to get around the island."

We bought the licenses and comforted the chief: "Chief. Fear not. As beguiling as your island is, tourism will shortly come. You will be wealthy and happy."

Of course no scooters were available so the smart-looking chief pocketed the money as he asked, "Would you and your daughter like a ride to the hotel? It's the only place for lunch."

"Chief," I said, "if my daughter were here she might accept, but this is my wife, and we need a good walk anyway, so thanks, but we will pass."

Little scammer. I had a life-size picture of the chief all over Denise while I sat frustrated in the back seat separated by an iron screen.

Denise and I hoofed it to the hotel for one of life's worst lunches. We complimented the chef with smiles and an outrageous tip, and raced to the inflatable before we both puked.

A dance was scheduled that evening, to which we were invited. Tom had not been ashore and looked forward to it. Denise and I hadn't shared with Tom the sparse feminine population situation so he had high expectations for island ladies.

Going ashore about 1900 we found our scooters still unavailable, however, promised for tomorrow, along with a picnic lunch for island sightseeing. To get to the dance we took a ride in the paddy wagon with the chief, Denise on my lap in the front seat. It went ok, but if the chief's hand had strayed while shifting gears there would have been a major problem.

The dance fizzled like an outdated sparkler, and for the first time in modern memory I didn't spend a dime. Beer was 'on the house' all evening. Tom and I had plenty. Denise sampled spiked fruit drinks, which I found too sweet. To return to the seawall and our inflatable, Denise and I got in the cab and Tom hopped into the bed of a pickup truck that was part Toyota, small degree Chevy, and rear canopy from a jeep. The truck was filled with generously overweight, giggling, giddy women, smelling of booze, and oh so happy to be with Tom.

The night's powerful drinks packed a punch. At morning's light, Tom was waving from shore, weaving dangerously, and still propped up as he stood on the rocky shore polluting the water before returning to *Endymion* for a full-day recovery.

Denise and I took the available excuse for rented motor scooters to investigate the island. We found the Chief's 'X-spot' magical lagoon in a volcanic rock chasm leading down to gentle waters with brilliant hues of blues and greens. It was a tough climb down uneven steep rocks to the sheltered pond. We stayed for hours, saw not another soul and had no fear of shedding swimsuits. Everywhere we swam or lounged the water was crystal clear to the bottom. Lush bushes clung to reddish brown rocks and cascaded toward the lagoon, clusters of fragrant multi-colored flowers hanging from them. Frangipani for sure and orchids I'm certain, added breathtaking scents. Birds pecked at flowers and sang to us while butterflies applauded with flapping wings. Multi-colored topical fish darted in and out of clusters of coral. One small opening led to the ocean and the shimmering blue Pacific. Pleasantly warm water pushed softly against our naked bodies, as the gentle ocean surge ebbed and flowed from the mystical spot. *Go ahead*, I thought, *ask me why we sail to uncelebrated islands.* This setting would be worth millions in the United States, yet we were enjoying it free—and privately. We couldn't imagine a more romantic setting. How, I wondered, could anyone have been sacrificially given to any God in such a serene, peaceful place—and if they had, in some pagan existence—what a place to go. We savored our lunch, made slow passionate love in paradise, and fully refreshed—hit the scooters again.

Nuie had no carnivorous animals, except poisonous snakes, so we ventured on, but with a wary eye. The blowy windward side of the island was void of buildings. Views across the wide-open South Pacific Ocean clearly showed the curve of the earth, and were astonishing. Hues of blue blended so intimately the horizon appeared neither as ocean nor sky. Further around and high on the cliffs we came to a deserted village. Spooky. Through glassless windows we saw tables set with dinnerware and waiting chairs. Who had not come to dinner? The church altar was surrounded by candleholders, several appearing to have been snuffed halfway. Why, we wondered? Was it a person—the wind—or the spirits the chief had warned about? Vines in tangled death grips tightly clutched abandoned houses. Empty streets were dusty and without tracks. Even the schoolhouse had chalk marks on blackboards. One could homestead here and have a choice of buildings.

No thanks—not us.

Denise wrote home today: *Mom and Dad, It's hard to believe such an intoxicating place as the lagoon we swam in even exists. I never would have believed it, and the island is almost deserted. This might be the most beautiful place on earth but it's also lonely. Someday this will be a big tourist place. I hope we can come back.*

During breakfast at the uncomfortable anchorage the next morning Tom told Denise and me about a fascinating pod of whales he had seen from the same cliffs we had visited. Growing up on the Great Lakes, Tom learned to dive and had explored shipwrecks beneath Lake Superior's frigid surface. It intrigued me. Lingering over another coffee I was asking Tom more about the wrecks and mighty storms that claimed them, when Denise jumped up sending her breakfast airborne—screaming, "Whale . . . whale, right there, whale—no—TWO whales! Holy crapola."

Passing between Tantivy lll and us were three humpback whales, two adults protecting their calf swimming between them. Ray shouted, "I'm swimming with them," and dove from *Tantivy III.*

Circling us once the whales came around again making Ray, who swam without fear, look like a tiny rag doll. Ardent photographer Tom was manning his camera but the moment got the best of him. Handing his sacred camera to Denise, he said, "I gotta do this. If anything happens to me tell my mother it was worth it!"

Cornball to the end, I thought. We didn't know who his mother was, and didn't need to. Tom was a strong swimmer. Huge untamed mammals and tiny fearless men, the likes of which I'll relish forever entertained us for fifteen minutes. When an exhausted Tom climbed aboard *Endymion* I heard him say, "I can die now." But he didn't and many years later he wrote to me:

I'm not sure what deep chime inside me sent those words to the surface, but I do know this much: My encounter with the three humpback whales, including close eye contact with the mother—was so raw and primordial that I felt as if I had touched something essential and everlasting in the world—something so real and authentically enchanting that were I to experience nothing else in my life, I would be satisfied to have lived because I've experienced it.

Fiji was our next major destination. We could sail north touching the Solomon's, or go south by way of Tonga. The Solomon's offered interesting World War Two history. "Maybe in Tonga we could meet the king from Bastille Day," suggested Denise.

The three of us sprawled out in the cockpit, charts spread across our backgammon table, discussing routes as if it were a democracy. Ultimately a ham radio weather report of typhoon potential to the north was our decision maker. We chose Tonga.

It was time to leave. We were ready and tired of rolling at anchor. We happily watched the anchor come up clean through the seventy feet of crystalline water while on hundred feet away a whale played in our yard.

CHAPTER 38

INTERNATIONAL DATE LINE

The International Date Line follows the 180th parallel of mother earth, except where it weaves eastward to enable Tonga, situated in the midst of a vast empty sea, to boast of being the first nation to greet a new day. Well—guess what? We happened to be six nm from the dateline at midnight—so while the earth spun on its axis, hurtling time forward, we were closer to the date line than any anyone on earth, excepting potential fishermen—none of whom were visible on our radar. I had never previously paid any attention to the date line, but it's possible Denise, Tom, and I were the first three of the world's seven billion people to etch our carbon footprint into September 19th, 1987, though probably not a soul but us cared.

Arriving at Tonga via the archipelago's northernmost island of Vava'u, should have, by this stage of our voyage, become a mundane event—another typical palm-fringed channel with white sandy beaches. But the old is forever new and every entrance was memorable. We threaded our way through the many petite islets into Vava'u in daylight for the beauty and because it wasn't well marked, evidenced by a dismasted fifty-foot sloop, abandoned on a slab of coral, remnants of sail still clinging to a portion of the mast.

Tied to the municipal dock in Neaifu's Port of Refuge harbor, I was struck by the extent of damage from a recent tropical disturbance we hadn't even heard of. Trees were down. Stately palms were headless and a few storefronts boarded up.

Officials with attitude came aboard, we thought to clear us. In a kingdom, without a democratic process, they unfortunately don't have to be pleasant, and they were not. Clearing a yacht into a country normally takes an hour, maybe less. Sometimes officials don't bother to come aboard at all. These overbearing presumptuous agents all but strip-searched us during a three-hour interrogation in our steamy, humid salon, with a blazing midday sun overhead.

We were ordered to surrender all liquor and cigarettes. We had none. They practically tore us apart, even stripping our refrigerator and tossing the 'black hole' (storage compartment). We had not lied. Our fishing gear caught one civil servant's eye. He boldly declared, "I'll take these, and these," and stuffed his bag with five hundred dollars' worth of our lures and hooks.

Denise was fuming. Tom was visibly uncomfortable. I strained to keep my fuse from detonating. This was blatant robbery—by representatives of the king.

With pockets stuffed they found our video collection, and took them all. I was shaking when they left with our best Penn deep-sea fishing reel as dessert.

"They may, at least, return the videos," Tom mused. "If memory serves me, the states uses NTSC format and the rest of the world uses the PAL system. Your tapes so won't play in Tonga."

284

Denise added, "Yup—and you know what, boys—it's their country, they can do as they damn well please, so dial down the temper, especially you, Skip."

Tom proved correct. One dark night a soiled laundry bag containing our tapes was unceremoniously tossed onto our deck.

We didn't stay long in Tonga. The chemistry wasn't right and I had this dark cloud, a sense of impending doom hanging over me. Aside from a luau and native dancing on a remote beach, Tonga held little joy.

Denise's thoughts were reflected in this letter home:

We're in Neaifu now, it's Sunday. Everything is closed because everyone is in church but I'm not sure why. A Governors' wife died so there's a weeklong ban on drinking, dancing and I'm sorry to say, shopping. The wife story is odd. They carried the poor sick woman around from island to island trying to get her help, and in the end that's probably what killed her! Yuk!

I was glad to leave Tonga.

CHAPTER 39

FIJI JOE

As the Tonga shoreline disappeared in the misty morning light, my sense of safety grew, as did the warmth I felt for both Denise and Tom.

Denise popped up the companionway. "Hey guys. Looks like life's not so bad after all. Pot of coffee here—any takers?"

Light wind, smooth seas, and a steady ride. It was glorious, gratifying sailing for the next 380 nautical miles, when on a densely dark night we entered the reef-infested waters of Fiji's Lau Group. We hove to until daylight.

I'd worried about navigating in Fiji because the available charts were last surveyed nearly one hundred years ago. Numerous new reefs had developed, either by oceanic action or natural reef growth. We had seen several wrecks. I didn't want to add *Endymion* to the list.

Well away from Fiji we checked by radio, as a coup was reported to be preeminent. Hearing the islands were quiet though tense, we decided to push on to Suva, another day's sail distant. By mid-afternoon clouds veiled the sun, wind was rising and seas building. It was another punishing night for our short-handed crew, who I believe rose to the occasion, though Denise confided, "Sometimes I'm so tired I could cry."

It was my habit at first light to walk the decks checking equipment and rigging. In turbulent conditions I sometimes crawled, but I believed in the ritual and performed it diligently. That morning I was astonished. Our stainless steel bow pulpit, through bolted to the deck, had been ripped from the deck by some powerful force, and bent nearly fifty degrees. *Endymion's* solid teak toe rail was in splinters. "What the hell!"

The night before had been rough, lifting and plunging us into the next rolling wave as we fought our way to windward, the wind howling like a banshee. But not to have felt or heard anything was odd. We may never know what twisted the bow pulpit, but this is what we collectively decided must have occurred:

Amongst the ocean's dangers, or treasures depending on one's viewpoint, there are many partially submerged floating containers, dislodged from cargo ships by storm or carelessness. Most eventually sink. We suspect a container, with a corner slowly rising on a wave, connected like the pointed end of an arrow, with *Endymion's* bow, as we came off a wave. The impact had been quick and powerful—but—had it been a millisecond later it could have put a hole in us, and sunk us. Had God given us a warning, or had he been our co-pilot too?

We had to lay over in Suva, political unrest or not. We entered the principal harbor of the 320-plus islands of Fiji about 1500, Friday, September 25th. Before Tom could fetch the dreaded Q flag, a fast-approaching small naval vessel with a man behind a fifty-caliber cannon, hailed us to come alongside. We co-operated.

Smartly uniformed, polite seamen came aboard wanting our papers. These men were handsome giants with broad shoulders, square jaws, and expansive smiles, but they asked serious questions about our intentions in Fiji, and they had a bundle of forms for me to complete. Denise reminded me, "We are in their country . . . show respect," adding in a whisper, "I don't like their boots on my teak decks!"

One of them overheard Denise and lifted his rifle high across his chest. His smile faded and he used menacing sign language with piercing direct eye contact as he advanced—backing Denise to the companionway where she stood fast. I watched protectively, secretly smiling. I admired her expression 'my teak decks.' It demonstrated pride. Once satisfied, the naval skipper ordered his charges to 'stand down' and explained all waterways were under military control. We were to anchor at The Royal Suva Yacht Club. We were not allowed anywhere else.

"Sounds good to me," said a bright-eyed Tom. "Tell me Sir," I asked, "why such restrictions?"

The official glanced at his watch and said with pride, "A transition of the government is happening as we speak. Colonel Rabuka (then third in command of Fijian forces) has peacefully assumed power to return our government to ethnic Fijians—but you needn't worry, the Colonel assures safety to all foreign visitors. Bulah, Bulah (Fijian expression of greeting or leaving)." He saluted, boarded his ominous patrol boat and quickly sped off.

"In other words," Tom exclaimed, "a bloodless coup."

We were drop dead exhausted when finally, late in the day, our pick settled on the muddy floor of the crowded Royal Suva Yacht Club anchorage.

"I'm whipped," commented Denise, "and looking at your tired eyes, Skip, I would say you are too."

We all were. The mental strain of the gunboat encounter and tap dancing with Tonga's thieving authorities had gravely frayed some nerves.

Tom, who would be leaving us to pursue his writing, said, "I have an idea—let's party!"

"Tom, excellent idea. Let's do it—but let's be cautious about going ashore permanently, right now. It seems a tense place, and you're sincerely welcome to stay aboard."

Typically optimistic, Tom semi-seriously said, "What could be better than partying over twenty-five-cent beers during a developing coup? I won't find better subject material!"

So we fired up the Avon. Destination: stress-releasing bargain-priced booze at the Royal Suva Yacht Club, a melting pot for Pacific voyagers. The club bar was packed, but with little "bulah" in the conversations' hushed tones, centered on politics and impending doom. We listened. There was trouble afoot in Fiji.

Our customs clearance was by appointment the following afternoon. First I had to find people capable of working with stainless steel to repair the bow pulpit. Joe, a short, wiry Fijian with a sharp eye, skilled hands, and an arsenal of tools was the first and only person we needed to connect with. By himself, in two days, he removed, straightened, and refitted the bow pulpit—and replaced the toe rail with such perfection an inspector general could not find flaw. We called him "Fiji Joe." He charged a whopping one hundred dollars . . . and earned this chapter in his honor.

CHAPTER 40

A MILITARY COUP

D enise and I hailed a taxi to the Australian embassy. A solemn
military presence lined the roads, including an occasional heavy
tank. Guards were posted every few feet around the Australian Embassy,
looking intently at all who entered. A line of concerned ethnic Indians
and Chinese seeking exit documents stretched for blocks.

"Thank God for our invitation," said Denise, as a guard acknowl-
edged our appointment.

Once inside, having again shown our passports, we were escorted
to the Office of Frank Johnston, First Secretary of the Australian
High Commission.

"Now, aren't you glad we dressed properly?" asked Denise.

As participants in the upcoming Bicentennial celebration and Tall
Ships Race, we were treated as rock stars. Mr. Johnston presented us
with copious amounts of publicity surrounding the race including
an article from the *Canberra Times*, announcing the "participation
of *Endymion*, a superbly sailed thirteen-meter sleek racing yacht

from America, expected to arrive in Sydney before the Christmas holiday." "How 'bout that," Denise chuckled. "Make you feel good all over, Skip?"

It did. In appreciation of our participation, Denise and I were given eighteen-month visas for Australia, including work permits. Over coffee, the High Commissioner explained more of the nautical heritage of Australia, from establishment of the first settlement by English prisoners to the reverence the country feels for Captain James Cook and his ship *Endeavour*.

"The United Kingdom," he told us warmly, "is gifting Australia a replica of Captain Cook's vessel to be known as *Young Endeavour*. It will be sailed, in part, by youngsters interested in our nautical heritage—and who write the best essays."

Those not selected would be directed to *Endymion* and other participating yachts.

Handing me a packet of letters from thirty-plus aspiring youths, the Commissioner suggested, "Please contact these individuals as soon as possible. Good luck!"

Our heads spun. We hadn't forgotten about the race invitation. Nor had we considered ourselves celebrities, but we'd become a focal point for an entire nation, a minor one perhaps, but none the less a position we hadn't asked for—and were uncertain we wanted.

Suddenly we had deadlines. Skippers don't like deadlines. Deadline pressure evokes poor decisions, like neglecting maintenance or leaving port in foul weather. But the opportunity was legitimately once in a lifetime—and challenging. We had three months to get to Australia and choose a crew from youngsters who were probably dreaming big, while counting on us to pick them. We would have to disappoint young people we hadn't even met. We could take only three. Denise and I shook hands on this one. We would do this as partners and we would do it right.

Returning to the yacht club, our so-called coup confinement center, we enjoyed a leisurely parting lunch with Tom. He was excited and moved ashore knowing there was always a spot for him aboard *Endymion* and in our lives.

"Tom will be OK," commented Denise. "He'll do well."

The next day, our friend and stateside attorney, Larry Dent and his buddy from Oakland, California, who we had never met, would come aboard, and sail with us to Australia.

Denise and I upped anchor and headed for our 1400 appointment at the Customs dock. We jabbered with Paul, a young athletic Customs officer, aspiring someday to be an Olympian. We showed him videos of the 1984 Los Angeles Games.

Paul was drawing Denise and me a map on a scrap piece of wood I was holding when an armored truck roared around the corner, lights flashing, horn honking. It was packed with soldiers, standing or on bench seats—all brandishing automatic weapons and hanging on as the vehicle ground to a noisy halt before us.

"Crapola! Here we go again," Denise said.

"Halt! Stop! Don't move!" commanded a zealous officer leaping from the front seat, nearly knocking Paul over.

We were surrounded in moments. Paul said something in the native tongue to the officer in charge and was brushed aside. Denise and I were inside a tightening circle of big, weapons-toting Fijian soldiers, who were not smiling. I was irritated. Drifting and blending wasn't intended to be like this.

"Papers—you the Captain?" I was asked.

"I am, and Bulah to you Sir. We cleared legally. We are a documented vessel of the US Government. What can I do for you—*Sir?*" Adding "Sir," with emphasis.

Paul had reacquired his sea legs and spoke to the lieutenant. "This is highly unusual, Lieutenant. There has been no wrongdoing. I've inspected the yacht, these people are cleared and are going to the Yacht Club for showers and a meal."

"Papers!" repeated the officer, his hand extended.

"These passports are the property of the United States of America. You may examine them but I cannot surrender them," I said, politely offering our passports and a folder of ship's documents, and hoping my ruse would work.

No response. He took his time looking at everything—departure papers from Tonga, crew lists, ship's inventory, ownership documents, and passports. We stood by tentatively in oppressive afternoon heat, sweat seeping through every inch of cloth touching me. The sky was about to explode. A soldier leering at Denise was bringing me into a slow fume. I'd had too much of this crap too many times. Denise saw it and signaled by expression 'not to worry.' I struggled to get into my two-foot zone—to concentrate.

The clouds let loose. The officer looked into the rain, rolled up our papers, and handed them to me. "You are free to go—only to the Royal Yacht Club. We will be checking. All non-Fijians must be inside by 8:00 tonight. National curfew. No exceptions, except church."

CHAPTER 41

CHILD THIEF IN AN INNER TUBE

Moving around Suva during the coup was difficult. The depth of the disagreements between indigenous Fijians and a large Indian population was substantial. The coup had accentuated prejudice, the roots of which came from Fijian traditions. Indian people directed most of the economy, and it wasn't sitting well with the Bulah crowd. The newspaper had been shuttered, movie houses and restaurants closed, even sporting events cancelled. People couldn't go out at night. Aside from inconvenience, we were not seriously affected, and never once pulled aside for inspection, though frightened friends were.

Larry and his buddy Mike Mulholland arrived without mishap, stepping aboard one day after Tom's departure. We paid Fiji Joe his one hundred dollars and sailed on to less inhabited islands. We kept a low profile, and were prepared to duck if we heard gunfire, feeling it best to be neither involved nor vocal.

Mike Mulholland was a character and born-again fisherman, with a mouth attached to a bragging line I'm confident reached God.

Denise and I agreed to silence it by out fishing him, though Mike had a suitcase full of gear and a spiffy new telescoping pole he swore not to share with any person, any time, anywhere. His line was in the water, whether we were moving or still. We powered occasionally in waters where islands were close, often needing to throttle down to enable Mike to clear precious lures he repeatedly snagged in shallow water. We feigned sympathy.

Denise wrote home:

It's hysterical Dad . . . Three grown men trying to catch the first fish—any fish. They have "secret lures," special weapons and killer's lures—but no fish! Wouldn't it be funny if the little beginner's pole you gave me were first to hook up? I hope so.

We anchored one night at Malolo Lai Lai, a wisp of an island. We were not more than one hundred feet from the Musket Cove Yacht Club. Correction—it's really a bar. There were neither yachts nor club, but the people—humongous, towering Fijian men of stone and their equally massive wives made sure we had a whopping good time. Denise, assisted by a lovely native lady, six foot two, tenaciously struggled to free a monster fifteen-pound clam from the shallow bottom. Once beached, Denise's new friend showed Denise how to cut the poison sack free. It was ugly. Stunk too. For the first time, using spices from America, Denise made savory clam chowder. We roared our approval. Mike, always up for a party, couldn't find the boat that night and slept on the beach.

Colonel Rabuka, now presumptive dictator, proclaimed October 11th Independence Day. Humph! We heard the announcement while anchored in a bug-infested bay near Lautoka, Fiji's western port of entry where twin-engine mosquitos hung out in heavy air. After securing *Endymion* we piled into the Avon to seek relief in town.

We lingered, even had ice cream cones we had to slam into our faces before they became puddles at our feet. Mike, dodging armed combat flies, bought a good size water buffalo steak in the open-air market. Larry, more parsimonious in nature, thrust forward enough coins for steak about the size of a watchband.

Back in the inflatable approaching *Endymion* I asked, "Which of you knuckle-heads left the swim ladder down? Denise—I thought you secured the ladder."

"I did," she said. "I always do—it's my job."

"Hey, look—the hatch is open." Larry pointed to the large foredeck hatch. "Looks like we've been robbed."

We slowed the Avon, coming up on the yacht from astern for the best view in case there were boarders—or someone trying to escape. Quietly Mike grabbed the swim step.

"Me first," I said, climbing aboard, oar in hand. Mike followed.

"Got your six," he said and Larry followed Mike. Denise manned the inflatable.

Everything on deck was secure except the hatch, a supposedly theft-proof French "Goiot" model, selected for its opening size to hurriedly stuff sails below, and for strength against dropped equipment or nasty weather.

"Larry—Mike," I whispered, pointing the boat hook I held. "Be sure someone doesn't try to get out the companionway or aft hatch. I'll go below first. I'm faster and I've done this many times."

Facing aft, I stealthily crouched over the hatch putting myself in my two-foot zone, and then suddenly thrust myself through it yelling "*Oorah*" as fiercely as possible.

My cry all but echoed. I was alone below decks. The threat was gone, but we had been robbed—just small things. Taking personal inventory, $300 cash from the chart table drawer had disappeared, yet Larry still had his wallet with cash in his forward berth. My stopwatch and coveted hand-bearing compass were gone, as was Denise's small bag of antihistamine pills but not her cosmetics. Mike was not victimized.

We took to the radio, asking others in the anchorage, "Have you seen anyone aboard *Endymion*?"

No one had, but one yacht reported, "There was a small kid on an inner tube a while ago. He paddled around, knocking on hulls and greeting people. Probably asking for candy—something like that. We thought it was cute, but he didn't come this way."

"Can you describe him, and how long ago?" I asked

"Oh, half hour ago, maybe a little more. Indian kid. Looked to be about ten."

"What was he wearing?"

"Bathing suit, blue as I recall. He had what looked like a small cooler tied to the tube."

We'd heard enough. Denise remained aboard while Larry, Mike, and I went ashore to file a police report. Speaking with the police, we weren't thinking coup, or that every cop was island-born Fijian and may have been prejudiced because of the coup. We know they never found the culprit and it's likely good they didn't. Mike put it this way, "The one thing you didn't want to be today was a little Indian kid running down the street in a wet bathing suit, with an inner tube and a small bag that looked like candy."

CHAPTER 42

DEAD ONE HUNDRED DAYS

The Outer Fijian islands called the Yasawa Group make one forget any hardships of cruising. We anchored close ashore to a village called Yalobi, on the small island of Waya. Same story: picture perfect swaying palms, white sandy beaches, patches of coral brimming with colorful parrot fish, and jagged volcanic mountains jutting to God behind the village. Bulah-shouting village officials greeted us with fists pumping the air. Denise wrote home:

All the islands in Fiji have one guy who is chief and absolute boss. We must offer him a gift to go ashore, often a few stalks of this awful kava root someone grinds into a nauseating drink they think is delicious. Sometimes we have to drink it with them, which isn't fun. It makes my mouth numb, fries your brain and slows you down like a handful of tranquilizers. It's strong and awful, looks like muddy water. Anyway, if the chief likes our present, and he always does, then we are free to roam around his village.

Mike & Skip prepare Kava for the Chief

Strolling to the end of the path at Yalobi we met Mere (Mary), a multi-tasking woman of middle age, sweeping dust from the entrance to her burr (house) while stirring a massive kettle over an open fire. Mere was engaging. She invited us to stay for dinner with her and her six runny-nosed children. We said OK. Mere batted her eyes and smiled coyly, focusing her attention on Mike. At about five foot ten, thin and muscular, horny Mike was an attractive alternative to the massive Fijian men, under the wings of whom Mere had grown up. Besides, Mike's bald spot was a magnet to Mere. She liked to kiss it.

Denise, Skip, Mike, Mere and her six kids

Over dinner and kava, Mere explained her recent separation from her husband, who had moved to another village for work. She was happy we had come to visit. She didn't enjoy being a single mom, and *seriously* wanted Mike to come back that evening to "make a new baby with me." We teased Mike unmercifully—even throwing a celebratory bachelor party for him in the cockpit. Mike blissfully went from kava to scotch, telling us, as he became more plastered, he would rename the island "Mulhollandland," when he became chief. Shortly thereafter he passed out.

At sunrise we noticed frenzied activity along the beach. Two pigs were roasting on spits, the heady aroma already tantalizing. Tables were set, flowers were everywhere, children frolicked and it appeared there would be a beachfront parade. We found today was the one-hundred-day death celebration for an elderly lady, whose body rested in a tree house visible from *Endymion*. She was wrapped in a ceremonial shroud, perhaps more for odor control than anything else. Today, as custom required at the one-hundred-day mark, her body would be paraded through the village and publicly cremated in a traditional fiery ritual. The soul is set free during this joyful event. Close to the crack of 10:00 a.m., Mike, burdened with a sledgehammer hangover, and still somewhat laced, rose slowly. Larry, Denise, and I faced him, looking unusually concerned.

"What are you going to do about this?" asked Larry, pointing to the festivities ashore.

"You must have had one whopper of a tanking to bring this on," added Denise.

Mike, in a mental fog, looked toward shore with a puzzled expression. It was my turn: "Mike, apparently you visited ol' Mere last night. You proposed to her! She accepted. This beach extravaganza is for *your* wedding, Mike—you and Mere are getting hitched!"

Denise chimed in: "Mike, see that big tree up the hill there, at about three o'clock, the one with the platform?"

"Yeah?"

"Well," continued Denise, "the Chief said the dead lady that's been roosting up there for a few months is gone now. That's your honeymoon house! The Chief gave it to you and Mere. He paddled out last night to tell us."

Larry's turn: "They are so pleased, Mike, that you took a poor woman like Mere, with all her bumbling kids, and are making an honest woman of her. And you're a white guy to boot. There's already talk about you holding a village office."

We poured it on. Larry told Mike the huge Fijian guy cutting bamboo with the machete was Mere's cousin. He will personally be looking after Mike.

Mike thought we were joking at first. Then, he wasn't so certain, saying, "There is no way damn way I'm going ashore."

We told him it was OK, we could bring Mere to him, we understood being a bridegroom made him nervous.

In the end it was Mere who spared Mike. Coming aboard she told Mike she had made a sad but wise decision. It would be OK for Mike to return to America if she could, instead of Mike, have a bottle of Captain Morgan rum and pack of cigarettes.

Done deal!

CHAPTER 43

AGROUND

A *ground!* Few words strike fear as rapidly in the minds of mariners. Groundings, universally dreaded and probably inevitable at times, are usually in the category of 'this can't happen to me.'

From San Diego to Manzanillo, through the Marquesas, Tuamotus, Societies, Rarotonga, Savage Island, Tonga, and now the Fijian islands, we'd sighted countless wrecks, on reefs and rocky outcrops or sandy beaches—so many we stopped taking pictures.

Every wreck had its moments of drama, in some way ending hopes and dreams. Each served as a poignant silent reminder to be prudent. It was our turn. We departed tiny Yalu Island, bound for a small anchorage forty nautical miles upwind. No big deal, except it was tricky navigation start to finish—and by departing late morning we had lost much advantage of the sun. We should have prudently stayed put, but we didn't.

Our course that day often took us within a mile of reef islands, the slim channel between them less than a thousand feet wide. They twisted like a snake on a mountain switchback. Larry and Mike spent the day in the rigging high enough to read the reefs. By late afternoon, the light had gone flat, making submerged reefs difficult to determine by color. Mike and Larry clambered back to the deck.

Making it worse, navigation markers had gone astray, not unusual in these parts. In their absence, I carefully lined up two charted prominent points of land, slowly turned *Endymion* between them, heading toward shore, and what I thought was the entrance to a small secluded bay.

We relied on our depth indicator. I slowed *Endymion*, five knots, four point five knots, four km, three point five—I was afraid to go less. We needed momentum to counter wandering crosscurrents. It was challenging, tough going. The charts showed a channel I couldn't find. I considered anchoring and waiting for sun tomorrow but decided it was too shallow. If I anchored with enough scope to be safe we could swing widely enough to get stuck in nasty coral. Plus, a nation of clouds was building to the east. It hadn't rained in this part of Fiji in months. We could get it—in buckets and soon.

Sitting behind me Denise had been reading *My Way*, Frank Sinatra's biography. She put it down to read me depths: "Forty feet . . . thirty-five . . . forty-two feet . . . steady at forty-four feet, down to thirty-seven, no trouble yet, slow and easy there, Captain.

"Thirty feet . . . Skip—slo 'er down," cautioned Denise.

I eased the throttle forward, and forty five thousand pounds of yacht reclined gradually to three knots. It was dead flat calm, and dark—like just before a storm.

"Twenty-eight . . . twenty-six . . . twenty-eight . . . twenty-one feet," Denise said firmly. "Nineteen . . . eighteen . . . eighteen . . .

going down fast." Cold sweat on a hot humid day broke on my brow. Then came three almost simultaneous "*snap*" sounds. Our trolling lines with weight and lures, dragging bottom because of our slow pace, scraped sharp coral and we kissed farewell to several hundred dollars' worth of precious gear.

Oh well, I thought, *we got us a nice twenty-pound fish this morning.*

"Eight . . . seven . . . eight . . . six," Denise said in a frightened voice.

Crunch! It was the sickening sound of fiberglass meeting coral. We bounced. *Thud*—then stillness. We were aground.

"Hard astern!" Larry was on the bow, signaling and yelling.

"Little late, Larry." My reflexes already had the Perkins in reverse.

Denise and Mike jumped to tend the inflatable line so it wouldn't tangle in the prop.

Endymion bounced. I thought God sent the gentle swell that followed, lifting us momentarily from our unwanted coral home. I pulled the throttle hard.

We moved aft a few meters—

Crunch! We were again gripped by coral. A rising breeze pushed our bow to port. Larry waved his arms frantically motioning me to go to starboard, avoiding collision wity a huge coral head. Sweat poured from me as the first storm in months swept over us, bullets of rain sizzling the sea. Visibility dropped to zero.

Could this possibly be worse? I wondered if this was the end of the ride, would we be another statistic in an almanac of near-miss navigation. My adrenalin juiced. I throttled *Endymion* harder in reverse.

"By God I hope not!" I shouted to God and all present. Suddenly, like a kid on a slide, I sensed freedom.

"Seven point five . . . eight . . . seven point five . . . fifteen feet depth!" Hope rang clearly from Denise. "Yes! We did it, Skip!"

Larry danced on the foredeck as I slowly maneuvered *Endymion* astern, my hands still shaking. *Endymion* had worked free of the coral with only minor scratches to her quality hull.

Not five minutes had elapsed since we first aligned ourselves with objects on the chart. I realized my error—what a "dumb shit" I'd been—hasty and careless. Looking at the chart again I saw I had lined us up with two chart objects—but the wrong ones, eerily similar to the correct one a mile distant. *Was this*, I wondered, *what begot derelicts we've seen, wrecks caused by skipper error and remembered only by their unsalvageable skeletons along the way.*

CHAPTER 44

MIKE LANDS AN UNKNOWN SPECIES

First we had to wade through Mike's never-ending bullshit, and it hurt sometimes, to be completely honest, but I do admit—Mike was a superb fisherman.

Anytime we had more than two inches of water between our keel and the bottom, Mike had two active lines, one line in the water for fish, the other for insulting Larry and me as 'Junior Varsity' fishermen.

Two catches I'm confident Mike will someday describe to spellbound grandchildren, happened during our passage to New Caledonia. Two and a half days out of the Yasawas, wind had been constant at eighteen to twenty-four knots. We steadily cranked out seven to eight knots—perfect trolling speed. Mike had the only line in the water. Denise called Mike below. He liked to help the ladies, though Denise's problem was trumped-up fictitious.

While Denise engaged Mike, Larry and I adjusted his gear, increasing the drag on his reel and engaging a strike alarm Mike had rigged. We reeled off a couple hundred feet to give the object on his hook time to absorb the seawater, and tossed it over. The wait was short.

The alarm sang out and the line screamed, running from the large Penn reel. Mike bolted from the cabin. Larry and I shouted, "Fish on the line, fish on the line!"

"Yes there is," said Mike triumphantly enunciating and separating every word for emphasis, "and you'll note, it's *my* line. You guys go back to your knitting. I got this one!" Mike was half stammering, fighting for breath as he slowly raised and dipped his pole, knowing something huge had swallowed his hook.

"Boating this monster is going to be tough," Mike said. "Can't you slow us down, Skip?"

"I'll try Mike." But I didn't.

"I'll get the net and fish bat," offered Larry.

"And I've got the camera," said Denise. "Reel him in, Mike. You'll be famous."

Mike was near muscle fatigue and exhaustion. He was certain, because the fish wasn't fighting that he had hooked a giant octopus, or perhaps a heavy award-winning bottom feeder like a halibut.

At thirty meters from *Endymion*, the 'catch' broke the surface for the first time. "What the f! You bastards! You dirty bastards!"

The giant, extra-heavy, thoroughly soaked vibrant color beach towel had surfaced. Mike took our howling laughter in stride, claiming he now held the world record for "rag-fish."

Later, in calm conditions, we had another first for *Endymion*. I was at the wheel and saw what looked like a line of breakers in the distance. *But it can't be*, I thought, there's *no land within forty miles in any direction.*

I was sitting to starboard, steering with my left hand and some-times my feet. It was easy going, no pressure sailing. I poked my head around the edge of the jib, took a bit of spray in my face, and when my eyes cleared, I clearly saw a line of breaking waves several miles ahead. I shouted below, "Larry—give me course verification. I'm showing 130 degrees up here."

"One hundred thirty degrees, same here," Larry reported. "Some-thing wrong?"

"Sounds right, but it can't be," I said. "I'm making 130 degrees. I know breaking seas when I see them, and these are breaking all across the horizon. Something's wrong. Come up—take a look."

Larry popped into the cockpit just as it dawned on me. There was no reef. A clear air gale was headed right down our throats. Breakers were the front line. I called "All hands" to shorten sail.

Fifteen minutes later the first winds smacked like a fraternity pledge paddle at twenty-five knots. Within minutes we had forty knots. I had to yell to be heard even across the cockpit. I bore off twenty degrees looking for comfort. Denise crouched under the dodger, ducking seas that began to sweep the deck. She never feared unless she saw it first in my eyes. She was looking at me when her attention was drawn aft. Our Avon had flipped. Our Honda four-stroke engine was under salt water, the gas can held only by its filling cord. Oars, shoes, shells, bailer, and bucket—all were gone. I was momentarily helpless, only able to watch and pray our towing line would hold. It did.

The mini gale, like so many nerve-testing events at sea, was shortly over. Denise took the wheel and brought *Endymion* head to wind, stopping our progress.

Mike and I dove overboard, managing with effort to right the inflatable. We field stripped the engine on deck and to our surprise, got it running again.

We tossed our fishing lines over again—Larry's to port, Mike's at mid-stern, and mine to starboard. Stiff competition was reignited with one rule, no fishing at night—too many dangers on a moving vessel in darkness. Hours passed. The sun was waning. No fish.

Denise was on watch and heard "*click*," followed by "*click click clickity-click click click*." Mike's line exploded with sounds of a powerful, hungry predator gobbling up his lure. "Fish on the line," she yelled.

Three grown men nearly trampled Denise getting to their lines. Mike's had the action and he let we 'pussies' know with conviction that he was king. Larry suggested we check the almanac for sunset because Mike may be in default of rules. To be polite, I started reeling in my line. Mike continued his unabated litany of profanity, dressing down his competitors.

I felt a tug on my line, followed by a more urgent pull. "Hey dickheads," I yelled, "I've got one, too. Feels like a strong one."

"Too bad, Captain, I got mine first. I win—you lose."

"Maybe you both have the same fish," chuckled Denise, turning to look over the wheel.

And we did! The claims to ownership became brutal when we found Mike and I fought for the same morsel. Eventually, five feet of kingfish was boated.

Mike went to work. "Your line was out 200 feet, mine only 125. Skip, listen up! There's no way this beauty would take my lure, and swim backwards to get your dopey lure. Besides, as you all can see, Skip's crappy lure doesn't have a single tooth mark on it."

"I see it this way," I said. "The fish swallowed my lure on first gulp. Then it spotted yours and thought—ahhhaa a mediocre dessert. As you point out, it didn't swim back for mine, so it obviously had to take mine first, on its way to yours."

"You settle the argument, Captain," Denise nodded at me, "and be fair."

"OK, and I'll be diplomatic," I said with deliberate pacing, "*I am* the Captain. *I own* the boat. *I win.* Case settled."

A restaurant on Isle De Pins, New Caledonia, made a superb meal of the fish for us. Mike chose beef, saying, "I want something that had parents."

Larry with the disputed fish

CHAPTER 45

LIGHTNING ACROSS THE TASMAN SEA

Our anchor was firmly connected to the bottom at Ile Des Pins (Island of Pines), a most unusual island in the southernmost part of New Caledonia.

What I saw over my morning "Joe" was classic palms fringing a powdery white sand beach, backed by ramrod straight, majestic pines of a proud variety found nowhere in the world, except here—this island had an exclusive. Orchids, daises, morning glories, and six-foot ferns as wide as a truck grew wild everywhere. The sea rippled calmly at the sand's edge. Colors ran deep blues, through aqua marines, culminating in greens. Fish lunged at every scrap thrown into the sea, viciously competing for our bait-disguised hooks. Mostly we caught exotic "parrot fish," their lives extended by Denise's warm heart. Birds hidden in majestic pines sang from a thick songbook, their mosquito abatement program a success.

We were alone in this magic—no hotels, fast food, or car rentals. The sound of a jet would be as foreign as nuclear fission. We saw no other boats.

There was once a dreaded French political prison here, first occupied in 1872. We couldn't fathom these beautiful surroundings being a place of punishment—until we saw it. The prison ruins, the eerie chilling stillness of these chambers of horror, even one hundred years later, sent shivers down my spine. Though overgrown by jungle, a rough trail hacked through the dense brush enabled we snoopy visitors to envision the torturous hell on earth awaiting those who had dared to speak or act against their rulers. Prisoners were always shackled to walls. There was a small graveyard. No one ever went home.

Natives here were brown, as in all Pacific Islands, though, it's more cocoa-brown. We noticed they didn't laugh much and seldom spoke unless spoken to first. Wide-eyed children looked at us as if an oddity. Denise broke the ice with dime store toys and a healthy supply of hard candy. There's nothing as fun for a child as having someone pull a toy car or piece of candy from his or her ear, a trick Dad taught me years ago. It worked well too, with toothless old ladies. We soon had a town full of new friends.

As much as we enjoyed Isle Des Pins, we continued to Nouméa, capital of the French Collectivity of New Caledonia and a busy port for military, commercial, and occasional cruising yachts. We were assigned a prime spot at the Port Moselle Yacht Club. Larry and Mike went to explore the islands, leaving Denise and me alone and happy to be so.

We had the good fortune one afternoon to be introduced to Commander Pierre Fostora and his wife Sarah as they strolled arm in arm along the docks. Denise had been taken by their sophisticated appearance. Pierre, second in command of the French Navy in New Caledonia, also directed rescue operations for vessels in trouble. He shared local knowledge about areas to avoid.

When Larry and Mike returned to *Endymion* several days later we completed provisioning. Both guys had a plane to catch in Australia and pushed me to leave right away, but like sailors the world over discourage Friday departures, I had a strong aversion to yachts meeting deadlines because this is where trouble lurks. Our one thousand nm passage across the Coral and Tasman seas would be our second longest depending on where we touched the Australian coast. No problems please.

Commander Fostora shared his weather fax maps with Denise and me, expressing now as an OK time to leave, but warned we shouldn't delay. "Weather," he said, "will likely deteriorate the following week."

Denise had enjoyed our stay and posted a brief note home: *New Caledonia has been wonderful. We will sail for Australia shortly, so I'll wish you Happy Thanksgiving today. Skip thinks we will be approaching the Australian coast on the real Turkey Day.*

That departure didn't happen. I worried about Mike. Personally he's more interesting than a best-selling book, but he was on my "injured reserve" list, with a seriously infected foot. We were on temporary hold as I pondered his condition and the weather.

Regarding weather, we would be sailing further south, meaning cooler temperatures, fewer flying fish, and fewer dolphins. However, nasty seasonal storms race across the "Roaring Forties," a portion of the Indian Ocean funneling through the Bass Strait separating Tasmania and South Australia. These storms can become full gales as they roll into the Tasman Sea. It was also summer in the Southern Hemisphere. Low-pressure areas, developing near the Equator move south morphing into full cyclones that become thoroughbred devas-tating hurricanes. Best to stay well clear of anywhere these weather systems could collide.

As for Mike, he purchased new sandals back in Fiji. Bragged about them, too. The sandals caused a blister that caused an infection. The leg swelled. Doctors prescribed medicine. The medicine didn't work. The Doctor told Mike, "Stay off the foot." Mike didn't listen. He went to the zoo. Now Mike couldn't put his foot in a shoe.

Three doctors visited *Endymion* last night. They inspected Mike's feet and sandals. Then they huddled. Their unanimous opinion—a fierce infection was spreading rapidly.

I said, "Mike, you're a dope."

Denise patted herself on the back: "See, I told you it was bad. It could become cellulitis."

It was now Thursday, November 19th. I knocked on Commander Pierre's door. In somber tones he now advised wind would be on our nose, meaning a slow, uncomfortable passage. His predictions were for the next seventy-two hours. Beyond that it was a SWAG (scientific wild-assed guess). He was not encouraging.

Mike was holding us back. Concerns crept into my two-foot concentration zone because we needed to depart to make their air flight, in spite of my better judgment. Mike, thinking it might improve my mood, held a dockside funeral service for his sandals. It was humorous but didn't answer my concerns about Friday sailings. We waited for prescriptions to be delivered for Mike late Thursday evening.

Denise made omelets for Friday breakfast followed by thick steak sandwiches for lunch. Reluctantly, we cast off for Australia at 1600, Friday November 20th, powering through the reef channel with engine assist. A Friday departure into a long crossing was unlucky and I didn't like it.

The first few hours beyond the reef and into the Coral Sea were magical however, with *Endymion* moving smoothly in a warm whisper of breeze. In the distance, far on the horizon, lightning f lashed continuously, a fascinating display of orange and white streaks across the sky, some diving toward the distant sea accentuating the curve of the earth and outlining ominous distant storm clouds. I had never seen such a panorama of far off storm clouds and it held us spellbound. It was romantic—but sinister. Then the wind died completely. Hours later we still lay virtually becalmed. It was spooky. Just as I was considering how strange this was, apocalyptic lightning illuminated *Endymions's* deck, providing a glimpse of advancing dense black clouds streaming plumes of rain before them. There are thunder squalls and there are thunderstorms—and for us the once-distant lightning was now close artillery. A few big drops splashed on deck, a hot wind puff struck our faces and *Endymion's* sails filled, followed by brilliant cockpit observations:

"She's gonna blow."

"We're in for a humdinger."

Twenty-five knot headwinds quickly pounced. No one but me wanted breakfast, so I fixed my own while being tossed around in the galley by rapidly building seas.

Sailing close hauled in force six winds (twenty-two to twenty-eight knots) is unpleasant. Our course was 220 degrees magnetic. To fetch it we had to sail at 210 degrees because of current.

Larry piped up with a queasy-sounding, "This is freaking miserable!"

"Larry, this is nothing. Learn to like it. When miserable comes, if it does, it will be easily identifiable."

Near the forty-eight hour mark, misery won. Larry unhooked an arm from the rail and puked over the side losing everything since departing. We felt for him, but didn't like cleaning up for him because he couldn't. Seasick crew burdens any yacht, not only by not functioning—but getting in the way, often bringing shipmates down mentally. Larry curled up in the lee cockpit corner, a place I preferred reserving for well people.

Into our third evening (Sunday), seas and the wind had calmed but we sailed hard to lessen time at sea and exposure to danger. Conditions rapidly improved.

An *Endymion* rule was new watch must relieve old watch on time, meaning don't make the tired, worn-out person on watch hang around while the new watch puts on a jacket, adjusts a harness, or gets coffee. The rule was tested that night.

Denise relieved me at midnight on a night so calm we could see twinkling stars reflected on the surface. We were both tired. Mike and Larry had shortened watches due to their health issues. I was on edge. The soft reassuring hum of our Perkins engine blended with the gentle sound of the bow knifing through the calm, throwing off an overload of brilliant phosphorus.

Her fragrance leading the way, Denise arrived on deck with coffee, ready to take her shift. Dead tired, I started below to make my log entry and collapse on a bunk, any bunk.

Denise called behind me, "Hey Skip—would you get me another dry toast?"

Apparently she didn't get my guttural response. She upped the ante. "Make it two pieces, please—a thin spread of butter on each?"

I was about to lose it when she cooed, "Would you sprinkle a little fake salt on them for me, please?"

I blew. "Damn it, Denise. I'm tired. Get your own stupid toast!"

Not smart! This petite beautiful person would do anything for me. "I'm sorry—sure, I'll get your damn toast. You got my coffee."

I couldn't sleep, so after tossing, turning, and a hefty dose of feeling guilty I rejoined Denise in the cockpit as she listened to classical music and munched her dry toast with the casual air of someone who had done this for centuries.

In the distance, maybe fifty miles ahead of us, it looked like someone had turned on the lights. More lightning, lots of it, flashed in the sky, often three bolts at a time. We watched with detached feelings—how good it was that it was so distant, and how nervous even distant lightning makes sailors.

Red sky at morning—sailors take warning. Sunrise was awesome with flaming colors. We continued under power, aware of a building sea and watching distant storm clouds approach.

"Here we go again." Larry lamely commented.

Around mid-morning the wind freshened to twenty knots—on the nose of course. By noon thirty knots crossed the decks with gusts just shy of forty—still on the nose. Low turbulent clouds erased the sun.

Then the sky fell apart, raining so hard I felt we were under water. The good side—heavy rain flattens angry seas. The wind howled. We shorted sail, taking the main to one-quarter size and lowering the mizzen completely. We rolled the jib to hanky size, making uncomfortable headway at five knots.

A patch of pleasing sunlight streaked across the water. The sky became scattered nimbus clouds by mid-afternoon. The storm appeared short lived. Seas were down so we upped more sail while congratulating ourselves—a dreadful premature mistake.

321

By nightfall Monday it was twenty-five knots, again with shorted sail. Fatigue set in, adding to our depression at making little headway. We wore safety harnesses, were miserable in damp foul weather gear. Stinging spray bashed us continually. The barometer dove to a low of 996 millibars. Serious stuff. The situation was becoming difficult to manage.

That moment of *"knowing what miserable is"* ' I had mentioned to Larry had arrived. Beating to windward, we lurched and pitched through solid walls of wave, twenty feet from trough to tip, with greenish white foam spray filling our vision. Tonight required one-hundred-percent-plus concentration from the helmsman. Boats break apart blasting into monster seas as we were, plunging the bow five feet under. Waves were striking the bow as a blue-gray wall, rushing aft burying anyone on deck, burning our eyes, making breathing difficult and talk impossible. The wind no longer just howled—it shrieked and screamed, wrapping around the rigging, assisting the waves attempting to knock us down. While it was rough on deck, it was chaotic below deck.

I saw Denise through the companionway, one hand clinging to an overhead grab rail and a foot braced against the settee, attempting to get into a berth with a strong lee cloth. As we crested on a wave, *Endymion* would hesitate for a second—and rocket down the backside, slamming the trough below, often rolling forty to fifty degrees, making objects below lethal missiles. Denise was tossed around like a doll in a washing machine but she wouldn't give up. Below deck procedure was to strap ourselves into a bunk, take cover, and try hard to think about places we would rather be—like the lagoon on Niue. Sleep was impossible.

Things deteriorated as the night dragged endlessly on. I excused Denise from midnight watch. I watched her move from a bunk to curl into the navigation station. Figuring someone, somewhere, must know something, she fired up the ham radio. Though unlicensed, Denise kept at it in spite of numb hands and near impossibility of keeping her slender fingers on the dials. She eventually caught snippets from a Darwin-based ham operator who quoted the *Australian Sun Herald*:

Friday, November 20th will be remembered as Black Friday. Houses lost roofs in NSW (New South Wales), 2-centimeter hail and flying debris killed cattle, and sheep were thrown into trees. Crops were flattened. Squalls were reported at 100 KPH. Pilots were warned not to be sucked into the turbulence.

This was the weather that Pierre had cautioned us about. The lightning show Denise flipped over eating dried toast a few watches back was upon us. I slipped further into my two-foot zone. Concentration.

Lethargy was inching aboard. Mike was toughing out substantial pain in his foot and had been firmly warned not to get it in salt water. While on watch he kept a plastic bag tightly wrapped to his leg but he couldn't move freely. I relieved Mike but he refused to go below. This was approaching survival sailing and Mike knew every able body we could muster was essential—but I couldn't allow him even to crawl around a pitching deck like this (not that he volunteered) so he huddled under the cockpit dodger, in pain but alert.

Forward deck work fell to Larry and myself—mostly me, as Larry had plunged again into seasickness. My stomach lurched at the very thought of going to the foredeck—but we did what we had to.

Before dawn Wednesday something happened that many have heard about but few experienced. Within a minute, maybe less, the howling wind fell almost silent. Our anemometer dropped from fifty to fifteen knots in seconds. The ocean swells were still monsters—but the angry wind waves that had blown from the tops of the giant rollers, dropped off. No spray or wind-whipped scud was drilling us, causing our eyes to bleed. We could hear each other without yelling. *Endymion* stood nearly straight up.

"Listen up!" I said. "I believe we're in the eye of a depression. Not sure—never been in one—but it makes sense. Grab a little rest if you can. Let's eat."

We ate like savages, and Larry, God bless him, overcame his burnout and managed to scramble eggs.

Gradually, as daylight broke, without allowing ourselves to become comfortable, we became acutely aware of our situation in the relative calm we languished in. Confused seas came from every direction. Our instruments indicated the wind was clocking. The eye was about to pass. Shortly, we heard the rising roar of wind. "Get ready—harnesses on!" I shouted, watching three anxious heads turn.

Coming at us was a curtain of black. I couldn't define sea from sky. I'd totally lost the horizon. For a few alarming moments I couldn't determine up from down.

Wham—the wind slammed from the opposite direction. Hello again misery. Battle-tested *Endymion* groaned, answered the wind, and sailed out of the eye.

We had not anticipated the relentless thunder and lightning— chillingly close. Larry and Denise were below. Mike, his foot still wrapped, was double harnessed in the cockpit. He might as well have been through bolted. I had the wheel. Though Mike and I were only four feet apart we had to scream over the din to communicate.

Mike, always the ships clown hollered, "I'm thinking it's time we confess our sins. We gotta do something to get outta this jam."

My eyes stung so badly from spray I could hardly see Mike, much less understand him.

*Storm in Tasman Sea-such photos are hard
to get as pictures tend to flatten the ocean*

"Whad ja say?" I shouted.

"I said confess captain. What in hell ja do to get us in this mess? Fess up. Must be something you want to make right with God."

"Me?"

"Yeah, you!"

"Mike, back in Huahine—I switched price labels on a Chinese guy's rot gut wine—several times. Does that count?"

Before Mike could respond, a ferocious bolt of lightning struck so close it lit up the ocean, almost blinding us. Thunder cracked so deafening and brutal it would have shaken *Endymion* were we not already being tossed about.

"Mike, this is serious. I need to check our grounding system. Can you take her—for maybe ten minutes?"

325

Mike knew I meant business and half crawled, half butt-walked to the wheel, refastening his harness as he moved. A large breaking sea drenched us, hitting waist deep, but it allowed me to seize enough of the following moment to get into the black hole (our storage locker).

Back in Mexico a service tech told me about a boat sinking from a lightning strike. "You have a nice boat, Senor," he warned me, "you need insur—you know what I mean insur?"

He sold me twenty feet of heavy truck battery cable and couplers to attach to our rigging and throw overboard, grounding ship to earth if in a serious electrical storm. So there I was a year later, in piercing rain with towering waves breaking over our bow, inching my way forward on a pitching deck, attempting without assistance to attach a battery cable that probably weighed more than I did to cold, wet, stainless steel rigging while lightning flashed at my fingertips. I crept forward a few feet, said a prayer, clipped my harness, dragged the cable and somehow managed to get to the lower shrouds (wire rigging) holding up the mast. The first U-bolt connector I pulled from my pocket was ripped from my hands and washed overboard. Lightning struck not more than a mile away. I could hear Mike yelling but couldn't understand him. *No way*, I thought, *am I going lose this boat.*

Ten minutes later, fatigued and shaking from fear and exhaustion, with two U-bolts connecting cable to shroud, I threw it overboard, relief sweeping though me like divine deliverance. I crawled and clipped my way back to the cockpit and took the wheel from Mike. Time had lost all meaning. Seldom wearing a watch, I measured hours by the ships bells that hadn't pierced my ears through the din of the weather. I didn't know it then but I had been awake and on deck for nearly forty hours.

Time blurred and I fought drowsiness with activity. My world was threatening waves, howling wind, foul-tasting foam and a pitching yacht. Eventually and ever so slowly the storm began to lose its punch. I knew we would make it. Denise came up to relieve me on the wheel.

"You're whipped!" she said, helping me move my aching body.

"I am. Thanks."

Securely strapped in below, I lay awake listening to the racket continue as each helmsman in turn, rocketed *Endymion* off a wave to fall with a thundering crash into the next trough. I felt safe, secure, and crazy as it may seem, I thought how spectacular this had been—a tiny ship with four highly individual souls aboard in a vast, storm-riddled ocean. We will all one day have a hell of a story for our grandkids.

As I looked back, I'd done what I had to do. It surprised me having no fear during the storm. I had to stay focused, stay in my zone, concentrate, and stay awake. I had been too busy to be afraid—hadn't even given it a moment's thought, but when it was over there was time to be thankful—and I was—to God—to Henri for building a sound yacht. A lesser yacht may have foundered in this storm.

By ham radio we were contacted by boats all the way from Hawaii to Valparaiso, near Cape Horn. While weather maps, forecasts, or crystal balls hadn't predicted this fluke weather, ham operators everywhere knew of *Endymion's* struggles, and those of other yachts spread across the Tasman Sea.

We also received weather updates from Penta Comstat, a private radio service in Australia. After a wave jolted open a cupboard sending cups flying, Denise yelled from her heavily padded berth, "Ask em when it's going to end!"

Comstat replied, "It will be over when it's over."

"Crapola," said Denise rolling over and ducking.

Around 0530 Thursday we entered a strong two-point-five-knot southerly East Coast Australia current. Wind from south-southeast forced us to sail 070 degrees, almost directly away from our course. At least the wind was down and barometer up.

At noon we calculated our position as one hundred nm from Coffs Harbor, our New South Wales, Australia destination. In fading evening wind we could see the coast. Strong current played havoc with our navigation and we were in busy coastal shipping lanes. I stayed up all night.

When Mike took the watch at 0400 Friday, we had Coffs Harbor clearly in our radar. Mike knew this landfall was important to me. As dawn broke the coast was close. Mike turned *Endymion* over to her skipper—thus giving me the honors.

I would never have imagined it being so emotional. As land drew close I choked and fought back tears thinking of my family (especially Dad), friends, and crew who had worked so hard and cheered so much for us to have this landfall.

Coffs Harbor lay directly ahead—maybe a mile or so. Small fishing vessels were headed seaward. Tall, puffy cumulus clouds, tops burnished pink by the rising sun, rose majestically over the harbor. Traffic was beginning to awaken the town, and behind us to the east, thunderheads towered to the heavens.

"Douse the main," I quietly ordered.

"Aye aye, Skipper."

The Perkins came to life as we passed the harbor channel number one entrance buoy. Mike looked at me, a broad congratulatory smile spread across on his face. I'm sure he saw the rain in my eyes. I had not expected this. I was swelled with emotion and pride, the kind only a sailor can know when all are safe following a long ocean passage.

At 0542 GMT (0442 local) on 27 November 1987, with Denise at my side, we let fly our anchor close to the customs dock. It was Thanksgiving Day in America, which seemed fitting.

"How about we have some rum?" queried Mike.

Captain Morgan and diet Pepsi. No abstainers.

EPILOGUE

Thanks for reading *No Return Ticket, Leg One.* I hope you enjoyed your time on deck. Before tantalizing you with a preview of *No Return Ticket, Leg Two,* allow me please to touch on what became of crew who were important in this first read.

TONY ROWLAND-BELOVED SON

Shortly after arriving in Australia Denise and I received a letter from my dad including the following heart-breaking news:

I am sorry to report that over Thanksgiving weekend your x-wife Barbara called. Tony is back in California and in jail. Her details were sketchy but apparently a supply boat he worked on in Tahiti was part of a drug ring and Tony became addicted. I know this isn't the news you want, but I would be guilt ridden not to keep you informed.

If it's any comfort to you I'm told his sailing with you, and later Denise was the best time of his life.

Affectionately, Dad

I sat paralyzed, the letter in my lap and recalled; *I smelled a rat in the woodpile when Tony first wanted to work on the alleged 'work/ supply boat for the fishing fleet.' Why—why hadn't I spoken up right then? Maybe I could I have prevented this? Was I too headstrong? This must be what was bothering him when we argued in Raratonga. Why had I not put it together.*

I began to weep. Denise came to my rescue; "I see the rain in your eyes Skip. I love Tony too. Even my trained nurses eyes didn't see signs of drugs. Tony hid it well my captain."

Denise held me close helping my world begin to heal.

As I edit this material for publication in 2016 Tony continues to battle the demons of drugs but is leading a reasonably healthy life in California with his wife and two fine youngsters we are pleased to call our grandchildren.

KYLE-TONY'S FRIEND AND PACIFIC CREW

Kyle left us in Tahiti to permanently work on the 'supply ship' we later learned was an integral part of a major international drug ring. About the time we crossed the International Date Line DEA officers busted the boat, Kyle was arrested, and for all we know still remains in a Tahitian grey bar hotel wearing blue striped pajamas.

TOM PEEK-VAGABOND FROM MINNESOTA

After voyaging with us Tom settled on the volcanic Big Island of Hawaii where along with being a mountain guide, firefighter and exhibit writer at Hawaii Volcanoes National Park, Tom also taught writing and editing to islanders while working on his own fiction. When writing this book Denise and I found Tom's old business card from Bora Bora and tracked him down through the Internet. Still in Hawaii Tom is an award-winning author (*Daughters of Fire)* and became my writing coach for what you have just read.

MIKE MULHOLLAND-OAKLAND NURSERY OWNER

Mike was surely the biggest 'character' ever to walk our decks. He didn't get enough of the Rowland's and returned to sail with us aboard *Endymion* from Darwin to Singapore adding his wit and wisdom (?) to further enrich the lives of everyone he encountered. Mike eventually sold his Oakland nursery, married a Thai lady and lives happily retired in California. To this day he remains a crappy fisherman—but we still love him.

Moving on I continued writing this true story because readers remarked there never seemed an end to our adventure—that so many unusual, sometimes frightening, sometimes humorous, but always interesting events involved *Endymion* and her crew. We didn't ask for these things—they just happened. And they continued in Australia.

In my second book *No Return Ticket-Leg Two* we race with Tall Ships, rocket down a flooding Australian river and are attacked by pirates in the Malacca Strait. Love conquers all and there are humorous moments of course. I'm told it's a compelling read. I hope to have you aboard.

Captain Skip Rowland
Box 1194
Northport, WA 99157
skip@skiprowland.com

GLOSSARY

Aft: Rear of vessel, as in *aft* end. Non boaters call it the 'back end.'

Avon: Brand of inflatable boat made of PVC or Hypalon.

Binnacle: Ship's compass and a useful thing to have.

Bosun's chair: a board fitted to a harness with compartments for tools. One sit's in the *bosun's chair to be* hoisted up the mast. Usually not much fun.

Bow: Front end of a vessel.

Clew: Lower aft corner of a sail, usually with metal eye where lines may be attached.

Chubasco: Violent short duration squall. Used in Spanish-speaking countries. Also known as "Willie Walls."

Eskie: same as an American cooler; an Australian term.

Gaff: An iron hook that could have several claws.

Gunkholing: Cruising along a coastline and anchoring in sand or mud anchorages.

Halyard: Line used to raise or lower a sail.

Head: Toilet, but then you knew that already—didn't you?

Heel: Indicates how far a boat is tipped, eg. on a *heel* of 20 degrees. A 90 degree *heel* would be lying sideways, which is not a good idea. (see *Knockdown)*

Jenny: Nickname for Genoa Jib, the forward sail. Reference to 150% means it covers 100% of distance from headstay to the mast and 50% additional further aft.

Ketch: Two-mast sailboat with the aft mast shorter than the forward mast and placed aft of the rudder post (if anyone cares).

Knockdown: When *w*ind or sea conditions lay a yacht on its side possibly causing severe damage or sinking.

Knot: One knot equals one nautical mile per hour, or 1.1508 statute mile per hour, or 1.852 kilometers per hour (Thus 5 knots = 5.75 mph or 9.26 km/h. Confused?

Knuckle: The area below the waterline in the bow (front) of the boat that we reinforced in case we hit something...like a rock.

Koh (or Ko): Thai word for Island

Lee: Away from the wind. The side of the boat closest to wind is *windward* side, farthest from wind is *lee(ward)* side. A *lee shore* means the wind is blowing onto it instead of away from it, and is therefore often dangerous. *In the lee of* means "sheltered from the wind by" perhaps and island. Ie: "I sat to the lee of his bad breath and was disgusted.")

Longtail: Narrow canoe-shaped Thai vessel used for passengers or light freight. The helmsman steers by holding a long rod connected through a motor to a propeller that skims the waterline keeping it from snagging coral, seaweed or mermaids.

Luff (as part of a sail): The forward edge of the sail

Luffing: Refers to a shaking or flapping of a sail, such as heading the boat closer toward the wind causing sails to shake.

Mizzen Mast: The aft (back) mast on ketch or yawl.

Mizzen Sail: Sail that goes on the mizzen mast. (see above)

nm: nautical mile; equal to 1.15 statute miles. Based on the circumference of the earth, and used in navigation.

Painter: A rope used to tie a small boat (dinghy or inflatable) to a dock or a mother ship.

Perkins: Brand of diesel engine. We had a 4/102 meaning four cylinder- 102 horsepower model.

Port (side): Left side of vessel when looking forward from aft.

Scope: Indication of the length of anchor line relative to the depth of water when anchoring. *Scope* three times would indicate 3x as much chain (or rope) as the depth in which the boat is anchored.

Shroud: Stainless steel wire rigging used to hold a mast in place. (good stuff)

Sheet: Line used to adjust the shape of a sail. Thus, *trim* the sheet to bring the sail tighter or *release* the sheet to give the sail more belly. Older schooners had a topsail. A watch commander might yell; "Hoist the top sheet and spank 'er," frightening feminine passengers.

Spinnaker: Wind gathering balloon sail seen in many pictures. Used when the wind is aft of abeam. Causes problems and occasional divorces.

Spinnaker pole: Metal pole attached to the mast at one end and spinnaker at the other end, helping to prevent the sail from oscillating.

Starboard (side): Right side of vessel when looking forward from the stern

Stern: Back end.

Tinny: Small open aluminum boat. We got a 12-foot outboard powered tinny, to replace our stolen inflatable tender.

337

Tuk Tuk: Thai bus carrying more people than it should, their luggage, animals, groceries and grand-parents. No express routes.

Two foot zone: An expression adapted from rock climbers, who, with vast vistas to enjoy, must concentrate on what is before them at the moment. Hence, in the *two foot zone.*